Moyra Bremner has had a lifelong lov[...] was born and brought up in Britain, [...] spent many years abroad, she grew u[...] continental food and learnt how to cook it long before its flavours were popular in Britain. She has collected recipes since she was a young child and her delight in cooking has been warmly encouraged by three highly appreciative children, now grown up. Originally she trained for the theatre, but later read psychology at London University before becoming a journalist, broadcaster and author. She was the first woman presenter of BBC Television's The Money Programme, and is the author of the bestselling book *Supertips to Make Life Easy*.

Liz Filippini was born in Yorkshire and trained to be an actress at the Royal Academy of Dramatic Art. For the past twenty-five years she has been living in Rome with her husband, who is Italian, and they have two grown-up children. During all the time she has lived in Italy, she has travelled to every part of the country: one of her major hobbies has been learning about regional food and wine, and she has collected recipes wherever she has travelled. Unlike most Italian women, who tend to remain faithful to the regional cooking they have known since childhood, she enjoys every aspect of Italian food, and pasta especially is her passion. Culinary skill runs in her family – her brother is a prize-winning chef and has a three-star restaurant.

a great... love affair with good food. She
... but because her mother had
... up on continental food and

Moyra Bremner
and
Liz Filippini

Pasta for Pleasure

Fontana Paperbacks

First published by Fontana Paperbacks 1984

Illustrations by Conny Jude,
except pages 19, 21 and 24 by Ken Lewis

Set in Linotron Pilgrim
Reproduced, printed and bound in Great Britain by
Hazell Watson & Viney Limited,
Member of the BPCC Group,
Aylesbury, Bucks

*

To my family and friends
whose unfailing appetite for pasta
and invaluable comments made
this book possible

To Barbara and John

Contents

Introduction

In Italy pasta is not one of the favourite national dishes, it is the one and only. Common to rich and poor, by both equally enjoyed, for a costly sauce is not necessary to the tastiness of the dish. One never tires of it and no other dish in the world satisfies so completely.

The Pleasure of Italian Cooking, Romeo Salto

Pasta is probably the most versatile and satisfying food man has ever created, and the sauces and ways of preparing it, which have been perfected over the centuries in the kitchens of popes, princes and peasants alike, have a range few other foods can boast. Infinitely varied in shape, colour and texture, it can add an extra dimension to soups, make the lightest and most delicate of first courses, be the basis of rich dishes to satisfy the heartiest or the most discerning eater, or create unexpected cakes and sweet dishes. Yet, despite its growing popularity, the range of dishes it offers is little appreciated outside Italy. Indeed pasta is probably as much misunderstood as it is popular.

The roots of the misunderstanding lie in the fact that we tend to think of cooking in national terms – we go out for a Chinese or Italian meal without bothering to consider whether we are in the mood for the cooking of Canton or Szechwan, Lombardy or Abruzzi, even if the choice is available. Twenty years ago Elizabeth David pointed out that Italian cooking as a unified entity didn't exist, and, remarkably, that is still true today. The cooking in Italian homes remains, as it has always been, deeply regional and the contrast of styles and flavours is remarkable. In parts of the south you can find pasta sauces as fiery with chillies as any Indian curry; in the Three Venetias pasta may be spiced with cinnamon and curiously sweet; in Tuscany they have game sauces, and in the plains of Lombardy they make pasta dishes of

7

melted cheese or onions with the same creamy richness which is found in the cooking round Lyon in France. Even the pasta itself changes from region to region, each area having its own particular preferences and many having local specialities which are found nowhere else; but because few people expect such a range it is seldom found either in local Italian restaurants or on visits to Italy.

Paradoxically the dish which has done most to popularize pasta – spaghetti bolognese – has done most to prevent the widespread appreciation of the wonderful variety of other sauces. Originally it was tourism which converted non-Italians to the pleasures of pasta eating, and at one time the discerning tourist could find a whole range of excellent local specialities among the pasta dishes on the menu of any good trattoria in Italy. But as tourism has grown, tourist after tourist has asked for the one dish he or she knows – spaghetti bolognese – blissfully ignorant of the fact that the sauce is only a speciality of Bologna, and as foreign to Naples or Florence as fish and chips. So, increasingly, up and down the country the Italians, always eager to please, have abandoned their regional specialities and filled their menus with spaghetti bolognese, spaghetti and tomato sauce, and a few other ubiquitous dishes. These are often poorly made because they are cooked without the loving attention to detail which an Italian will devote to the regional dishes he prides himself on.

The purpose of this book is to introduce people to the immense range of pasta dishes which are eaten in the different regions of Italy, and at the same time to show them how well such dishes fit into a non-Italian household. The recipes have been collected during twenty-five years of travel in every part of Italy; some come from restaurants which have managed to resist the tourist trap, but most of them represent the typical home cooking of their area. To reflect the regional nature of Italian cooking, and the extraordinary differences in flavour and style from one region to another, this book is unusual in being divided by region rather than by type of dish. And since the aim of each chapter is to reveal the characteristic cooking of that region there is no set pattern to the way recipes are arranged within it, though the most typical recipes tend to be towards the beginning and sweet pastas and substantial dishes towards the end.

This is not a book of *haute cuisine*; it is good provincial food, with all the homeliness and practicality which that implies, and because few of the dishes have any real pretensions to sophistication, it is good food which requires the very minimum of skill and effort from the cook. Many of these dishes were originally devised by women cooking on a single hob, and though Italian mothers will go to great lengths to feed their families well, and will make very elaborate dishes for special occasions, they tend to have large families and are expected to provide two large meals a day. So they have found ways to make dishes which are both quick and excellent. This means that regional pasta cooking is equally suited to the needs of the working woman, the student cooking on a single gas ring, or the novice cook who likes good food but doesn't know where to start.

Few people realize how many excellent and unusual pasta sauces use ingredients which can be found in any store cupboard – eggs, bacon, peas, mushrooms, or even walnuts – the only exotic touch being the way they are combined. Most of the recipes in this book need only ingredients which can be found in any good delicatessen or greengrocer, but where dishes do require special Italian ingredients we have included an explanation in the Methods and Ingredients chapter and have also tried to suggest the cheapest way of obtaining them. Wherever possible, satisfactory substitutes are suggested – although if you can get the real thing it will always be better to do so.

Sauces usually use only a little of each ingredient, so it is worth buying the best possible so that each one makes its full contribution to the flavour of the sauce. Even when a costly ingredient is called for, it is unlikely to make the dish expensive, for one of the great advantages of pasta is that you can use it to stretch luxury ingredients between far more people than it would otherwise serve – carried on a heap of buttery tagliatelle 200g (7 oz) Parma ham will feed five people, served on its own or with melon you would need at least twice as much.

Though the regions of Italy vary so widely they have one thing in common – essentially cooking in Italy is thrifty cooking: not mean or parsimonious but prudent and well planned, and nowhere is this more so than in the matter of pasta. Not only are small quantities of good ingredients combined to make a sauce which will serve a fair number, but thrift is also found in what you might call serial cooking. For example, the sauce from a round of pot roast beef is used to dress pasta – so creating two dishes from one lot of cooking; then the leftover scraps of meat will go into pasta sauces, or be used in the stuffing of cannelloni or ravioli, according to the particular tradition of the region; then the ravioli will be cooked in the broth from some other dish. And if any ravioli are left over, there is a simple sauce for reheating them for another meal. Even the leftover fragments of broken pasta and rinds of Parmesan are put to use in pasta soups, so nothing is wasted.

You don't have to cook many genuine regional pasta dishes before you realize how easily they assist the household budget, how they enable a few eggs or sausages to feed unexpected guests, or how conveniently this style of cooking creates good meals out of oddments which can be found in any refrigerator. A special heading for leftovers has been included in the Index, but when these are used it is not the thoughtless shoving together of leftovers which depresses the families of the super-thrifty the world over, but a gentle art in which really good food is produced from very little.

Faced with the extraordinary range of dishes which can be made with pasta, it can be difficult to know how to fit them into a non-Italian pattern of eating. To get over this we have indicated both how many people a dish will serve and the type of meal it is best suited to. In the section called The Pasta Menu the recipes are also listed, with their key ingredients, showing whether they are soups, salads, light or main dishes and indicating how substantial they are. Of course all these are only guidelines. For pasta can be eaten at any time and in any way, which is part of the beauty of it, and one person's substantial meal may be another one's snack. If anything, we have erred on the side of generosity, for leftovers can be used up, but there are few things as dispiriting as an inadequate meal.

The one problem with pasta can be the confusing variety of names, and the fact that any one shape may be called one thing on one box and another on the next. Sometimes the different names indicate a genuine, if marginal, difference – for the ribbon-shaped fettuccine of Rome are fractionally wider than the equally ribbon-shaped tagliatelle of Emilia-Romagna – more often the different names are simply a matter of regional preference, or the decision of a particular manufacturer. This flexibility may be annoying, but then one would hardly expect a country which has had forty-four governments in forty years to be consistent in the names that they give to their pasta! The names used in this book are those which are generally used in the region we are writing about, but to assist readers in buying the correct type of pasta, various shapes are shown inside the front cover together with some of the names they are often given. The best policy is to go for the right shape and not worry too much about the name, and if the right one can't be found choose something similar. Italian cooking is concerned with the look and feel of food, as well as the flavour, and anyone who experiments will soon get a feeling for what goes well with what.

When buying pasta, the most important thing is its quality, for there is a world of difference between good makes and bad ones, and we have gone into this in greater detail in the chapter on Buying, Making and Cooking Pasta. For, although Italians eat pasta with an endless variety of sauces, the sauces are only part of their pleasure; the pasta is eaten as a delight in its own right, not just as the vehicle for the sauce, and only when you have a pasta which is good enough to give you that pleasure will you enjoy it to the full. In some cases the Italian delight in the pasta itself means that they use very little sauce and let the pasta itself provide the principal flavour of the dish. In dishes with very light sauces, which will mainly be eaten as a first course, we have retained the Italian proportions, but where the ingredients of a sauce suggest that outside Italy it will be a main course, we have increased the proportion of sauce to pasta, to make a more nourishing meal. Even so, the pasta itself remains important in any pasta dish and it is well worth paying the few pence extra for a really good brand.

Set against the fact that pasta provides one of the cheapest, quickest and easiest ways to create good meals, the common criticism of pasta is that it is fattening. In Italy they have a saying 'That which chokes not, fattens'; only in *that* sense is pasta fattening. The proverbially well-rounded Italian mammas acquired their ample curves in the same way that the Victorians acquired theirs, not from eating pasta, but from eating too much of all kinds of food, and Italian women today are no fatter than their counterparts in Britain, France or Australia. The idea that pasta is fattening arose from two fallacies: the puritan belief that anything which is really enjoyable has to be bad for you, and the old-fashioned idea that all starchy foods were fattening – an idea now discredited by modern medical knowledge and proved wrong by the success of the F-Plan diet, which positively encourages the eating of starch. In fact, there is now a pasta diet, and current medical thinking is that there are two central issues in losing weight – the total intake of calories, and the form those calories come in.

In both respects pasta is an ally for anyone watching their weight. In addition to starch, it contains proteins and minerals and has only half the calories of the same weight of meat. Most important of all, pasta is made of durum wheat which is digested more slowly than many other foods, providing a slow, steady release of energy which delays the return of hunger pangs and so reduces the desire for fattening nibbles between meals. This slowing down of the digestive process is even greater when the pasta is left slightly firm – '*al dente*', as the Italians say – which is why Italian doctors are as insistent on this style of cooking as Italian gourmets. But the ultimate proof of this pudding really is in the eating – neither of the authors of this book gained weight while testing these recipes even though they were eating at least two pasta meals a day, and though one of them has always had to watch her weight.

For general health the emphasis nowadays is on more fruit and vegetables, and more fibre; but smaller quantities of high-protein foods like meat or eggs, and less sugar, salt, animal fats, and food additives. Here again, pasta scores: it is a natural food which doesn't need additives and preservatives, its sauces are made with fresh natural ingredients, and the meat used for them is usually lean and in relatively small amounts. Looking at the recipes it may seem that quite a lot of fat is used, but a dish for four usually contains less fat than one person uses to fry bacon and eggs and, for those concerned about cholesterol, there is the advantage that many dishes use olive oil rather than butter, and that a regular pasta eater would encounter plenty of dishes containing butter's natural antidote – garlic. By being such a filling food, pasta also banishes the desire for sugary puddings, and fatty cakes, so the crisp salads and fruit which doctors recommend are just what you feel like eating afterwards.

Anyone who feels they are getting too little dietary fibre in the rest of their food can use wholemeal pasta instead of white pasta – for the range of wholemeal pasta is increasing all the time and pasta can easily be made at home with wholemeal flour – and though some sauces are not at their best with wholemeal pasta, many taste even better. But perhaps most important of all, pasta is a deeply satisfying food which allows you to reap the rewards of its dietary virtues while giving as much pleasure as any dietary vice.

It is always said that Marco Polo discovered spaghetti in China and brought it back to Italy; but it was not new to him. He wrote that 'they are very good and similar to certain lasagne which we eat'. Nevertheless, it was in China three thousand years ago that pasta, a paste of flour and water cooked by boiling, was made for the first time. Exactly how and when it arrived in the Mediterranean is a mystery. Etruscan frescoes portray the making of *lagane* in what is now Tuscany, something similar was made by the Greeks who settled in south Calabria, and the Roman menu certainly included pasta. At Roman banquets it was served more as a titbit or sweetmeat, dressed sometimes with vinegar, cheese and spices, and sometimes with honey, and often fried not boiled; a method which could still be found in Sicily until relatively recently.

With the fall of the Roman Empire the art of cooking was also swept away, but not all the culinary secrets of that time were lost. It is said that when Saint Guglielmo's enemies mocked him in the eleventh century, they took him ravioli filled with dry bran which, by his saintliness – with a little help from the Almighty – he changed into delicious ricotta cheese. In the twelfth century we find lasagne and maccheroni mentioned in monastery household accounts, and there are references to slotted ladles for lifting the pasta out. By the fourteenth century Boccaccio was writing in the *Decameron* of 'mountains of macaroni cooked in capon broth and served with Parmesan'.

Long before Marco Polo's time, Sicily was familiar with spaghetti, for it had been introduced by Arab invaders who were thoughtful enough to bring along aubergines as well, so setting the scene for the aubergine sauces for which the island is justly famous. Saracen tribes then spread the new pasta shapes to other parts of the peninsula and by the Renaissance pasta was widely popular. The first pasta factory of all was built in Campania, in the south, where the climate, and especially the *ponentino* wind which blows each afternoon near Naples, is ideal for drying pasta, and in those days a pasta man was a better weatherman than a sailor and knew exactly when it would change.

In the mid-eighteenth century a group of well-heeled and ostentatious young Englishmen, just back from Italy, opened the Macaroni Club in London at which they served that 'new-fangled' food, and its members – the fops who delighted in drinking, gambling and duelling, and were the curse of Vauxhall Gardens – soon became known as 'macaronis'.

Despite this slightly disreputable start, pasta has been eaten in Britain ever since, exported from the pasta factories of Italy which mushroomed in the nineteenth century. But it has only been in the last ten years that it has gained real popularity, as pressures on both money and time have caused more and more people to move away from traditional eating patterns with their large and expensive hunks of meat, slowly peeled potatoes, and fattening puddings. In pasta, people have found a food as quick to prepare as most fast food but far more satisfying, inexpensive and varied. Recently it has become the biggest area of growth in the whole of Britain's food industry, but the potential of pasta is only just beginning to emerge. It is in the infinite variety of pasta dishes that the full pleasure of pasta lies, and these can only be found in the regions of Italy.

Buying, Making and Cooking Pasta

Buying Pasta

AMOUNTS

It is difficult to predict how much pasta is needed per person – it varies enormously with the individual appetite, and the richness of the sauce. But, as a general guideline, in Italy they allow 100g (3½ oz) of packet pasta per person, but small eaters may need less and hearty eaters may need 125g (4½ oz). Fresh pasta is heavier so you need about 125–140g (4½–5 oz) more per person. However, the rustic pastas, of farms and villages, are far more filling than other pasta so you may need rather less. Stuffed pasta is even more variable but in Italy they calculate 20–25 of the very small tortellini or cappelletti in broth, or 35–40 when served with a sauce. With ravioli, agnolotti and tortelloni you need about half that number, but this does depend on their size and their filling. When buying these it is wise to ask the shop what quantity they recommend per person.

CHOOSING PACKET PASTA

Although the different brands look alike, there is a great difference between the best pasta and the least good, for pasta should have a flavour of its own, not simply be a vehicle for sauce. The makes which are among those most highly regarded in Italy include Agnesi, Barilla, de Cecco, Ponte and Spigadoro.

Some lasagne sheets claim to need no pre-cooking. As they cook in the sauce they require far more liquid than any of these recipes would supply and simply do not give the same results as other lasagne. It is far better to use normal lasagne, which is very easily cooked by the method on page 23, and is far more versatile.

Cannelloni tubes are a bad buy; they break easily and are fiddly to stuff. The easy, Italian way to make cannelloni is simply to lay the filling on cooked sheets of lasagne, cut in squares, and roll them up. For this you need *wide* rectangles of lasagne like those on the inside cover, *not* narrow strips.

CHOOSING FRESH PASTA

Good fresh pasta should be better than its counterpart in a packet and more and more shops now sell fresh pasta. But it shouldn't be assumed that all fresh pasta is good pasta; some makers are using poor recipes, others excellent ones. So it's worth asking about the ingredients and about the proportion of eggs to flour in egg pasta, and whether they use fresh eggs or dried. Or you can simply try the makes available until you find one you really like. A great deal depends on the way the 'dough' is handled by the machines. See also page 17.

Making Pasta

PASTA-MAKING EQUIPMENT

Pasta is much easier to make than pastry, and it's a delightfully satisfying occupation. For most pasta you need nothing more sophisticated than a board and a pair of hands, and if you also have a food processor the mixing of any pasta is done in an instant.

For rolling pasta by hand, you need a really long rolling pin, shaped like a log, with no handles. But it is often easier to use a machine which squeezes the pasta between two adjustable rollers which are brought closer and closer together. Such machines usually have a second set of rollers which cut the pasta into perfect tagliatelle, and some have a range of additional ones which cut other widths. There are numerous different makes and the things to watch for are that the rollers will adjust well and will roll the pasta almost paper thin, for stuffed pasta. Also, make sure that the machine is really sturdy and can be firmly clamped to your work surface, for these machines are impossible to use if they slide about.

There are electric pasta-making machines which mix the flour with the liquid and extrude the dough through holes of various shapes, but they usually omit the resting period, which is a pity for it makes a difference to the flour. They also fall between two stools, being neither as labour-saving as buying fresh pasta ready made, nor as much fun as making the pasta by hand or with the aid of a hand-operated machine.

There are various sizes of pasta cutters for pressing out the tiny circles for certain stuffed pastas. They work well, but a very small biscuit cutter or the sharp rim of a glass will also do the job.

One piece of equipment which is not recommended is a sectioned tray for making ravioli. It looks a splendid idea, but the results are very disappointing.

PASTA FLOURS

It is only in the manufacture of packet pasta, which is dried, that *semola* – a coarse durum 'flour' – is almost invariably used; where fresh pasta is concerned different types of pasta require different types of flour according to how they are made. Plain flour is usually used for handmade pasta which contains eggs, but durum flour has a better flavour for rustic pasta made with only flour, salt and water. Buckwheat flour is used for pizzoccheri in Lombardy, around Venice they made bigoli with wholemeal flour, while in Apulia they make orecchiette with ordinary semolina, of the sort used in milk puddings, for semolina is made of durum wheat.

MAKING EGG PASTA

For egg pasta the standard proportions are 1 large egg for every 100g (3½ oz) plain flour and a pinch of salt, and these proportions should be used unless others are given.

To make pasta by hand you simply put the flour in a mound,

add a pinch of salt, and make a well in the top. If spinach or other moist ingredients are included, they should now be drained as dry as possible, chopped thoroughly, and mixed with the flour. The eggs should be added one at a time: break each one into a cup and tip it into the centre of the flour, and work it in with a fork or your fingertips. If necessary add just enough water to make a soft pliable dough without a trace of wetness. But if it does become too wet just add some more flour until you have the right consistency. Then knead it thoroughly for 15 minutes pushing it away from you with the heel of your hand, then folding it back on to itself time and again. Rest it for 30 minutes under an upturned bowl. See page 21.

MAKING NON-EGG PASTA

The method is exactly the same as for egg pasta except that water replaces the eggs, and it needs rather less time to rest.

PASTA ROLLING

When pasta dough becomes dry it is almost impossible to handle. So large quantities of pasta should be divided into several balls, and the balls kept moist under a basin or in a plastic bag while they wait to be rolled.

Not all homemade pasta needs to be rolled, but when it does place the dough on a well-floured surface, and press it out into a circle with your hands. Then roll it smoothly and evenly, turning it as you work and occasionally lifting the edge of the pasta back over and around the rolling pin, smoothing and stretching it gently outwards from the centre, then unrolling it, turning it, and repeating the process, until the pasta is really thin. For filled pasta it should be almost as thin as paper, but for lasagne, cannelloni and tagliatelle it can be slightly thicker. At first you may find it difficult to make it thin enough, but don't be put off; the knack is easily acquired with practice. If you are making stuffed pasta, cover each sheet, as soon as it's rolled, with a clean teatowel wrung out in water, to keep it moist.

The easy way is to use a pasta machine which passes the pasta between adjustable rollers, see page 19. Start with the rollers at

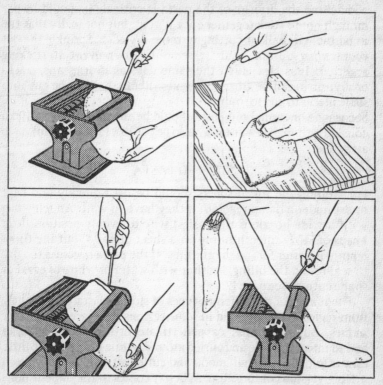

their widest and pass the pasta through several times, folding it in half each time. Then, to roll it thinly, bring them a little closer together each time you pass the pasta through. The trick here is to keep turning and folding the pasta in three so you end up with straight folded edges to either side and a neat strip to work with.

PASTA CUTTING

Pasta which is to be cut by hand into tagliatelle, or similar pasta, should be sprinkled with flour and left to dry for about 30 minutes. Then cut it with a very sharp knife into whatever type of pasta you require. The easy way to make long ribbons, like tagliatelle, is to fold it over and over, into a flat roll, then cut the roll into 'slices' of the width you want. If it is going to be cut by a machine the dryness of the pasta is critical. It should be dry enough not to stick together once it's cut, but not so dry that the machine will balk at cutting into the dry edge. Sprinkle the cut pasta with durum flour or semolina to prevent it sticking together. It is best eaten the same day, as it dries and cracks easily, or it can be frozen in boxes. Remnants can be cut into little pieces to add to soups.

Lasagne or cannelloni pasta should be cut into sheets 8×10cm (3×4 in), though lasagne may also be cut 10×15cm (4×6 in).

STUFFED PASTA

For stuffing the rolled sheets should be used quickly and kept moist under a damp teacloth if they have to wait. An icing bag with a wide nozzle is the easiest way to evenly position little heaps of fairly smooth filling on a sheet of pasta, but the tip of a knife is better for rough mixtures. If the pasta becomes too dry to seal round the filling, brush it with water or white of egg. For shape cutters, see page 17.

The names of the different types of stuffed pasta vary slightly from region to region, and in some regions there are also dialect names. But, generally, cappelletti are little squares of pasta folded into a triangle and curled around, while tortellini are little circles folded into a half moon and curled around, and tortelloni are big versions of tortellini. When it comes to the flat cushions of pasta the names become less predictable: small squares are generally called ravioli, but they can be called agnolotti; bigger squares are generally called agnolotti; half-moon shapes and triangles often have dialect names but can also be called agnolotti; whereas circles may have dialect names but can also be called ravioli! As to why one shape is used rather than another, it is largely a mixture of tradition and of certain shapes holding certain types of sauces, but you can make the shapes you find easiest, if you wish.

When any of these are stuffed with meat they are usually cooked in good broth and may then be served *in brodo* – in the broth – or be lifted out and served *asciutti* – dry – with melted butter and Parmesan or with a classic tomato, cream or mushroom sauce.

20

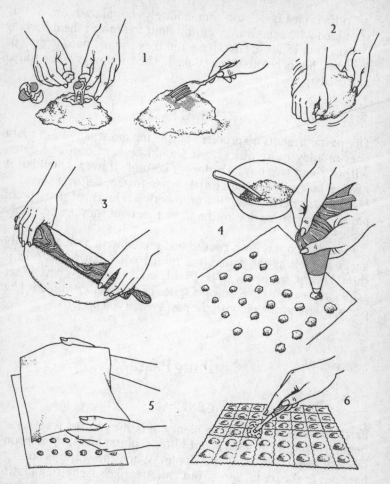

The Making of Ravioli

1 Making the pasta
2 Kneading
3 Rolling
4 Filling on pasta sheet

5 Covering with second pasta sheet
6 Cutting ravioli

Stuffed pastas should immediately be placed on a tray sprinkled with semolina or durum flour to prevent them sticking – plain flour is not so effective – and they usually need to dry out for a few hours before being cooked. The trimmings are re-rolled and used up.

KEEPING PASTA

Dry pasta presents no problem but, being moist, any fresh pasta goes mouldy quite quickly. It should be kept cool and eaten within about two days. For longer keeping, it freezes well but it needs a box as it becomes brittle when frozen. Leftover sheets of cooked lasagne can also be frozen between layers of greaseproof paper – the process doesn't improve them but they are certainly usable.

Pasta which has been cooked and mixed with a sauce usually keeps as well as the sauce it is mixed with, but to taste as it should do, pasta needs to be freshly cooked. So it is best to set aside, and even freeze, surplus sauce or soup *before* you add the pasta, then combine it with the pasta when you need to.

Cooking Pasta

GENERAL

Pasta needs to be cooked in plenty of boiling salted water. Per helping of pasta you need about 1 litre (2 pints) and ½ tablespoon salt – added when the water ripples. When the water is boiling hard put in the pasta. Spread out varieties like spaghetti, and stir smaller ones, so they won't stick together, bring the water rapidly back to the boil, and boil steadily, stirring occasionally to separate the pasta. Stuffed pastas are cooked in the same way except when cooked and eaten in boiling broth, and fine strands of pasta can be cooked straight from the freezer. For lasagne and cannelloni, see below.

All pasta should be cooked *al dente* – so it is still slightly firm (literally, '*al dente*' means 'to the tooth'); it should never be soft.

The finest tagliolini may take only 1 minute, an average packet spaghetti around 7 minutes, while large homemade rustic pasta could take 15 minutes or more; but tasting frequently is the only way to judge when pasta is perfectly *al dente*, as every make and shape takes a different time to cook, and even packet instructions cannot be relied on.

For a generous sauce drain the pasta well by shaking the colander, but when the sauce is very simple a few drops of water should remain on the pasta and the colander should be put over a bowl, so some pasta water can be added to the sauce if the pasta is too dry.

It is important to warm the serving bowl or dish you put it on, and to serve it on to warm plates – pasta cools easily, and tepid pasta can be most unappetizing.

LASAGNE AND CANNELLONI

Sheets of pasta for lasagne or cannelloni are cooked like other pasta but considerably more water is needed, and a drop of oil should be added to the water to stop the sheets sticking together. Cook them a few at a time, and stir frequently, so they won't cling to each other. Lift them out as soon as they are al dente and lay them out individually on a damp teacloth. When cut in half most long sheets of packet lasagne make the ideal squares for cannelloni.

When assembling a dish of lasagne, Italians usually place the sheets edge to edge, and in the same positions on each layer, so a portion the size of a single sheet can be lifted out without cutting. But they can just as well be overlapped to fit the dish. The important point is to use lots of thin layers of sauce and pasta rather than thick slabs.

With cannelloni the secret is to choose an oblong dish in which they will fit exactly – then the sauce won't slide off and allow the tops to dry up. (See page 26.)

REHEATING PASTA

In general pasta does not reheat well, as it tends to become overcooked, but, if necessary, pasta which is really *al dente*, and

The Making of Cannelloni

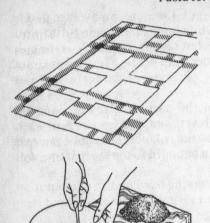

1 The pasta sheet is cut into squares, cooked and laid out on damp teaclothes

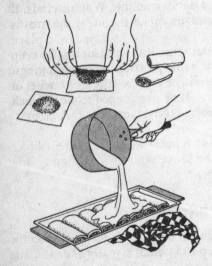

2 The filling is prepared

3 The pasta squares are filled and rolled

4 The rolls are placed in an oven dish and covered with sauce

has not been mixed with sauce, can be reheated dy dropping it in boiling water and draining it almost immediately. Thrifty Italians, needing a quick snack, often heat yesterday's leftovers quickly in a pan, but sauces with cream in, for example, separate to a greasy mess on reheating. Baked pastas, such as timballi and lasagne, reheat rather better, but are never quite as good as at first cooking. To make one lot of preparation give two meals, it is better to assemble two small dishes of lasagne and heat each when it's needed. To heat, or reheat, lasagne from cold, cover it with foil and heat it in a moderate oven, removing the foil towards the end. See also page 22, and Mozzarella, pages 31–2.

EATING PASTA

The correct way to eat pasta is sometimes a puzzle – perhaps because the method which is correct in Italy is not exactly tidy. Unless it's in soup, pasta is eaten with a fork; large strips of pasta like pappardelle are cut with the edge of the fork and eaten in pieces, but most long thin forms of pasta are wound round the fork into a bundle. The way to do this is to catch a couple of strands of pasta between one prong of the fork and the next, then twist the fork with its tip against the plate until the bundle is formed – then you whip it into your mouth before it unwinds. If that fails, the next best method (though not quite etiquette) is to hold a spoon close to the plate with your left hand, and place the point of the fork against it as you twist – not having to keep the fork so upright makes it easier to keep the pasta on the prongs. It is worth mastering the knack of pasta-winding, for the feel of the food is part of its pleasure, and little stumps of spaghetti lack the delicious sensuality of a long slippery strand.

Methods and Ingredients

ALMONDS To blanch almonds drop them into a bowl of boiling hot water, leave them for 1–5 minutes, then take them out individually and squeeze off the skin.

AMARETTI These are very hard Italian macaroons, made with sweet and bitter almonds, which are popular in Italy after meals with coffee or a liqueur. The cheapest are often sold loose.

ANCHOVIES The quantities given are for tinned anchovy fillets in oil. They can be drained and used straight from the tin. Those left over keep well in a refrigerator, or you can freeze them individually for long storage. Whole salted anchovies are used in Italy. Their flavour is stronger, so use only half the number and rinse and bone them.

ARTICHOKES For these dishes buy the smallest artichokes you can find and use only the inner part. To prepare them, remove the dark leaves, and slice off the tip, and the woody part of the stem. Then, from the top, cut round in spiral so that only the fleshy part of the leaves remain. Halve lengthwise. Remove any fluffy seeds and cut them into thin slices. Leave them in cold water and lemon juice to stop them darkening – and clean your hands with the leftover lemon. Tinned or frozen artichoke hearts can be substituted, but taste slightly different. See also page 00.

AUBERGINES Aubergines need to be cut up and salted for an hour or so before use, otherwise they drink up oil when fried and become greasy. Even so, test that the oil is hot enough to quickly turn a piece of bread golden before frying them – slow-frying could still turn them oily. This does not apply to dishes in which they should melt into the sauce.

BACON   Italian smoked bacon, *pancetta affumicata*, tastes just like British smoked bacon. In the ingredients it is given simply as 'bacon', streaky bacon should be used unless a recipe says 'lean bacon'.

Pancetta   Italian unsmoked streaky bacon, is used more often in sauces. It has a far stronger flavour than its British counterpart, but British unsmoked streaky bacon can replace it and, where necessary, we have increased the quantity to allow for its milder flavour. When thickly sliced lean unsmoked bacon is needed unsmoked gammon works well.

BEANS   In Italy many types of beans are combined with pasta, especially in soups. Chickpeas and borlotti beans are among the most popular. Borlotti beans are plumper than most, and their pale pinkish-brown skin is flecked with burgundy. When borlotti are unobtainable, use red kidney beans, although the flavour is different; the little knobbly chickpea has a unique flavour which nothing can replace. In Tuscany black-eyed beans, white with a distinct black blotch, are popular but they taste very much like ordinary white haricot beans. All these beans must be soaked overnight before use. If tinned beans are substituted, they should be drained and added to the dish for just long enough to heat them. Dried kidney beans must be *boiled rapidly* for 15 minutes, and drained, after soaking.

In Italy varieties we know only as dried beans are also sold fresh in their pods, to be shelled like broad beans. So, 'fresh haricot beans' means the fresh version of dried packet beans. Substitute the pale green frozen flageolet beans by 'Bonduelle'.

Broad beans should only be used in sauces when young and tender, but young frozen beans may be substituted.

BONE MARROW   This is the fatty substance found in the centre of bones, especially the shin bone of beef. The bone should be sawn into short lengths so that the marrow can be scooped out.

BRAINS   Brains of any kind need to be eaten the day you buy them and thoroughly cleaned. Put them in a bowl of cold water under a gently running tap for at least 4 hours. Then pull off the outer membrane and leave them for a while in tepid water to remove any remaining blood. Then put them in cold salted water with some lemon juice, bring them slowly to the boil and cook for 1–2 minutes. Drain and dry.

BREADCRUMBS Two kinds of breadcrumbs are used. Crumbled fresh bread is referred to as 'fresh' or 'soft' breadcrumbs. 'Dry' or 'oven-baked' breadcrumbs are made by baking pieces of bread slowly in a low oven, until golden, then crushing them almost to a powder with a rolling pin, or bottle. *The dyed packet breadcrumbs sold for frying cannot be used.*

BROTH   In Bologna they cook and serve stuffed pasta in a rich broth made from boiling both chicken and beef with bones, vegetables and herbs. But the broth from a good boiling chicken can be used. A cheap broth, for using in sauces, can be made by putting chicken, turkey or game bird carcasses in cold water with their cleaned giblets, an unpeeled onion, 1 carrot, ½ stick of celery, a few peppercorns, a bay leaf, salt, a little thyme and some parsley. Bring this to the boil and simmer gently for 2–4 hours, then strain. The packs of chicken pieces sold by some supermarkets for stock can be used instead of carcasses. Many sauces need only a small amount of broth, so it's convenient to have it frozen in small containers such as yoghurt pots.

Bouillon cubes vary greatly in their quality, and a bad bouillon cube can ruin a sauce, so it pays to choose carefully.

CACIOCAVALLO Pronounced catcho-ca'vallo. See pages 66–7.

CAPERS   These are the pickled buds of a Mediterranean shrub which have a deliciously piquant flavour, and also cut the richness of sauces.

CHILLIES   When a recipe simply says 'chillies', use fresh or dried chillies of either colour. It is impossible to say just how much to use, for different types vary enormously in their fieriness, so taste a tiny piece before deciding how much to put in.

Chilli powder must be pure chilli powder; check the packet to see it is not mixed with other spices.

CLAMS AND MUSSELS   Clams can be the size of a small coin, or as large as your palm, but Italian clams tend to be small with shells which are proportionately light. So if you have to buy large clams increase the quantity, to allow for the weight of their shells, and cut them up after cooking.

Clams and mussels are easy to prepare and cook, but to be safe they must come from unpolluted water and still be alive at the moment you start to cook them. Fortunately no self-respecting mollusc stays open when attacked. So tap those that are open sharply and put them aside. Those which close tightly are alive and well. Those which have failed to close in 1–2 minutes are dead and should be discarded.

The live ones should then be left in a bowl under running water for about 2 hours, to cleanse them. Then scrub the shells thoroughly, scrape off anything attached to them, and pull the beards and random strands from the mussels. Put them in cold water until cooking time, which should be as soon as possible – certainly within twenty-four hours of purchase. Recheck that they are all alive just before cooking.

CREAM   'Thick cream' is double cream, or any cream which will thicken when heated.

To 'cream' an ingredient means to beat it with the back of a spoon until it becomes like thick cream.

EQUIPMENT   No special equipment is needed for making the dishes in this book, but some things certainly make life easier.

Apart from a really sharp knife – which too few kitchens possess – one of the most useful implements is a small wooden bowl partnered with a crescent-shaped chopping blade on a single handle, called an 'hachinette' in France and sold in good kitchen shops outside France as a herb bowl and chopper. It is perfect for chopping tomatoes without their juice running everywhere, for the small quantities of vegetables and herbs which occur in so many pasta sauces, and for nuts.

Parmesan can be hard enough to break a normal knife, so the Italians have a special stumpy-handled knife with a short extra-strong blade which is most useful for cutting it.

A food processor is invaluable, but not essential. Some have a grating attachment specially designed for hard cheeses like Parmesan and pecorino, which is a great time-saver. They are also excellent for sieving tomatoes, and for making the finely chopped fillings for some stuffed pastas, but beware of using them to chop cooked meat for a sauce, for they can reduce excellent meat to the consistency of the most repellent baby food.

It looks like a gimmick, but the implement like a flat wooden spoon with stumps of dowelling sticking out, which is sold as a spaghetti server, is a godsend for fishing out slippery spaghetti to taste if it's al dente – and for serving it quickly to a hungry family. Equally, a flat wooden spatula is best for lifting lasagne sheets from the water, and a perforated spoon is best for stuffed pasta.

See also Pasta-Making Equipment, pages 16–17.

FONTINA   A smooth rich table cheese, with a brown rind, which is made in Piedmont, especially in the Val d'Aosta area. It has a delicate but distinctive taste, and melts very easily. When it is unobtainable other mild-flavoured melting cheeses can be used; *taleggio* is probably the best, but St Paulin is also good and so is Port Salut, while Gruyère melts in a similar way but has a far stronger flavour.

GORGONZOLA   This strongly flavoured blue cheese with a rich creamy texture is made in the plains of Lombardy. Its milder form, *Gorgonzola dolce*, or *dolce latte*, is most used in sauces. Some also use equal amounts of Gorgonzola and another Lombardy speciality, *mascarpone*, a white buttery cheese like rich cream cheese. This is seldom found outside Italy, but a cheese called *Gorgonzola al mascarpone* is quite widely sold. As it combines the two cheeses in alternate layers it can be used whenever a recipe requires equal amounts of each. *Mascarpone* goes sour rapidly, so it must be used when fresh.

HAM   Italian ham, *prosciutto cotto*, is similar to the best York ham. It's convenient to buy the cheap off cuts of good ham from shops which slice it freshly, then chop and freeze them. They can then be used straight from the freezer when you need to make a quick sauce, and the same applies to bacon. Ham bones are an excellent addition to soup and some recipes use the fat from ham to cook other ingredients.

HERBS   Basil is the herb of Italy *par excellence*; a perfect partner to tomato, its aromatic leaves can turn a simple sauce into something special and they are essential for some dishes. Dried basil tastes very different and can only be substituted when long slow-cooking is required. But basil will grow happily on an indoor windowsill, and more than pays for its keep. It can even be chopped up and preserved in fine vegetable oil for winter, though it needs refrigeration, and easily goes mouldy. A better method is to freeze it. The leaves lose their texture but retain that elusive aroma and can be used in most sauces.

Other fresh herbs are also used with pasta and many are very different when dried, particularly thyme, oregano and marjoram. When dried, these should only be put in dishes which take long slow-cooking; and use less, for drying concentrates their flavour. Briefly cooked dishes are better with no herbs at all than with dried ones, and we have tried to indicate where the flavour of a herb is so important that a dish would be unsuccessful without it. Bay, juniper and rosemary can be used either fresh or dried.

Borage is an old-fashioned herb which tastes rather like cucumber. It's a classic ingredient of Pimms and can be tucked into a border in any temperate garden.

LARDO   Used in country districts of Italy this is a slab of cured pig fat, not packet lard. It is worth looking for as it lends a very particular flavour to sauces, but when it is unobtainable substitute fat from ham or unsmoked bacon, plus a little lard.

MEASUREMENTS   A 'tumbler' is an average tumbler holding 150ml (6 fl oz). A 'cup' is a standard Imperial cup, which is 280ml (½ pint).

MORTADELLA   This speciality of Bologna is a distinctive sausage; extremely large, it is made of pork minced to a creamy paste with herbs and spices, mixed with diced pig fat, then cooked. Its name comes from the Latin *murtatum*, myrtle, with which it was once flavoured.

MOZZARELLA   These little balls of fresh white cheese were originally made in Campania from buffalo milk but are now made commercially, both in Italy and elsewhere, from cow's milk. The best-flavoured mozzarella is still made from buffalo milk and sold as *mozzarella di buffalo*; this is best for salads but the cheaper cow's milk variety is better for pasta sauces.

Paper-wrapped mozzarella must be stored in a bowl of water or fresh milk, and should be rinsed before use. It will only keep 3–5 days in a refrigerator. It cuts most easily when chilled and it can be frozen for use in hot sauces, though not in a salad. Unfortunately, dishes containing mozzarella do not reheat well, for the cheese becomes leathery when reheated.

MARSALA   A fortified dessert wine from Sicily, darkly coloured with boiled grape juice, and immensely popular in Britain in the nineteenth century. There is no real equivalent, but if really necessary a medium sherry may replace it.

MOSTARDA DI CREMONA   Made in Cremona and eaten all over Emilia-Romagna and in Lombardy, this is a curious preserve: mixed whole fruit in a mustard-flavoured syrup. An unexpected combination which goes particularly well with Emilia-Romagna's famous boiled meat.

NUTMEG   The hint of nutmeg which is found in many Italian sauces makes an enormous difference. To taste its best, nutmeg must be newly grated, so it's worth looking for whole nutmeg and keeping them in an airtight jar ready to grate freshly.

OIL   The flavour of oil is important in Italian cooking, and it will make a difference if you use good-quality olive oil. The best Italian oil is a clear yellowy green sold as Extra Vergine. For basic frying – of aubergine for example – a pure oil, such as sunflower or corn oil, should be used.

OLIVES   Choose large olives if they need to be sliced: it's much less work to stone a few big ones than a host of tiny ones. But don't be tempted to leave in the stones and serve them whole in recipes which ask for them to be chopped – they simply roll off the pasta. Whole olives keep well under olive oil in a cool place.

PARMESAN   This very hard cow's milk cheese is a vital element in many Italian dishes. But, to work its magic, it must be freshly grated: ready grated, pre-packed Parmesan does not have the same vividness of flavour. If you dislike the chore of grating it each time, a whole chunk can be grated then frozen: it keeps its flavour well and can then be used straight from the freezer, and the rinds can be kept for use in soups, see page 78. Or find a shop which sells it freshly grated.

Created in the towns of Parma and Reggio, and made since at least the twelfth century, its great straw-coloured discs, big as a wheel, are stamped in black with the words Parmigiano Reggiano. Without those words it is not true Parmesan. It must age for two to four years to reach the full flavour and hard, almost dry, texture which are so characteristic.

See also page 89.

PASTRY   To make the short pastry needed for pasta pies: cut the fat in small pieces, rub it into the flour until it looks like fine breadcrumbs, add a pinch of salt, mix in the egg yolk (if used) with a palette knife, then very gradually mix in enough cold water to make a firm but pliable paste. Form it into a ball and rest it in the refrigerator for 30 minutes before rolling.

PECORINO   *Pecore* are sheep, and the name *pecorino* can describe a wide range of Italian sheep's cheeses. Most are local cheeses found only in their own region, and usually, if you ask for pecorino, you will be offered either pecorino romano or percorino sardo, and these varieties are also exported. Pecorino romano is a pale hard cheese, with a dark rind and a strong tangy flavour. Pecorino sardo is similar but smaller, with a pale rind. When young, and relatively soft, they can be eaten as table cheeses. Mature they may be too strong for some palates but are excellent with pasta. Without their skins pecorino rinds can be used in soup, like those of Parmesan. No other cheese tastes quite like them, but if they can't be found provolone can successfully replace them in some dishes, and Caerphilly in others.

PIMENTOS   These are also called peppers, or sweet peppers, and if no particular colour is specified any colour can be used. For skinning they must be grilled until all the skin blisters or turns black: it can then be pulled off under a tap. The stalk and seeds need to be carefully removed, for the seeds can be as fiery as chillies. Frozen pimentos can be used in most sauces, except where the skins needs to be removed.

PINE KERNELS OR PINE NUTS   These tiny cream-coloured nuts have a delicious, slightly resinous, and unique flavour, and many delicatessens stock them.

PORCINI   These are the wild ceps or boletus mushrooms most used in Italian cooking. The *Boletus edulis* is the one most often picked. Large, with a shiny brown top (hence its common name, 'penny bun'), and curious honeycombed underside, quite unlike other types of mushroom, it has a rich, almost meaty taste which enriches many pasta sauces. It grows in Britain but only those who know their mushrooms should try their hand at mushroom-picking, for even this distinctive family has poisonous members. If you do have fresh porcini wipe them clean with a damp cloth, and cut off any dirty or damaged parts before use.

Dried porcini are sold in some delicatessens, and though expensive, a very few will make a difference to a sauce. Porcini are not always well cleaned before drying, so the water they are soaked in can be gritty and should always be strained through muslin, or a paper coffee filter, before being added to a sauce.

PROSCIUTTO   Pronounced prosh-ōō-toe, this is a leg of raw pork cured by salting and drying. The meat is chilled and a small quantity of salt massaged in to produce a firm sweet ham with a distinctive flavour. Prosciutto is also called Parma ham, for it originated in Parma, and the best prosciutto still comes from round there. Eaten raw, in very thin slices, good prosciutto makes a beautiful antipasto to start a meal, but it is expensive. Luckily, only the delicate pasta sauces need prosciutto slices, for the rest use the off cuts which most shops can be persuaded to sell very much cheaper. They can then be cut up and frozen until needed. Where possible, the substitute which best suits that recipe is given, but there is no equivalent.

PROVOLONE   A hard cheese with a nice tangy flavour, similar to that of caciocavallo (see pages 66–7), but far more widely sold.

RICOTTA   Ricotta is similar to curd cheese: soft and white with a fine, slightly granular consistency. There are two sorts, both called ricotta. Ricotta in the north of Italy is made of cow's milk, but in central and southern Italy a more fragrant variety is made of sheep's milk. In Italy, sheep's ricotta is used for the pasta sauces of those regions, but we have only included those which can equally well be made with cow's ricotta. This is widely sold in Britain and should taste as fresh and sweet as new milk and be eaten very fresh. Curd cheese is a good substitute where ricotta is not a main ingredient.

Hard or salted ricotta is used for certain dishes in parts of southern Italy, and is closer in flavour to pecorino. Little is exported and there is no real substitute, but the Greek feta cheese is slightly similar.

See also page 183.

SAFFRON   As it is the pistil of an autumn crocus, saffron is sold both as little dried filaments and as powder. The filaments ensure it is real saffron and should be steeped in a little water to draw out their colour, but powder is easier to use so only powdered saffron is given in the ingredients. Insist on genuine saffron for its flavour is needed as well as its colour.

SALAMI   All kinds of salami are made in Italy but only two are used in these recipes. The basic 'salami' is Milan salami, a long sausage which is widely sold and has slices over 5cm (2 in) across, finely speckled in red and white. The 'peppery salami' is much slimmer and shorter, weighing only some 300g (11 oz), tinted red and strongly flavoured with chilli. Although fairly difficult to find, small Italian salamis strongly flavoured with black pepper (such as those of Negroni) can be used instead, as can Spanish *chorizos*, though the flavour will be different.

SAUSAGES   Sausages in Italy are made of pure coarsely ground meat, usually pork, with no filler. They are plump, full flavoured and well seasoned and, typically, weigh about 100g (3½ oz) each. Some good shops stock them and they are well worth looking for. The nearest equivalent are often German bratwurst.

SAUTÉ   This is the process by which food is placed in a small amount of moderately hot fat or oil and cooked gently, while constantly being moved so it does not fry or overcook: this is often the preliminary to other kinds of cooking.

SCAMORZA   See page 39.

SEASON   When we simply say 'season to taste', we mean 'add salt and pepper, while stirring and tasting to check you are adding the right amount'. The tasting is important: many ingredients, such as cheese or bacon, release saltiness into the sauce; others, such as sugar and wine, reduce saltiness, so adding a fixed amount of seasoning never gives good results.

SQUID   Squid are one of those rare foods which come through the process of freezing without changing their taste or texture, so frozen squid can be used in any of these recipes. Whether it is fresh or frozen, remove the eyes, ink bag, beak and the flat bone inside the body, and rinse the squid thoroughly in running water, removing any yellow matter and pulling off any loose or tough bits of skin.

STRAINING   The liquid from cooking shellfish or soaking dried mushrooms needs to be strained to remove pieces of grit. A piece of muslin laid in the bottom of a sieve is the usual method but any clean fine white cloth can be used, so can the paper filters sold for filtering coffee.

SWEETBREADS   Sweetbreads, whether from lambs or calves, need to be eaten the same day, and they must be cleansed before cooking. Soak them for 2–3 hours in a bowl of water under a slowly running tap, so that the water is changed constantly. Drain, place in cold water, bring slowly to the boil and simmer them for 6 minutes. Drain, rinse in fresh water, remove as much membrane and fat as possible, and pat them dry.

TOMATOES

TOMATO CHOOSING Most Italian sauces use sweet, deep red plum tomatoes, so, when richly flavoured fresh tomatoes are unobtainable, Italian tinned plum tomatoes are often the best choice whenever a recipe says tinned tomatoes can be used.

TOMATO PASTE This is a concentrated tomato purée, sold in tubes and tins, most often used in recipes which need long cooking and have only a hint of tomato. Large tins are cheapest and can be frozen by the tablespoon for future use. Some brands are more concentrated than others, so add tomato paste gradually, tasting as you do so, or it may accidentally dominate the other flavours. It is not a substitute for chopped tomatoes.

TOMATO SKINNING To skin a tomato quickly, simply cut a nick in the skin and drop it in a bowl of boiling hot water. When the skin splits open lift it out, then drop it briefly into cold water and the skin should peel off easily. The water must be really boiling, so large quantities of tomatoes are best done in batches. Beware of leaving ripe tomatoes in hot water for so long that they become pulpy; unripe tomatoes will not peel even by this method.

WHITE SAUCE If no other quantities are given the quantities for a basic white sauce are 40–60g (1½–2 oz) butter: 40–60g (1½–2 oz) plain flour: 575ml (1 pint) milk.

To make basic white sauce: gently melt the butter and stir the flour smoothly in. Cook it gently, stirring constantly, until it becomes pale and slightly frothy. Then add the milk little by little, stirring all the time with a loop whisk until you have a smooth thick sauce which no longer tastes of flour. Then season it to taste. If you have no loop whisk use a spoon, but it will be harder to make a lump-free sauce.

When chopped onion is used, it is softened in the butter before the flour is added, and when bay leaves, thyme or nutmeg are included they go in just after the milk. If the recipe uses both broth and milk the broth is added first.

37

WINE   Using wine in cooking may seem extravagant, but adding a little wine to make a really tasty dish costs no more than adding sauces and ketchups to less interesting food. In Italy wine is cheap, and it's used lavishly in cooking, often being almost cooked away so that the sauce is flavoured with the aroma of the wine more than with the wine itself. We have given the quantities used in Italy, but this is a matter for your judgement. In sauces which are highly flavoured, for example with tomatoes and chillies, the wine can be reduced, or replaced with a little water; though the sauce will be better with the full amount of wine. In more subtle dishes, such as the *Spaghetti all'Isolana* of Sicily, it makes a big contribution to the flavour and the quantity cannot even be cut. The wine does not have to be expensive but it should be sound and genuine – undrinkable wine only produces uneatable food. The most convenient way is a good wine box but remember that, once opened, even these deteriorate with time.

Italy exports little wine, compared to France, and rarely her best, but when buying Italian wine to drink with pasta there are points worth looking for. A little black cockerel, or a cherub, on the label indicates a good chianti. Bottles with corks are almost always better than those with screw tops, and look for the words 'casa vinicola' on the label. They tell you that it has, at least, been made at one single vineyard.

ZEST   The zest of citrus fruit is the thin outside layer of the peel which carries the volatile oils and the flavour. It should be thinly pared with a lemon zester or potato peeler, for the pith underneath can be bitter.

1 ABRUZZI

Abruzzi, and its tiny companion region Molise, straddle the wooded Apennines, which run down the leg of Italy, and descend to the Adriatic. A harsh, isolated region, Abruzzi is dotted with little villages and peasant farms which provide the lamb which is such a feature of the cooking.

The customs and tastes belong to southern Italy: the local cheese, scamorza, is similar to Campania's mozzarella, and chillies – beloved throughout the south – are much used. The 'little red devils', as they are called, grow in all shapes and sizes – and degrees of heat. Each household keeps a flaming pot, and the chillies are threaded on strings in autumn and hung in shining scarlet garlands in kitchens and doorways. For according to Abruzzi's folklore, chillies are not just a spice but a talisman against bad luck.

Here, they produce beautiful pottery bowls. You find them on

39

market stalls, between brightly woven blankets of red, white, blue or green, waiting to be bought and filled with the delicious *maccheroni alla chitarra* which is a speciality of this region. This homemade egg pasta is pulled out in sheets across a wooden frame with steel wires rather like a loom, or, to the romantic mind of an Italian, like a *chitarra* – a guitar. When a rolling pin is passed across it the pasta falls through in long threads which are not round like macaroni, or flat like tagliatelle, but like golden square-sectioned sphaghetti. Delicious and substantial sauces smother this homemade pasta as it is served in patterned ceramic bowls. A delight to tongue and eye.

Pasta once had fewer names than it does now and all kinds of pasta went by the single name *maccheroni*. But if you buy the Abruzzi *maccheroni* in packets, you will find some manufacturers now call it *spaghetti alla chitarra*, though to those in Abruzzi it remains *maccheroni* to this day.

Maccheroni alla chitarra con peperoncino
Chitarra Spaghetti with Chillies

The combination of lamb, sweet peppers, red hot chillies and cheese makes this one of the best sauces for Abruzzi's traditional pasta, and those who lack the Abruzzi taste for chillies need only put in a fraction of the amount. In Abruzzi this fiery dish is especially welcome in winter when the *tramontana* – the biting north wind – blows over the mountains. A light main course for 5–6.

450g (1 lb) maccheroni alla
   chitarra or spaghetti
4 tablespoons olive oil
1 large onion, finely chopped
1 garlic clove, finely chopped
400g (14 oz) minced lamb
2 large red or yellow
   pimentos

2 fresh or dried chillies
400g (14 oz) fresh or tinned
   tomatoes, skinned and
   chopped
1–1½ tumblers dry white
   wine
a handful grated pecorino
   romano cheese

Warm the oil in a heavy casserole and cook the onion, garlic and meat over a moderate heat, stirring, until the meat browns slightly. Clean the pimentos with a damp cloth, remove the stem and seeds and cut them into thin strips. Slice the chillies finely and taste them, cautiously, before deciding how much to put in. Add the tomatoes, pimentos and chillies to the pan and season them with salt. Cook the sauce over a low heat for 45 minutes, stirring occasionally, and adding some of the wine from time to time until it has all been used.

When the sauce is ready cook the pasta in boiling salted water. Drain when *al dente* and transfer it to a warm pasta bowl. Add a good handful of pecorino then pour over the sauce. Mix lightly before serving, and pass round more cheese at table.

Master Peppe had kept a maccheroni shop in his youth and grown up in sweet slow wittedness amongst the lovely fringes of pasta, amidst the steady noise of sifters and rollers, enveloped in the warm air thick with clouds of flour . . . and . . . having abandoned the food trade, took to selling ceramic and earthenware crockery – jars, plates, jugs, all the bright flowery pottery with which the craftsmen of Castelli adorn the tables of Abruzzi. Amidst those rustic, one could almost say religious, shapes, unchanged throughout the centuries, he lived, very simply – sneezing continually.

Tales of Pescara, Gabriele d'Annunzio

Maccheroni alla chitarra e sugo di agnello
Chitarra Spaghetti with Lamb Sauce

Although this is simpler and more economical than the previous lamb sauce, it's very tasty and is often served with *spaghetti alla chitarra* (see page 40) on Sundays. A main dish for 3.

400g (14 oz) chitarra spaghetti	*1 tumbler dry white wine*
200g (7 oz) lamb, minced or chopped in small pieces	*200g (7 oz) fresh or tinned tomatoes, skinned and chopped*
2 tablespoons good olive oil	
1 clove garlic	*1 fresh or dried chilli (or less)*
a pinch of rosemary – fresh is best	*1–2 tablespoons grated pecorino romano cheese*

Brown the meat gently in the oil with the crushed garlic and chopped rosemary. Pour in the wine and let it bubble and evaporate a little. Then add the tomatoes, and some chilli, and simmer the sauce slowly for 30 minutes or more, seasoning with salt to taste.

Have ready a large pan of boiling salted water and cook the pasta *al dente*. Drain, place it in a warm pasta bowl, add 1 or 2 tablespoons of cheese, then the sauce, and mix lightly at table.

Maccheroni alla chitarra con pomodoro

Chitarra Spaghetti with Tomato

This recipe is unusual in that it uses smoked bacon. It makes a nice homely dish for 5–6 – a good quick lunch.

600g (1 lb 5 oz) chitarra spaghetti or macaroni	*600g (1 lb 5 oz) fresh skinned and chopped tomatoes*
100g (3½ oz) smoked bacon, in a thick slice	*1 fresh or dried chilli*
2 tablespoons olive oil	*grated pecorino romano or provolone cheese*

Put a large pan of salted water to boil for the pasta. Cube the bacon and fry it in the oil until it begins to take colour. Add the tomatoes and as much sliced chilli as you wish. Cook until the sauce is no longer watery, but not for too long; the

Methods and ingredients which may be unfamiliar are explained on pages 26–38.

tomatoes should not become a smooth purée or lose their fresh sweetness. When partly cooked, season to taste with salt.

Cook the pasta *al dente*. Drain, place it in a warm bowl, add the sauce, toss lightly, and serve, passing round the cheese at table.

Fusilli in salsa

Fusilli in Sauce

Another typical dish is *fusilli in salsa* made with chillies, tomatoes, and scamorza cheese: a cheese similar to mozzarella, but harder, which can be found hanging by its raffia cord in many Abruzzi kitchens, and melts to lusciousness among the coils of pasta.

With full-flavoured tomatoes and fresh basil, this classic sauce makes a delightful first course for 3–5, but, like most simple sauces, it depends very much on the quality of the ingredients.

*400g (14 oz) fusilli, long ones
  if possible*
1 garlic clove
1 handful parsley
3 tablespoons olive oil
*1kg (2¼ lb) fresh tomatoes,
  skinned*
a few fresh basil leaves
a piece of fresh or dried chilli
*150g (5 oz) fresh scamorza or
  mozzarella cheese*
*grated pecorino romano or
  Parmesan cheese*

Cook the finely chopped garlic and parsley gently in the oil until they colour slightly. Add the chopped tomatoes, basil, salt to taste, and as much chilli as you like – start with a little piece and taste, and add more if you want, for in Abruzzi they like their pasta fiery. Simmer this for 15–30 minutes, to thicken. Stir it occasionally, tasting and adjusting the seasoning.

Put a large pan of salted water to boil for the pasta. Slice the scamorza or mozzarella. When the sauce is almost ready, cook the pasta. Drain when *al dente* and place it in an oven dish. Add a handful of grated cheese, pour over the sauce, arrange the cheese slices on top, and pop it in a hot oven for just long enough to melt the cheese. Serve immediately.

*The flocks are kept by earth-coloured shepherds, too old to
go up any more to the high pastures. Singing comes up from
the valleys and the old shepherds and their fierce white dogs
under the trees seem the last guardians of Arcady.*

In the Abruzzi, Anne McDonell

Pasta alla pecorara
Pasta the Shepherd's Way

Rich, spicy and decorative: a dish such as shepherds might eat for
a family celebration. An informal main course for 6.

600g (1 lb 5 oz) long fusilli	dried or fresh basil
60g (2 oz) dried porcini	45g (1½ oz) diced aubergine
mushrooms or 150g (5 oz)	45g (1½ oz) diced courgette
button mushrooms	30g (1 oz) chopped pimento
70g (2½ oz) unsmoked bacon,	90g (3 oz) unsalted butter
thickly sliced	75g (2½ oz) pecorino or
8 tablespoons olive oil	Parmesan cheese
1 large onion, thinly sliced	45g (1½ oz) crumbled ricotta
150g (5 oz) minced beef	or curd cheese
1 fresh or dried chilli	30g (1 oz) stoned black
450g (1 lb) fresh tomatoes,	olives
skinned and chopped	

Soak the dried porcini in a little tepid water for at least 30
minutes, or rinse the fresh mushrooms and slice them finely. Cut
the bacon in tiny cubes, and gently brown in half the oil with
the onion and minced beef, stirring so the meat cooks evenly.
After 10–15 minutes add a piece of chilli, the tomatoes, a pinch
of dried basil or a few fresh leaves, and the mushrooms (including
any porcini water, strained through muslin to remove grit).
Season with salt, but no pepper, and simmer gently for 15
minutes.

Meanwhile, put a large pan of salted water to boil for the
pasta, and sauté the aubergine, courgette and pimento gently in
the remaining oil and a tablespoon of butter in a wide casserole.

When tender, remove from the fat and keep warm.

Cook the fusilli while you gently melt the remaining butter in the pan in which the courgettes cooked. Drain the fusilli when *al dente*. Toss them briefly in the butter over a low heat, pour over the sauce, add half the pecorino, mix and transfer to a warmed pasta bowl. Dress the pasta with the remaining pecorino or Parmesan, little pieces of ricotta or curd cheese, the olives, and the diced vegetables, and perhaps some fresh basil leaves.

A bottle or so of wine is needed with the next dish. Rich, and hot with chillies, it comes from near Chieti, a pre-Roman town on the low hills that slope down to the Adriatic. There the wheat grows luxuriantly, and at harvest time, the women used to take wine to the fields at the end of the day in great painted vases.

Fregnacce

Nonsenses

This isn't a sophisticated sauce but it is very good, and it's as fiery and colourful as the people of Abruzzi; a dish they serve to start lunch on Sundays and festival days. The sauce can be made in advance and reheated while the pasta cooks. It serves 4–6.

600g (1 lb 5 oz) lasagnette or pappardelle
1 clove garlic, chopped
10 tablespoons good olive oil
100g (3½ oz) chopped prosciutto ham trimmings
300g (10½ oz) thick unsmoked bacon, diced

1kg (2¼ lb) fresh or tinned tomatoes, skinned and chopped
1 large red pimento
1 fresh or dried chilli
grated pecorino romano cheese

Cook the garlic gently in the oil with the ham and bacon until golden. Add the tomatoes, and a pinch of sugar if the tomatoes are tinned. Simmer them for 30 minutes, adding a little water if it threatens to stick. Remove the stalk and seeds of the pimento, and cut into small squares. Add these to the sauce with as much chopped chilli as you like. Cook for 30 minutes, tasting and seasoning with salt and more chilli if you wish.

Have ready a large pan of salted boiling water to the boil and cook the pasta *al dente*. Drain and serve, as they serve it in Abruzzi, smothered with the sauce in a brightly coloured ceramic bowl, passing round the cheese at table.

Lasagne abruzzesi
Lasagne Abruzzi Style

A really robust lasagne, strongly flavoured with tomato and mushrooms, but without needing the work of those which have white sauce. It takes a little time but can be assembled in advance and heated when you need it. A main course for 4–6.

fresh lasagne made with egg pasta from 300g (10½ oz) plain flour (see pages 17–18) or 300g (10½ oz) packet lasagne

Filling

50g (1¾ oz) dried porcini mushrooms or 200g (7 oz) button mushrooms
1 small onion
1 small carrot
½ celery stalk
200g (7 oz) lean beef mince
a handful parsley
½ tumbler dry white wine
1.6kg (3½ lb) fresh or tinned tomatoes, skinned and sieved

a little unsalted butter
some fine oven-baked breadcrumbs
200g (7 oz) mozzarella or scamorza cheese, in small pieces
2 hardboiled eggs, cut in rings
60g (2 oz) prosciutto trimmings
3 tablespoons olive or sunflower oil

Methods and ingredients which may be unfamiliar are explained on pages 26–38.

Soak the dried mushrooms in a little warm water for 1 hour, till soft and full.

To make the filling, fry the beef gently in the oil with the finely chopped onion, carrot, celery and parsley, stirring, until the meat browns. Add the wine and let it bubble and evaporate a little. If you are using fresh mushrooms, rinse and slice them finely. Add the tomatoes and either type of mushroom. Cover, and simmer very gently, for at least 1 hour, stirring occasionally until the sauce thickens. If it thickens too much add some of the liquid from the dried mushrooms, strained through a muslin or a little wine or water. Season to taste when almost cooked.

Cook the lasagne, as on page 23. Rub a square oven dish, 25cm (10 in) across, with butter and sprinkle the sides and bottom very well with fine dry breadcrumbs. Shake out the excess crumbs, place a layer of pasta so that it comes well up the sides. Spoon in a thin layer of sauce, dot it with pieces of cheese, slices of egg, and fragments of prosciutto. Cover these with a layer of pasta. Continue these layers until the dish is full, finishing with just the sauce.

Dot the top with little pieces of butter and bake in a moderately hot oven for 30 minutes.

Millefoglie alla 'guardiese'
Pasta Layers the Guardia Way

A substantial dish for 8 which can be made in advance, and which heats up beautifully, so it is worth making this quantity and perhaps assembling it between two dishes. The large amount of cheese makes it creamier than *Lasagne abruzzesi*.

fresh lasagne made with egg pasta from 400g (14 oz) plain flour (see pages 17–18) or 400g (14 oz) packet lasagne

Filling

100g (3½ oz) fatty ham, chopped	150g (5 oz) fresh or frozen peas
3 tablespoons olive or sunflower oil	150g (5 oz) button mushrooms
100g (3½ oz) unsalted butter	1 garlic clove
1 tumbler dry white wine	2 scamorza or mozzarella cheeses
1.5kg (3 lb 5 oz) fresh or tinned tomatoes, skinned and chopped	150g (5 oz) grated Parmesan cheese
200g (7 oz) veal mince	

Sauté the ham in the oil and a 'walnut' of butter until golden. Pour in the wine and let it bubble for 5 minutes. Add the tomatoes, season to taste, cover, and simmer for about 30 minutes. Meanwhile, shape the mince into cherry-sized balls, dust them with flour and fry in a little oil. Add the drained meatballs to the tomato sauce.

While the meatballs simmer for 10 minutes, parboil the fresh peas (frozen ones need no pre-cooking). Then clean and slice the mushrooms finely and cook them briefly in a little butter with the whole clove of garlic. Add the peas to the mushrooms and season to taste. Cook together for a minute or so to mingle the flavours. Then remove the sauce from the heat, and add the peas and mushrooms, without the garlic. Cool it slightly before adding the scamorza or mozzarella, cut in little pieces, and three-quarters of the Parmesan. While the sauce cools, cook the lasagne as on page 23.

Rub a large oblong oven dish with butter. Line the bottom with overlapping lasagne squares so that they come up the sides to form a box. Cover them with a thin layer of sauce, then add a layer of pasta. Continue these layers, finishing with a layer of sauce. Sprinkle it with the remaining cheese and put the dish in a hot oven for 20 minutes, until the cheese turns golden. Serve the pasta from the pan.

Before Christmas, Abruzzi shepherds still come to Rome, in their breeches, cloaks and fleecy sheepskin waistcoats, to play traditional Christmas songs, in the traffic-ridden streets, on their *zampogne* – local instruments modelled on the pipes of Pan, but with a windbag of goatskin.

Winters are cold in Abruzzi, and warming pasta is prepared rich with melting cheeses, mince and ham. While on Sundays a succulent leg of lamb is often cooked with tomatoes, garlic and rosemary and its juices used to anoint a steaming mountain of fettuccine.

Cosciotto d'agnello all' abruzzese con fettuccine

Leg of Lamb Abruzzi Style with Fettuccine

An excellent way to cook lamb for a Sunday lunch for 6–8. This uses a complete leg, but the quantities can easily be reduced for a smaller joint. It is worth using fresh fettuccine if you can. Parmesan is traditional with this dish but in some ways pecorino goes even better, and even with no cheese at all this is an excellent meal.

600g (1 lb 5 oz) fettuccine
10 slices unsmoked bacon
2–2.5kg (4–5 lb) leg of lamb
fresh or dried rosemary
4–5 cloves garlic
5 tablespoons oil
1½ tumblers dry white wine
1kg (2 lb 3 oz) fresh or tinned tomatoes

2 tablespoons chopped parsley
fresh oregano (optional)
about 90g (3 oz) unsalted butter
Parmesan cheese
parsley to garnish

Drop the bacon slices into boiling water for 1–2 minutes, then drain. Make little holes all over the lamb with a sharp knife, and insert rosemary and little slivers of garlic, then brush it with oil. Heat the remaining oil in a large casserole and brown the lamb

49

all over with the bacon slices. Add the remaining garlic and the wine and evaporate it a little over fierce heat before adding the tomatoes, parsley, a pinch of oregano, and seasoning to taste. Cook for 1¼ hours over moderate heat, or in a moderate oven, for underdone lamb, or 1¾–2 hours for thoroughly cooked meat.

Have ready a large saucepan of boiling salted water for the fettuccine. When the meat is cooked, set the covered casserole aside while you cook the fettuccine *al dente*. Drain the fettuccine, and put them on a warm oval dish. Dot them generously with unsalted butter, toss to coat them, form into a nest, and lay the leg of lamb on top decorated with the slices of bacon and some chopped parsley. Pass the Parmesan and the sauce from the meat round at table in separate bowls. The most delicious fettuccine are those which lie under the joint and catch its juices as they run out: so, for once, the carver does best.

Up on this wild plain, open to all the winds of heaven, we find tempers of almost flower-like sweetness. We eat our macaroni with the contadini *and set off with our genial landlord as guide.*

In the Abruzzi, Anne McDonell

Ragù per maccheroni carrati
Meat Sauce for Macaroni

This is another very good dish for Sundays. The recipe provides two dishes – pot roast veal to eat at lunch with vegetables, and a meaty pasta sauce for the evening. Or you can start the meal with the pasta and follow it with the meat, as they often do in Italy. Each serves 4–6. You don't have to buy *chitarra* spaghetti; other egg pasta, thin tagliatelle for example, also suits this sauce.

500g (18 oz) chitarra
  spaghetti
½ onion, sliced
1 tablespoon oil
20g (¾ oz) lardo or bacon fat
1kg (2¼ lb) joint of breast
  of veal
½ tumbler dry white wine

120g (4 oz) mushrooms
60g (2 oz) unsalted butter
200g (7 oz) chicken livers
500g (18 oz) fresh tomatoes,
  skinned and chopped
good grated Parmesan or
  pecorino cheese

Soften the onion in a little oil in a casserole just large enough to take the meat. When it turns golden put in the chopped lardo or bacon fat, and the meat dusted with flour. Brown the meat nicely all over, season it and pour in the wine. Add a tumbler of water and simmer very gently for about 2 hours, or until it is really tender, being careful the liquid does not cook away. (Easier still – though it isn't traditional – cook in an oven at gas mark 3, or 325°F, 160°C.) Set aside the juices and 200g (7 oz) meat for the pasta sauce and eat the rest as a main course, with vegetables.

To make the pasta sauce, chop the reserved meat from the joint. Rinse the mushrooms, slice them finely, and sauté them gently in butter for 3 minutes. Add the well-chopped livers and cook them until they no longer look pink. Then put in the veal, the juices the veal cooked in, and the tomatoes. Season to taste, cover, and simmer gently for 45 minutes.

Cook the pasta in plenty of boiling salted water. Drain when *al dente*, place in a warm bowl and top with the sauce. Add a little pat of butter and some cheese to each serving.

2 APULIA

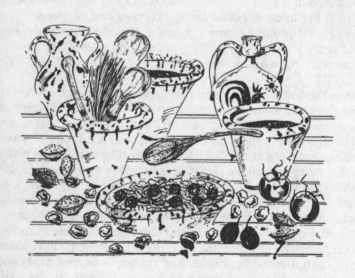

To visit Apulia's little coastal towns is to really see the south: white Moorish architecture, turrets, narrow alleys and hidden courtyards have an exotic air found nowhere else in Italy. Summer nights are warm, and garden trees waft their scent over white walls where brilliant bougainvillea softens to velvet in the evening light. Its whitewashed villages relieve a landscape which is harshly dry; a flat land where plantations of hundred-year-old olive trees form a seemingly boundless sea of silver green interrupted only by the brighter green of the vines grown *a tendone*, as tall as a man, then arched overhead to form a cool roof above the burning, bright red earth.

Here and there are dotted white islands – *trulli* – the characteristic houses of this area: circular, almost Eastern in style, their thick whitewashed walls are topped by curious cone-shaped roofs. These are the homes of farmers who tend vines, which produce heady wines, and olives yielding an oil so richly flavoured it is enjoyed only in Apulia.

Beside the *trulli* grow almond trees which, in springtime, hide each house in a foam of white blossom, and in summer provide the nuts for *latte di mandorla* – milk of almonds – the most refreshing drink for the burning heat of the south. At the same time, grazing in the shade of the almond trees, the family's goats wait, unwittingly, to be the pride of the table on the next feast day.

Sunk in the outside walls are ovens, domed like the *trullo* itself, where on special occasions succulent kid or lamb is roasted by the fierce heat of glowing wood embers, with slithers of garlic, on a bed of golden potatoes, the whole panful scented with rosemary sprigs nipped from the bushes that line the lanes. Surrounding the roast are pans of stuffed vegetables, and the sauce for pasta.

Feast days excepted, the food is simple, using excellent vegetables, fresh fish and abundant pasta. The speciality, made from semolina, being *orecchiette* – little ears – because of their shape. Semolina is made from durum wheat and Apulia was once one of the regions where it grew profusely so orecchiette are inherited from the cooking of that time.

Orecchiette
Little Ears

Making orecchiette is easy, and it's a slow, soothing occupation for a wet Sunday afternoon. They can also be found in packets – those made by Agnesi, for example, are very good. Alternatively, try the traditional sauce with other pasta the size of an average coin, such as shells. This makes enough for 4–5, but it may well feed more, for orecchiette are more filling than most forms of pasta.

600g (1 lb 5 oz) semolina

Mix as for non-egg pasta (page 18) to make a stiff mixture. After kneading for at least 15 minutes, roll it between your hands into long cords as thick as a finger. Slice the cords thinly and shape each slice into a little ear by hollowing it with your thumb or the tip of a knife – of course, they don't have to look exactly like little ears. Place them on a tray sprinkled with semolina to dry for several hours before cooking.

Cook them like any other pasta, remembering that the timing will depend on their thickness. Be prepared for rustic pasta to take far longer than packet varieties. Serve them with any of the following sauces, but whatever sauce you choose this is still heavy peasant food, not designed for a smart occasion.

Orecchiette

Orecchiette e broccoletti di rape
Little Ears with Turnip Tops (or Broccoli)

Those who grow their own vegetables can eat orecchiette in the way most typical of Apulia – with turnip tops – but this very simple sauce with its unusual combination of flavours also works well with broccoli. A first course for 4–5.

600g (1 lb 5 oz) fresh orecchiette or 450g (1 lb) packet orecchiette
1kg (2 lb 3 oz) turnip tops, or fresh or frozen broccoli

2 cloves garlic, sliced
6 tablespoons olive oil
4–6 anchovy fillets, drained of oil
freshly ground black pepper

Rinse the vegetables well. Remove any hard stalk from the turnip tops, or cut the broccoli heads into small sections and prepare the stalk by stripping off the woody outer layers and cutting the inside into diagonal slices. Cook either vegetable in a little boiling salted water till just tender and put a large pan of salted water to boil for the pasta.

Soften the garlic in the oil over gentle heat. Add the pounded anchovy fillets, stir, and add the turnip tops or broccoli. Cook this sauce gently, crushing the ingredients with a fork. Meanwhile, cook the pasta. Drain the orecchiette when just cooked and put them, in a warm bowl, in alternate layers with the sauce, seasoning each layer well with black pepper. Serve at once. No cheese is added, but a trickle of fine olive oil is a nice addition.

Orecchiette al pomodoro
Little Ears with Tomatoes

In this arid region, sheep and pigs are more common than cattle, and sauces are often made with pork or lamb rather than beef. Fresh meat is best for this, but it can also be made with the minced leftover meat from a joint. Although unheard of in Abruzzi, Cheddar goes very well with it. A final variation is to season with a little fresh or dried chilli. A good family meal for 4–5.

600g (1 lb 5 oz) fresh orecchiette (see page 53–4) or 450g (1 lb) packet orecchiette or short pasta
300g (11 oz) minced pork or lamb
2 cloves garlic, chopped

2 tablespoons olive oil
1 small onion, finely chopped
500g (18 oz) fresh or tinned tomatoes, skinned and chopped
1 tablespoon chopped parsley
grated Parmesan cheese

Brown the mince lightly with the garlic in olive oil. Add the onion, tomatoes and parsley, cover, and simmer gently for at least 1 hour. Stir the sauce occasionally, adding a very little water if it gets too dry, and add salt to taste towards the end.

Cook the pasta in plenty of boiling salted water. Drain, place in a warm bowl, top with the sauce and plenty of grated cheese, and serve at once, passing round more cheese at table.

Orecchiette del trullo

Little Ears Trullo Style

This is a most attractive rustic dish. It serves 6 or more, and makes a good family main dish.

500g (18 oz) orecchiette or similar pasta
a handful fresh breadcrumbs
a little milk
200g (7 oz) finely minced lamb
1 egg
thyme or chopped parsley
a grating of nutmeg
1 small onion
a finger-length celery
½ carrot
1 clove garlic
5 tablespoons olive oil
700g (1 lb 9 oz) fresh or tinned tomatoes, skinned and chopped
basil leaves (optional)
grated pecorino romano cheese

Soak the breadcrumbs in a little milk, squeeze them out and place them in a basin with the mince, the egg, and a pinch of thyme or a tablespoon of chopped parsley. Season with salt, pepper and nutmeg. Mix together well and, with floured hands, shape into meat balls no bigger than a hazelnut.

Soften the finely chopped onion, celery, carrot and garlic in the oil. Add the tomatoes and basil, season with salt, and simmer gently for 15–20 minutes, stirring and adding a little water if it threatens to stick. Add the meat balls and simmer for 15 minutes more.

While the meat balls cook, bring a large pan of water to the boil and cook the pasta *al dente*. Drain and transfer to a warm pasta bowl. Top with the sauce and a handful of grated pecorino cheese. Mix at table.

Fusilli della rivoluzione
Revolutionary Fusilli

They have a revolutionary way of making tomato sauce in a *trullo* oven. It's a great timesaver and tastes quite different from tomato sauces made on top of the stove. A light dish for 4–5.

500g (1 lb 2 oz) short pasta
800g (1 lb 12 oz) pulped
  tomatoes
3 tablespoons olive oil
2 cloves garlic, chopped
some basil leaves

a piece of fresh or dried chilli
½ handful oven-baked
  breadcrumbs
½ handful grated Parmesan
  cheese

Simply put the tomatoes, oil, garlic, torn basil and a little chopped chilli in a casserole, season to taste, sprinkle on the dry ingredients and bake in a hot oven for 25 minutes, without disturbing the crust. Cook the pasta *al dente* in plenty of boiling water, drain, place in a warm bowl and spoon over the sauce.

On special occasions in Apulia, when joints of meat are roasted in the *trulli* ovens, a really good broth is a favourite start to the meal. In it float little *grattatini*.

Grattatini di pasta
Little Pasta Gratings

A beautifully simple way to embellish a really good broth for 6.

75g (2½ oz) soft
  breadcrumbs
1.5 litre (3 pints) good broth
250g (9 oz) plain flour

30g (1 oz) good Parmesan
  cheese, grated
a pinch nutmeg
4 egg yolks

Soak the breadcrumbs in a little broth. Squeeze them out, and mix to a really stiff paste with the other ingredients. Then grate the lump of paste on a cheese grater letting the 'crumbs' fall on to a floured tray. Spread out and allow to dry a little before cooking in broth for about 5–8 minutes. Serve the broth with grated Parmesan at table.

If you make too many, dry the spare 'crumbs' thoroughly, and keep them in a jar to use another time.

Apulians make courgette sauces from various combinations of tomatoes, cheese, eggs and herbs, and the courgettes are cut in long slices, or rings or little dice, as the cook fancies. Whatever their shape, courgettes are at their best when lightly cooked: too much cooking spoils their delicate flavour. In Italy the flowers are sold separately, in bunches, to be stuffed with mozzarella and anchovy fillets, dipped in batter and deep-fried: a wonderful antipasto to enjoy while waiting for the pasta to be served.

Pasta con zucchine
Pasta with Courgettes

There are two versions of this delicate first course for 5–6. First the simplest, most economical version.

I

600g (1 lb 5 oz) spaghetti, or short pasta
1kg (2 lb 3 oz) tender young courgettes
8–9 tablespoons olive oil
2 garlic cloves, chopped
a pinch of fresh thyme
½ tumbler dry white wine (optional)
500g (18 oz) fresh or tinned tomatoes, skinned and chopped
fresh basil or parsley

Methods and ingredients which may be unfamiliar are explained on pages 26–38.

Rinse the courgettes and cut them into small dice. Warm the oil in a wide shallow casserole and sauté the courgettes gently with the garlic and fresh thyme (if you don't have fresh thyme leave it out, as dried thyme spoils the fresh flavour of the courgettes). Season with salt and pepper, and when the courgettes begin to turn golden pour in the wine and let it cook away a little. Add the tomatoes and simmer gently until the courgettes are *just* tender, tasting and adjusting the seasoning.

Have ready a large pan of boiling salted water. Cook the pasta *al dente*. Drain, place it in a warm bowl, add the sauce, and mix lightly. Serve, decorated with the fresh basil or parsley.

II

Alternatively, you can make the sauce using 700g (1 lb 9 oz) tomatoes but rather less oil, and put 300g (11 oz) diced mozzarella in a warm pasta bowl. Then, when the sauce is ready, it is mixed with the cooked pasta and tossed quickly with the mozzarella, which melts into long strings – delicious to eat but a devil to serve.

Apulia lies between two seas, so fishing is important, especially round the big ports of Bari and Brindisi, and at Taranto where oyster and mussel beds abound. On hot summer nights down on the waterfront, milk of almonds, delicious and refreshing, is sipped on terraces and at bars, while the smell of fish grilled on charcoal, or simmered with wine, wafts from the trattorias. On the menu a pasta dish may be indicated as *rosso* (red) or *in bianco* (white), meaning with or without tomato. The seafood is so good here it is usually eaten *in bianco*.

Spaghetti alla tarantina
Spaghetti Taranto Style

The simplicity of this dish makes it one for true mussel lovers. A first course or very light lunch for 4–5.

500–550g (18–20 oz) spaghetti	1–3 cloves garlic, chopped
1.5kg (3½ lb) mussels in their shells	6–7 tablespoons good olive oil
	fresh parsley, chopped
½ tumbler dry white wine	freshly ground black pepper

Clean and prepare the mussels, as on page 29. Put a large saucepan of salted water to boil for the pasta. When the water is almost ready put the mussels in another large pan over a fairly high flame. The water still clinging to the shells after washing should be enough liquid but you can add half a tumbler of water or, better still, white wine. Cover and cook for about 5 minutes, until the shells open – be careful, as overcooking makes them rubbery. Throw away any that refused to open and remove the rest from their shells. Strain their liquid through a muslin to remove any sand. Put the spaghetti in the boiling water to cook.

Meanwhile, soften the garlic gently in the oil and before it turns golden add the mussels, give them a quick stir, pour in a ladleful or so of their liquid, and then they are ready. Drain the spaghetti when *al dente*, add it to the mussel pan, mix briefly together over the lowest heat and serve, garnished with chopped parsley. Add freshly ground pepper at table.

Spaghetti ai frutti di mare
Seafood Spaghetti

Conger eel is a rich and unusual addition to shellfish pasta and well worth tracking down. A main course for 4–5.

500g (18 oz) spaghetti
1.25kg (2 lb 12 oz) assorted
   shellfish (e.g., clams and
   mussels) or 600g (1 lb 5 oz)
   frozen shellfish
500g (18 oz) peeled and
   chopped tomatoes

7–8 tablespoons good olive oil
2 garlic cloves, sliced
5–6 slices conger eel, each 5cm
   (2 in) thick
2 tablespoons chopped parsley
300g (11 oz) peeled shrimps,
   fresh or frozen

Clean and check the mussels and clams, see page 29. Then open them over a brisk heat and remove them from their shells as in the previous recipe. Thaw frozen fish as instructed on the packet.

Warm the oil and garlic in a wide pan. When the garlic begins to colour add the eel, tomatoes, half the parsley, and season to taste. Cover and simmer gently, stirring occasionally for 20 minutes, or until the eel is tender. Add the thawed shrimps and the shellfish and simmer gently for no more than 10 minutes, for shellfish become tough if overcooked.

Have ready a large pan of boiling salted water and when the sauce is almost ready cook the spaghetti. Drain when *al dente* and place in a warm bowl. Serve the spaghetti on to each plate, spoon over some sauce and top with a slice of eel and some parsley.

3 CALABRIA

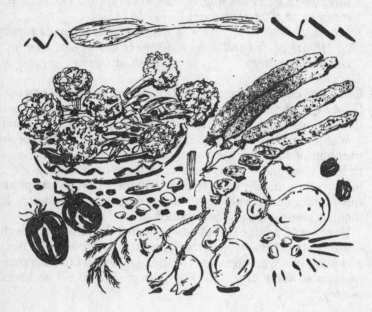

Calabria is a poor land; a place of lifelong feuds, with its own laws, culture and creed. The long magnificent coastline is bordered with Mediterranean evergreens – myrtle, agave and Indian fig – which withstand the long parched summers, while its mountains are wooded with pine and fir. The land is dramatically beautiful; not easily forgotten by those who visit it. In small villages women still wear black anonymous dresses and seem always to be waiting at the doors of their simple homes for fate to overtake them.

In spite of the poverty, Calabria's food is full of variety. The soil produces fruit and vegetables which are highly flavoured – small for lack of rain, but richly sun-drenched. Sweet tomatoes, scarlet pimentos, fiery chillies, deep mauve aubergines, resiny pine kernels, dusted purple from the cones, and local raisins all make wonderful ingredients for pasta sauces.

Calabria

There is an old Calabrian saying that a woman cannot marry until she knows fifteen ways to make pasta – the pasta itself, not the sauces which go with it – which shows how important homemade pasta is in this region. Here you find homemade *pizzicotti* (pinches), *schiaffettoni* (big smacks), *ricci di donna* (ladies' curls), *cappidu angilu* (angels' hair), *rascatelli* (scrapings), *stranguglia prieuti* (priest stranglers), *cannarouzzoli* (husband chokers), and even *paternostri* (our father's). The Calabrian housewife has a different pasta for every occasion and for all tastes, but you need considerable practice to make them, so we have not suggested that you try. The Calabrian passion for pasta may be reflected as much in the husband's eating as in the wife's cooking.

He does not eat them with deliberate mastication; he does not even – like your ordinary amateur – drink them in separate gulps; but he contrives, by some adroit process of levitation, that the whole plateful shall rise in a noiseless and unbroken flood from the table to his mouth, where it glides down his gullet with the relentless ease of a river pouring into a cavern.

Old Calabria, Norman Douglas

Vermicelli alla calabrese

Vermicelli the Calabrian Way

A typically Calabrian combination of flavours, and for this peasant dish the sheep's cheese, pecorino, is essential. Using the special Italian pig fat, lardo – not the same as lard – gives this the heavy, curiously comforting taste one finds in British lardy cake. A first course for 4–5.

500g (18 oz.) vermicelli, spaghetti or bucatini
3 large red or yellow pimentos
70g (2½ oz lardo or ham fat, chopped

4 tablespoons olive oil
1 clove garlic, finely chopped
5 tablespoons pecorino sardo cheese, grated

Rinse the pimento, removing the stalk and seeds, and cut it into stamp-sized pieces. Put the lardo in a heavy pan with the oil, garlic and pimentos. Cook very gently, stirring frequently to stop the vegetables burning, until the pimentos are soft.

Cook the pasta in plenty of boiling salted water. Meanwhile, add 2 tablespoons of pecorino to the pimentos, stir and remove from the heat. Drain the pasta when *al dente*, toss it briefly in the sauce, and serve, passing round extra pecorino at table.

A variation is to add 350g (12 oz) fresh tomatoes, skinned and chopped, when the garlic and lardo have softened and begun to colour.

Broccoli is popular and naturally finds its way into a number of pasta dishes – though it's often considered a peasant vegetable. A country rhyme goes:

> I've always eaten broccoli
> I've always worn clogs
> Few wits in my head.

Peasant or not, in Calabria they create unexpected combinations which make it worthy of any table.

Spaghetti chi 'vruoccoli arriminata'
Calabrian Spaghetti with Broccoli

In Calabria they use purple broccoli with large heads similar to cauliflowers – sometimes called cape broccoli in Britain – or large green broccoli. Cauliflower will do, but broccoli's contrasting colour and flavour makes it more interesting; with cauliflower you may prefer the contrast of wholemeal spaghetti. A light and easy first course for 5–6.

Methods and ingredients which may be unfamiliar are explained on pages 26–38.

600g (1 lb 5 oz) spaghetti
 or bucatini
1kg (2¼ lb) broccoli with
 large heads or 1 medium-
 sized cauliflower
3 cloves garlic, crushed
7 tablespoons olive oil

800g (1 lb 12 oz) fresh
 tomatoes, skinned and
 chopped
30g (1 oz) pine nuts
90g (3 oz) raisins
1½ tablespoons chopped
 parsley

Rinse the broccoli well in salt water, and divide the heads into very small florets. Put a large pan of salted water to boil for the pasta, and a smaller one to boil for the broccoli or cauliflower.

Cook the garlic gently in the oil till slightly golden, add the tomatoes, and simmer for about 10 minutes. Add the pine nuts and raisins and continue simmering while you cook the broccoli or cauliflower so it remains slightly crisp, and the pasta is *al dente*. Drain both. Put the pasta in a warm bowl, top with the florets and then the sauce. Sprinkle with parsley and serve, mixing lightly at table.

High among the beeches and chestnut trees, in the thickly wooded Sila region, grow pines. On summer outings whole families collect the purple pine nuts which spill from their fallen cones, to be treasured and stored in tins till needed, then cracked open to release the ivory kernel that adds its sweetly resinous flavour to many Calabrian dishes.

Vermicelli al sugo di carne
Vermicelli with Meat Sauce

A really meaty sauce from the Sila region to the north of Calabria – a main course for a family of 5.

500g (18 oz) vermicelli or
    spaghetti
a handful of pine kernels
60g (2 oz) button mushrooms
olive or sunflower oil
thyme
1 small onion, finely chopped
1 small carrot, finely chopped
a finger-length stalk of celery,
    finely chopped
2 garlic cloves, crushed

150g (5 oz) beef mince
150g (5 oz) pork mince
a bay leaf
1 tumbler dry white wine
½–1 tablespoon concen-
    trated tomato paste
a little broth
unsalted butter
grated Parmesan or pecorino
    sardo or caciocavallo
    cheese

Toast the pine kernels golden brown in a moderate oven – a matter of minutes. Rinse the mushrooms, slice finely, and sauté briefly in 1 tablespoon oil with a pinch of thyme. Set aside. Sauté the onion, carrot and celery in 2 tablespoons oil. When they begin to soften, add the meat, garlic and bay leaf. Cook, stirring until the mince browns slightly. Stir in the wine, half the tomato paste, the mushrooms and most of the pine kernels. Cover and simmer gently for 45 minutes, stirring occasionally and adding a spoonful or so of broth if it becomes dry, and more tomato paste if necessary.

Cook the pasta *al dente* in plenty of boiling salted water. Drain, transfer to a warm bowl, add the sauce, mix well, add the remaining pine nuts, and serve immediately. Parmesan or pecorino or, better still, caciocavallo (see below), can be added to each serving and a pat of butter is also a nice addition.

Hanging in the shops of Calabrian villages are wonderful hams, sausages dusted scarlet with paprika, salamis studded with peppercorns, and huge cheeses – like golden Aladdin's lamps – glowing above trays full of dried fruits, figs stuffed with white almonds, dried chestnuts, raisins, and jars of mountain honey.

The cheese – also made in Apulia and Lucania – is caciocavallo. *Cacio* is the general name for cheese of any sort, and *cavallo* means horse, but nobody knows for certain why the cheese has this name. Perhaps because it was once shaped like a horse – there are still cheeses shaped like animals in southern

Italy – or maybe because its characteristic pear shape with a string round its neck could hang from a saddle or across a peg in couples mounted or *a cavallo*. Buttery yellow with a slightly smoky flavour, it melts into finer, less rubbery threads than mozzarella.

The ham is *capocollo*, made from the back of the pig near the head, salted, rinsed in wine, enclosed in a membrane, tied like a large salami, and smoked. It must then age for at least six months before being eaten. It is a real delicacy and, like prosciutto, usually eaten in thin slices as an antipasto, but the off cuts are used in cooking. This recipe uses both these specialities but it works well with the substitutes.

Maccheroni alla calabrese

Calabrian Macaroni

An excellent lunch dish for 4 which can be made with cheap off cuts of prosciutto.

400g (14 oz) long macaroni, bucatini or ziti
100g (3½ oz) capocollo or prosciutto
5 tablespoons olive oil
½ medium-sized onion, finely chopped
1 handful chopped parsley
½ garlic clove, crushed
a piece chilli
600g (1 lb 5 oz) fresh tomatoes, skinned and chopped
200g (7 oz) caciocavallo or provolone cheese, diced

Put a large pan of salted water to boil for the pasta. Chop the prosciutto, and sauté in the oil, with the onion, parsley, garlic and enough chilli to make the dish slightly peppery. When they soften and colour slightly, add the tomatoes, season with salt and cook gently for about 10 minutes.

Cook the pasta, broken in thirds, and drain when *al dente*. Place a layer on a greased oven dish, dot with cheese, then with spoonfuls of sauce. Continue for three or four layers, ending with sauce. Put the dish in a hot oven for a few minutes, to just melt the cheese. Serve at once.

Maccheroni alla carrettaia

Wagoners' Macaroni

Rustic pasta like this tastes even better off wood, and shallow, rectangular, wooden dishes, the size of a chopping board, are sold in local markets and fairs in many parts of Italy. Failing such a platter, a peasant dish like wagoners' macaroni is best suited to a pottery bowl rather than delicate china.

This sauce uses a minimum of ingredients and equipment but it makes a good simple meal for 2–3, and is almost as good with packet pasta.

egg pasta made with 250g (9 oz) plain flour but only 1 egg, see pages 17–18, or 250g (9 oz) packet macaroni, fusilli or orecchiette

Sauce
1 onion, finely chopped
unsalted butter, oil or lard
100g (3½ oz) good, coarsely minced beef
1 tumbler dry red or white wine

1 tablespoon tomato paste
grated pecorino romano cheese

Roll the pasta thinly and cut it in ribbons wide enough to wrap round a no. 7 knitting needle, cut these in 5–10cm (2–4 in) lengths, shape round the knitting needle and spread on a tray dusted with semolina to dry.

Shaping rustic macaroni

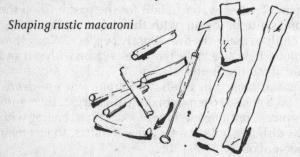

Soften the onion gently in the fat or oil. Add the beef and cook, stirring, till it browns slightly, then mix in the wine and tomato paste. Simmer very gently for at least 40 minutes, adding a touch of water, or better still more wine, if it becomes dry. Season to taste.

Cook the pasta *al dente* in a large pan of boiling salted water. Drain, add a generous amount of pecorino, then the meat sauce. Stir and serve.

Maccheroni alla salsiccia

Macaroni with Spicy Sausage

Sausages are *piccante* – spicy – in the south and combine well with cabbage for a quick, economical and very tasty family dish. If Italian sausages can't be found, substitute the meatiest sausages you can find (see page 36) and season well with ground black pepper before cooking. A simple main course for 5–6.

500g (1 lb 2 oz) long
  macaroni
200–300g (7–10 oz) spicy
  Italian sausages
4 tablespoons olive oil
½ tumbler dry white wine

a little broth
½ medium-sized green
  cabbage
2 handfuls grated pecorino
  romano cheese
freshly ground black pepper

Skin the sausages, break them into small pieces, and sauté gently in the oil till nicely brown. Add the wine, raise the heat and evaporate by half. Then add about a ladleful of broth (or water and a fragment of good bouillon cube), and simmer for 15 minutes, adding a touch more broth if the liquid cooks away.

Meanwhile, put a large pan of salted water to boil for the pasta. Shred and rinse the cabbage. When the sausages are almost ready put the pasta in to cook. Take a bite of pasta from time to time and when it's almost cooked add the cabbage to it. Cook them together briefly until the pasta is *al dente* and the cabbage still slightly crisp. Drain and place in a warm pasta bowl. Pour over the sausage pieces with their liquid, add the cheese, and a good grind of black pepper. Serve, mixing lightly together, with extra cheese at table.

Spaghetti alla Carmelina
Little Carmel's Spaghetti

This delicious recipe is for fresh baby squid, but you can make it with any good squid, and they don't have to be tiny. A first course or a light lunch for 4–6.

500g (18 oz) spaghetti
600g (1 lb 5 oz) fresh or frozen
  squid
6 tablespoons olive oil
½–1 clove garlic, finely
  chopped

1 chilli
1 tumbler dry white wine
3–4 fresh medium-sized
  tomatoes, skinned and
  chopped
1 tablespoon chopped parsley

Clean the squid, as on page 36. Then dry, and cut the squid into thin, finger-length strips. Sauté these in the oil in a shallow pan, for a few minutes, with the garlic, and a little piece of chilli (taste it before deciding how much to put in). Then add the wine, tomatoes and parsley. Season with salt and simmer very gently for about 40 minutes, until the squid is tender – stirring occasionally and adding more wine if it cooks away. Taste, adjust the seasoning and keep warm.

Cook the spaghetti *al dente*, in plenty of boiling salted water. Drain, and toss briefly with the squid over a low heat. Transfer to a warm serving dish, which will show off the little pinky-white curls of squid sitting prettily on the spaghetti. Scatter with parsley, and serve.

Another version omits the tomatoes, but the sauce is then thinner and you lose the charming pink and white of tomato and squid combined.

Methods and ingredients which may be unfamiliar are explained on pages 26–38.

4 CAMPANIA

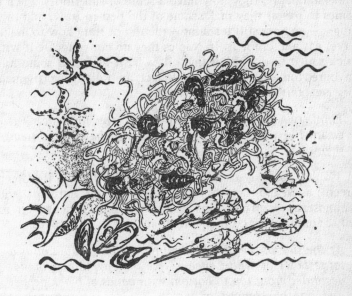

 Here southern Italy begins. The hills are sharper than in the gentle Roman countryside, and the impressive coastline is fringed with inlets, coves and jutting rocks; the jagged line broken only by the silver half-moon curve of the Bay of Naples. Its ancient honey-coloured buildings are backed by the imposing cone of Vesuvius.

Life in Campania is focused on Naples and on little coastal towns like Sorrento, and the cooking reflects this. The fertile black volcanic soil provides an abundance of produce: in particular deep-red plum tomatoes, wonderfully fresh and sweet, which, combined with mozzarella cheese made from the milk of cows and buffalo that graze inland, form the basis of Campania's cooking.

At one time the rest of Italy derided Neapolitans for being 'leaf eaters' who only ate pasta on special occasions: the laughter was short-lived. Aided by an ideal climate, the ingenious Neapolitans perfected durum-wheat pasta and built the first pasta factory. Understandably, they now have a sense of superiority when it comes to pasta: they make some of the best in Italy, and they taught – and are still teaching – the rest of Italy how to make, serve, eat and enjoy it. In Naples they do not suffocate it with thick sauce; a dribble of fine oil, a basil leaf, and some full-flavoured tomatoes are enough. In fact, an Italian advertisement for a Neapolitan brand of pasta reads:

> *Think twice before laughing at the way foreigners eat pasta. Every Neapolitan may smile at the way you eat them.*

In Naples pasta is cooked perfectly – *Verdi! Verdi!* (Green! Green!) as Neapolitans say. Not green in colour, but so *al dente* it almost stands on end. This is how street-sellers once sold it, for only a couple of pence, in squares from huge bubbling pans.

> *At the side of the great steaming macaroni cauldron is a large bowl of white cheese, like an Egyptian pyramid, decorated from top to bottom with bands of black pepper and on the summit of which is placed a tomato, or sometimes even a red flower.*
>
> *Neapolitan Ways and Customs*, De Bourcard

For an extra penny you could have a spoonful of fresh tomato sauce, cooked without oil, flavoured with basil – and in Garibaldi's time this bore his name. The spaghetti was eaten with the fingers, off paper, by workers in their break and by those who came to watch the singers and actors who busked in the streets of Naples. Now the macaroni-sellers and street-performers have vanished, and workmen return home for their midday meal, but the sauces they eat with spaghetti remain the same: simpler than in central and northern Italy and often vegetarian, and all the year round the summery scent of Naples's famous tomato sauce wafts from open windows, along alleys perpetually festooned with lines of washing.

Methods and ingredients which may be unfamiliar are explained on pages 26–38.

Spaghetti al pomodoro
Spaghetti with Tomato Sauce

The classic tomato sauce, which is found all over Italy, originated in Campania. Carefully made, with full-flavoured ripe tomatoes and fresh basil, it is excellent; but if the tomatoes are poor, or the basil dried, there is no concealing the fact. This quantity serves 5–6 and is the basic tomato sauce for other recipes, though some people may prefer one of the variations.

I

600g (1 lb 5 oz) spaghetti or other long, slim pasta
2–3 garlic cloves
4 tablespoons good olive oil

1.25kg (2 lb 12 oz) fresh ripe tomatoes
4–6 small fresh basil leaves

Put a large pan of water to boil ready for the pasta. Colour the crushed garlic lightly in the oil over gentle heat. Add the finely chopped and sieved tomatoes, the torn basil and some salt to taste. Simmer for about 10 minutes to evaporate the tomato water and thicken slightly. Cook the pasta *al dente*. Drain, top with the sauce, and decorate with a few more basil leaves. Cheese is not usually added.

II

Another version is to cook the tomatoes and herbs alone and only add the oil on serving.

II

Those who dislike garlic can use half a finely chopped onion cooked in 6 tablespoons oil. The sauce is simmered for 30 minutes and 3–4 basil leaves are added in the last few minutes. The long cooking means tinned tomatoes can be used for this recipe.

Any of these sauces are excellent with the spinach- and ricotta-filled pastas of other regions, but reduce the garlic and add little flakes of butter to the cooked pasta before dressing it with the sauce.

Spaghetti con salsa a crudo
Spaghetti with Raw Tomato Sauce

Cheap, quick, foolproof, cold tomato sauces are eaten all over Campania. The first, and classic, version is perfect with Italian tomatoes, but some other varieties lose their fresh summery taste when skinned, so the recipe using unskinned tomatoes may be better. Either will make an effortless first course for 4–6 on a warm evening.

I

500g (18 oz) spaghetti or
  similar pasta
500g (18 oz) full-flavoured ripe
  tomatoes, skinned and
  chopped

6 tablespoons good olive oil
1 clove garlic, crushed
10 fresh basil leaves, chopped

Put the tomatoes in a bowl and crush with a fork. Add the oil, garlic, half the basil and season to taste. Mix, cover, and set aside for a couple of hours for the flavours to mingle.

Cook the pasta *al dente* in boiling salted water. Drain, mix it with the sauce and serve decorated with the remaining basil. It will not be piping hot but Italians find food that is neither too hot nor too cold the most refreshing.

II

For an alternative version, the tomatoes are chopped with their skins on, and you need 7–8 tablespoons olive oil, 2 crushed garlic cloves, 3–4 torn basil leaves, salt, and either pepper or a little finely chopped fresh chilli.

Vermicelli all'isola d'Ischia
Vermicelli from the Island of Ischia

A sophisticated cold sauce, quite good enough to start a supper party for 4–6, yet child's play to make.

500g (18 oz) vermicelli or
  spaghetti
800g (1 lb 12 oz) fresh or tinned
  tomatoes, skinned and
  roughly chopped
1 sweet red (or ordinary)
  onion
100g (3½ oz) green olives
  stuffed with pimento

2 garlic cloves
2 tablespoons chopped parsley
80g (2¾ oz) capers
a touch of fresh oregano
  (optional)
5 tablespoons good olive oil
grated Parmesan or pecorino
  romano cheese

Strain the watery juice from the tomatoes. Slice the onion, stuffed olives and garlic finely. Put them in a bowl with the parsley, the capers (chopped if large) and oregano. Season to taste and pour over the olive oil – strong 'Extra Vergine' is best. Cover, and refrigerate for 24 hours.

Cook the spaghetti in plenty of boiling salted water. Meanwhile, squash any oversized pieces of tomato with a fork, and taste and adjust the seasoning. (Some Italians also remove the onion and garlic.) Drain the spaghetti when *al dente*, transfer to a pasta bowl, add the cold sauce, dust well with cheese and mix lightly. Serve immediately.

Vermicelli ai capperi
Vermicelli with Capers

In hot weather this is another cold sauce which makes a lovely start to a meal for 4–6.

500g (18 oz) vermicelli or
  spaghetti
100g (3½ oz) big black olives,
  stoned
100g (3½ oz) capers
50g (1¾ oz) tinned anchovy
  fillets

1 garlic clove
a handful parsley
freshly ground black pepper
6 tablespoons good olive oil
3–4 tablespoons grated
  pecorino sardo cheese

Chop the olives, capers, anchovy fillets, garlic and parsley together finely. Put them in a pasta bowl, with the olive oil, a good grind of black pepper, and pecorino. Stir, cover and refrigerate slightly.

To serve, cook the vermicelli in plenty of boiling salted water. Drain them when *al dente*, leaving a little water clinging to them. Mix them lightly with the sauce, and serve, handing round pecorino if you wish.

The simplest sauce of all is made with only oil and garlic. In this part of Italy they consider it the best stomach-settler at the end of an evening out.

Linguine aglio, olio are so light, so superb, that whoever gets home at dawn after dining out wishes for one thing only, and as a joke suggests it; then, playfully, actually asks the sleepy mistress of the house to make it. And then, very seriously, he eats it, twisting as much as he can round his fork, and this is no easy thing, even experts must put their minds to it, for these long, thin, tongues of pasta drained al dente and almost green – oh! the tenderest mother-of-pearl green, you understand! – dressed with oil that's just gently warmed with the crushed garlic clove, flee from all sides and those that stay, the survivors, are the most tricky to collect together – but they are also the most delicious.

Mario Stefanile

Linguine aglio
olio e peperoncino
Linguine with Garlic, Oil and Chilli

This excellent and unassuming mixture is found, with either linguine or spaghetti, all over central and southern Italy, and is as popular in Rome as in Campania. So much so that carousing Romans often eat it late at night, or even at dawn. To serve 4.

500g (18 oz) linguine or
   spaghetti
6 tablespoons best olive oil

2–3 garlic cloves, chopped
a piece fresh or dried chilli
chopped parsley (optional)

Cook the pasta in plenty of boiling salted water. Meanwhile, warm the oil with the garlic and as much finely chopped chilli as you like – it must soften without browning, or the garlic will become bitter. Drain the pasta when *al dente*, leaving a little water clinging to it. Place in a warm bowl, add the oil mixture and serve, decorated with parsley.

There are pasta fans who insist the pasta should be *saltati* – 'jumped' in the pan with the oil before serving. This method needs *really* undercooked pasta or the extra heat will ruin it.

Linguine con peperoni
Linguine with Pimentos

A simple sauce which makes an excellent and inexpensive first course for 3–4.

400g (14 oz) linguine or
   spaghetti
3 large red or yellow
   pimentos
2 garlic cloves

6 tablespoons good olive oil
1 very small onion, finely
   chopped
chopped parsley

Skin the pimentos, see page 34. Remove the seeds and cut the pimentos into strips – these are the roast peppers served, dressed and cold, all over Italy in summer. Let the garlic turn golden in the oil in a large shallow pan. Remove it, lower the heat, put in the onion and pimentos, and season with salt. Cook them for almost an hour, so gently that they simply melt in the oil. Keep warm.

Cook the pasta in plenty of boiling salted water. Drain when *al dente*, toss it briefly with the peppers, place on a warm dish, sprinkle with parsley and serve. The leftovers are quite good cold, with just a squeeze of lemon juice.

Pasta e patate

Pasta and Potatoes

Soups in this region are hearty, and so thick that the spoon stands in the pan. You can add more liquid if you prefer, but this is not so much a soup as a cheap and tasty meal in a bowl – and an excellent use for the cheese rinds which accumulate when you use real Parmesan. This amount serves 8, but it freezes well, see page 22.

400g (14 oz) short hollow pasta
cheese rinds from Parmesan or pecorino, or a slice of cheese
150g (5 oz) unsmoked bacon, in a single slice
1 large onion

1 small celery stalk
1 medium-sized carrot
olive oil
250g (9 oz) fresh or tinned tomatoes, skinned and chopped
800g (1 lb 12 oz) potatoes

Hard cheese rinds are often added to soups in Italy. First they are scraped clean with a serrated knife, then they are either left in warm water to soften before use or toasted briefly under a grill.

Sauté the finely chopped bacon, onion, celery and carrot in a soup pan with a little olive oil and cook until light brown. Add the tomatoes and cook for a minute or two before adding the potatoes, peeled and cut in small dice. Season with salt and pepper, add the cheese and enough water to cover the vegetables. Cover the soup and simmer, stirring occasionally, and adding enough water to stop it catching. When the potatoes are cooked add the pasta, and more boiling water and salt if needed. Serve as soon as the pasta is cooked.

The cheese should have given its flavour to the soup, otherwise add grated Parmesan at the table and freshly ground black pepper.

Methods and ingredients which may be unfamiliar are explained on pages 26–38.

Vermicelli alla Posillipo

Vermicelli the Posillipo Way

Posillipo is a charming crest of land between the gulf of Naples and Pozzuoli – Sophia Loren's birthplace. Always noted for its beauty, the ancient Romans built villas there surrounded with beautiful gardens. This dish, with its lovely blue-grey mussels and coral-pink prawns against the pasta, is a suitably impressive first course for 6, or main course for 4–5.

Each shellfish needs separate cooking, so it looks complicated written down, but the actual cooking is very easy, and the ingredients can be cooked in advance and combined and heated before the meal. With frozen shellfish, use half the quantity of clams and mussels, add their liquid as for fresh shellfish, and simply warm them in the tomato sauce just before serving. If the fresh shellfish are big, buy more to allow for the weight of their shells.

600g (1 lb 5 oz) vermicelli or spaghetti
250g (9 oz) squid, fresh or frozen
3 garlic cloves, sliced
3–4 tablespoons good olive oil
½ tumbler dry white wine
500g (18 oz) fresh mussels
500g (18 oz) fresh clams
a piece fresh or dried chilli (optional)
600g (1 lb 5 oz) fresh or tinned tomatoes, skinned and chopped
500g (18 oz) cooked prawns in their shells
parsley

Clean the squid, as on page 36, and cut into narrow finger-length strips. Sauté the garlic in 1 tablespoon of oil until golden. Add the squid and cook gently for 1–2 minutes before adding the wine. Cook it away slightly, before adding water to almost cover the squid. Simmer gently until tender, adding wine or water if the liquid cooks away. Young squid take about 25 minutes, old ones much longer. Cooked like this and dressed with lemon and chopped parsley, squid make an excellent cold hors d'ouevre so you can always cook extra for another meal.

Thoroughly clean and check the mussels and clams, page 29.

Put the clams in a pan with a splash of white wine or water, cover and cook over a brisk heat until they open. Add the mussels and cook quickly until they too open – being careful not to overcook. Strain the liquid into a jug through a muslin, to remove any grit, and take three-quarters of them from their shells. Keep them all covered until needed.

For the tomato sauce, sauté 2 garlic cloves in 2 tablespoons olive oil with a small piece of chilli (if used) until golden brown, add the tomatoes and most of the shellfish liquid (this is often salty, so stir and taste the sauce before seasoning). Cook rapidly for 5 minutes, then simmer gently for 20–25 minutes stirring occasionally. While it cooks, shell most of the prawns.

To assemble the dish, have ready a large pan of boiling salted water for the pasta. While it cooks, gently warm the shelled shellfish and the squid for 3 minutes in the tomato sauce, and heat those with shells a moment or two in a covered pan in the reserved clam liquid. Drain the vermicelli when *al dente*, transfer to a wide dish, pour over the sauce, and mix lightly. Decorate with the clams, mussels and prawns in their shells, and a sprinkling of chopped parsley. Serve immediately.

An old Neapolitan song extols the pleasures of pasta and clams.

> Give me, folks, any old job
> Hard or easy – I don't care,
> I'll do it singing.
> But when it's time to stop
> Let me find on the table top,
> Or on your lap, if fate desires,
> A bowl of pasta full of clams.

Vermicelli con le vongole is such a dish.

Vermicelli con le vongole

Vermicelli with Clams

In Italy there are clams with little, snail-like horns sticking out, called *vongole veraci* – true clams. They are served in what many feel is the only true way to savour perfectly cooked pasta and this delicious sea creature – sucked straight from their shells, between glistening forkfuls of pasta flavoured with oil and garlic. Whatever clams you use, this is a good light lunch or first course for 4–5.

550g (1 lb 3 oz) vermicelli or spaghetti
1kg (2 lb 3 oz) fresh clams, more if they are large
dry white wine (optional)

6 tablespoons good olive oil
2 garlic cloves, chopped
1 tablespoon chopped parsley
1 chilli (optional)

Put a large pan of salted water to boil for the pasta. Clean the clams well, see page 29. Put them in a covered pan over a brisk heat, with a splash of wine if you wish, shaking the pan occasionally until they open, which takes about 5 minutes. Remove from the heat.

Warm the oil in a wide pan with the garlic, parsley, and perhaps a touch of chilli. When the garlic colours slightly add the clams, in their shells, and a few spoonfuls of their liquid – strained through a muslin to remove any grit. Simmer for 5 minutes.

Cook the pasta *al dente*, drain, toss in the sauce and serve topped by the parsley.

Cannelloni alla moda di Partenopea

Cannelloni the Parthenopean Way

Parthenope was one of those sexy sirens who, failing to seduce Ulysses, threw herself into the sea with her sisters. Legend has it that the waves finally washed her body to a bay below the city that took on her name – Parthenope, later Neopolis or Napoli – Naples. So her name is given to many Neapolitan dishes.

These cannelloni are delicious: a soft cheese filling with a fragrant tomato sauce. A first course for 6, or light lunch for 4.

cannelloni squares of egg pasta made from 400g (14 oz) plain flour, pages 17–20, or 400g (14 oz) wide rectangular packet lasagne

For the filling and sauce

1 tablespoon olive oil	2 eggs
500g (17 oz) fresh tomatoes, skinned and chopped	200g (7 oz) mozzarella cheese, diced small
4–5 fresh basil leaves (optional)	50g (2¾ oz) good Parmesan cheese
200g (7 oz) ricotta cheese	a little unsalted butter
60g (2 oz) prosciutto, off cuts or good ham	

Warm 1 tablespoon of olive oil, add the tomatoes and basil. Season with salt and simmer gently for 15 minutes, stirring occasionally. Taste, adjust the seasoning, and set aside.

Cook the fresh or packet pasta as for lasagne, see page 23. Cut the packet lasagne in half to make large squares.

For the filling, cream the ricotta, mix in the prosciutto cut into small pieces, the lightly beaten eggs, and mozzarella. Season to taste, allowing for the saltiness of the prosciutto.

Divide the filling between your squares, roll each one up, overlapping the edges, and place in a single layer in an oblong buttered oven dish, the width of the cannelloni, with the overlapping side underneath. Cover with tomato sauce, sprinkle with Parmesan, dot with the remaining butter and bake in a moderate oven until the surface is lightly browned.

Neapolitans love festivals: no other region has so many, and they always end in the same way – with a macaroni meal. Even strictly religious festivals are an excuse to set off with baskets full of *pasticci* and *timballi* – pasta pies – that mamma has lovingly prepared since dawn, tucking into the mound of macaroni all sorts of delicious morsels to be hidden under the golden crust.

Making a *ragù*, which provides the sauce for *timballi* and for steaming panfuls of *ziti*, is almost a rite in these parts. In grandmother's time *ragù* was only made at weekends. It was a special affair, started on Saturday evening and finished on Sunday morning. A *conserva* of puréed tomatoes, dried in the summer sun, added a special flavour, and the slow six hours' cooking was often supervised by grandpa as he sat by the fireside. The best *ragù* was made from a mixture of pork and beef, in the following way.

Ziti co'o ragù

Ziti with Sauce from a Pot Roast

A complete meal for 6.

600g (1 lb 5 oz) ziti or similar pasta	*200g (7 oz) tomato paste*
6 tablespoons olive oil	*1½ tumblers dry red wine*
1kg (2 lb 3 oz) joint lean stewing beef	*400g (14 oz) tinned tomatoes, weighed and puréed, without the liquid*
6 pork spare-rib bones	*2 slices unsmoked bacon, chopped*
350g (12 oz) chopped onions	

Heat the oil in a casserole which just fits the ingredients and brown the meat and onions all over with the bacon. Remove the meat, stir in the tomato paste, and cook slowly adding wine now and then (or water when the wine is used up) until it darkens. Now add the tomatoes, little by little, so they too darken. This ritual of slow turning and stirring traditionally takes a couple of hours beside a wood stove, and the long cooking gives a very special flavour but today even Neapolitans may cut this to 30 minutes.

Return the meat to the pan, barely cover with boiling water, replace the lid leaving a crack open. Bring back to the boil, then cook over the lowest possible heat (or covered in an oven at gas mark 2, 150°C, 300°F), it must hardly simmer – *pippiare* – for about 4 hours, till the beef is really tender. If the spareribs are ready early, remove and return to the pan again before the end. Taste and adjust the seasoning in the last hour.

For the first course the ziti are broken in two and cooked in plenty of boiling salted water, drained when *al dente* and topped with the sauce from round the meat. To follow, the meat is sliced and served with green vegetables.

La genovese
The Genoa Dish

This dish is a curiosity: unique to Naples, and unheard of in Genoa – despite its name – it is a traditional Neapolitan Sunday meal. It seems that Genoese merchants brought the dish to Naples in the fifteenth century and only there has it survived, perhaps because its mellow oniony sauce tastes curiously un-Italian. The sauce dresses pasta for 5–6 and the meat is served with vegetables as the main course.

600g (1 lb 5 oz) long macaroni or bucatini
5 tablespoons oil
1kg (2 lb 3 oz) pot roasting beef or pork
a pinch of marjoram
1 celery stalk, chopped

2kg (4 lb 6 oz) onions, thinly sliced
1 small carrot, chopped
100g (3½ oz) diced unsmoked bacon
1–2 tumblers dry white wine
Parmesan cheese, grated

Heat the oil in a casserole just large enough to take the joint with the vegetables piled round the sides. Put in the meat, seasoned with pepper, salt and marjoram, and the vegetables and bacon. Cook over a moderate heat, browning the meat all over, and moving the vegetables constantly to stop them burning.

When the onions are golden and the meat brown, turn down the heat and cook slowly, adding the wine little by little until the sauce deepens to a rich brown. Then add a glass or two of hot water, cover, and cook in a very low oven for 2–3 hours until the meat is tender, adding more wine or water if the liquid cooks away. The tender meat should be surrounded by a dark, savoury onion sauce.

Cook the pasta in plenty of boiling salted water. Drain when *al dente*, and serve topped by the sauce and a handful of Parmesan. Pass more Parmesan round at table, and serve the meat with vegetables for the main course.

5 EMILIA-ROMAGNA

I went in, sat down and studied the menu: lasagne, tagliatelle, agnolotti, tortellini, ravioli with ricotta: rice was lacking, considered 'bog food' . . . the menu went on generously – turkey breast with sautéed mushrooms, stuffed pig's trotters from Modena, spiced sausage, kidneys, marrow bone. And all around flowed Albana wine or Lambrusco, exhaling perfume.

Italian Caprice, Giovanni Comisso

 At the heart of Emilia's gastronomy lies 'Bologna la Grassa' – Fat Bologna – so called for the abundance that surrounds her, but she is also 'Bologna la Bella' – the beautiful – and one of Europe's loveliest towns. Archways, domes, all the architecture is plump and female and the women are as bonny as their town –

buone, say the Italians, which also means good in bed. Only two of Bologna's ancient towers remain, and these, with time, have gently inclined – 'to better sniff the wonderful cooking', say the Bolognese. For, as the great chef Artusi remarked, 'When you hear Bolognese cooking spoken of bow down, for it deserves it.'

The perfect egg pasta was created here: for centuries pasta was only made with flour and water, then the Duke of Bologna ordered that the lasagne and lasagnette in that town be made with 'the best flour, to be mixed, by force of the wrist with eggs only and no action of water'. So began the dishes for which the region is famous: stuffed tortellini, ribbons of tagliatelle, and thin cream-coloured or green tagliolini.

Gone are the days when Bologna housewives rose daily at dawn to prepare tagliatelle, tortellini and panfuls of broth and *ragù* for their families. They like to be independent and go out to work: but in Bologna many women work in restaurants, trattorias and shops hand-making the pasta their mothers stayed at home to make. For the best restaurants and shops sell only pasta made by hand, not by machine. Robust grandmothers and young girls work side by side in teams, neatly dressed in white. They are called *sfogline*, and delicately they mix and knead the pasta till it shines like silk, before rolling it into sheets as thin as paper.

Since Roman times Via Emilia has run, as straight as a ruler, across the north, linking Bologna with other centres of gastronomy – Modena, Reggio and Parma – which provide delicacies known the world over – rosy Parma ham, surely the most delicious way of curing pork; *parmigiano reggiano*, Parmesan, in huge golden cartwheels; mortadella, the fat country sausage once flavoured with myrtle berries from which its name probably derives; and from these have come sumptuous pasta sauces, and the tortellini for which the region is justly famous.

Romagna, though officially combined with Emilia, is very different: old-fashioned villages drowse beside slow-moving waterways rich with eel and mullet, which were once fried and combined with pasta and white sauce to make a fish lasagne. But it is Emilia which has always lived 'on the pig's back', so to speak. The gently rounded hills and lush pastures feed livestock well: the rich milk is made into Parmesan, while its whey fattens the pigs – in fact, Modena's pigs are so renowned they are almost a public idol.

The traditional main dish is a selection of boiled meats. In the best restaurants this may be a mammoth array – ham, beef, poultry, pig's trotters, sausages, tongue – nothing is left out, and the steaming meat is served with preserved fruit spiced with mustard or a sharp green sauce. In the broth from the boiled meat, they cook pasta stuffed with delicate combinations of the meat and Parmesan: called tortellini near Bologna but cappelletti in Romagna. But, the following and best-known dish of the region is one which has been most greatly misunderstood worldwide.

Tagliatelle alla bolognese
Tagliatelle with Bolognese Sauce

It is curious that, the world over, the best-known pasta is spaghetti Bolognese. For in Bologna, where Bolognese sauce was created, it is eaten with tagliatelle – the pasta also created in Bologna. Moreover, the true Bolognese sauce often has little in common with its international namesakes. This is the true Bolognese sauce, as it is cooked at one of Bologna's top restaurants. For 4.

500g (18 oz) tagliatelle
15g (½ oz) dried porcini
mushrooms (optional)
60g (2 oz) unsalted butter
60g (2 oz) streaky unsmoked
bacon, finely chopped
40g (1½ oz) celery, finely
chopped
40g (1½ oz) carrot, finely
chopped
a small onion or shallot

300g (11 oz) excellent beef
mince
1½ tumblers good red wine
nutmeg, grated
1½ teaspoons plain flour
2 scant teaspoons tomato
paste
a little broth
a little milk
good Parmesan cheese,
grated

Methods and ingredients which may be unfamiliar are explained on pages 26–38.

Soak the porcini for an hour in a little warm water, if using. Melt three-quarters of the butter in a casserole with the bacon. When the bacon begins to colour add the celery, carrot and chopped onion and let them soften gently. Add the beef, and brown it. Pour in half the wine and cook briskly to evaporate most of it. Season with salt, pepper and nutmeg, sprinkle with the flour, stir, add the tomato paste, the porcini and a ladle of broth. Cover, and simmer the sauce *very* slowly for at least 1½ hours, stirring occasionally and adding a little porcini liquid, strained through a muslin, or some hot broth. Towards the end add 2 tablespoons of milk, to soften the flavour, taste and adjust the seasoning.

Have ready a large pan of boiling salted water. Cook the pasta *al dente*, place on a warm dish, add the remaining butter in little flakes, and top with three-quarters of the sauce – the rest is passed round at table, like the Parmesan.

This is the classic version, but some people add 2 tablespoons of thick cream to the sauce at the very end. In Bologna they also vary the recipe by using half beef, half pork.

Parmesan – *Parmigiano Reggiano* – the unique granular cheese which is the Midas touch on so many Italian dishes, comes from the towns of Parma and Reggio, where the ancient traditions and quality of the milk combine to make this unique cheese. For years the towns argued over which name the cheese should carry, eventually the dispute was settled by calling it *Parmigiano Reggiano* (or simply *Parmigiano*) in Parma, and *Reggiano Parmigiano* (or *Reggiano*) in Reggio. Its great golden cartwheels have been made since long before Boccaccio mentioned it in the *Decameron* in the fourteenth century. Nowadays it is artificially aged – the original three years reduced to one – but it is still handmade by men who can tell the precise ripeness of each cheese by touch and smell. Real Parmesan, from Emilia-Romagna, freshly grated, is utterly different from ready-grated packets, whatever their origin. Only good Parmesan will create one of the loveliest of all pasta dishes – *tagliatelle alla panna*.

Tagliatelle alla panna
Tagliatelle with Cream

This classic cream sauce is perfect with freshly made tagliatelle and many stuffed pastas. Yet it is one of the quickest and easiest of all sauces to make. A light lunch for 4 or a first course for 6.

500g (18 oz) fresh tagliatelle or 450g (16 oz) packet tagliatelle
250ml (9 fl oz) thick cream

nutmeg, freshly grated
70g (2½ oz) good Parmesan cheese
80g (3 oz) unsalted butter

Have ready a large pan of boiling salted water for the pasta. Warm the cream in a wide shallow pan over the lowest possible heat, and season to taste with white pepper and nutmeg. Add the grated Parmesan and heat, stirring until smooth and thick. Remove from the heat. Put the butter in a pasta bowl and warm the bowl while the pasta cooks. Drain the pasta when *al dente*, toss it in the cream, then mix it delicately with the butter. Serve immediately, with extra Parmesan at table, if you wish.

Tagliatelle al prosciutto di Parma
Tagliatelle with Parma Ham

Delicious, wonderfully easy, and an excellent way to enjoy the luxury of Parma ham without having to buy very much. Off cuts of prosciutto are quite good enough for robust sauces but this delicate mixture needs proper slices. A rich dish which serves 4–5 as a light lunch, and 6 as a first course.

Methods and ingredients which may be unfamiliar are explained on pages 26–38.

500g (18 oz) very good
    quality tagliatelle
200g (7 oz) prosciutto (Parma
    ham)

150g (5¼ oz) unsalted butter
freshly ground pepper

Put a large pan of salted water to boil for the pasta. Keeping the slices separate, so they don't stick together, chop the ham roughly. While the pasta cooks, melt the butter very gently in a wide casserole. Heat the prosciutto in it very gently, without cooking. Remove the pan from the heat. Drain the pasta when *al dente*, transfer it to the casserole, mix delicately and serve on a warm dish. Cheese is not needed but a little freshly ground pepper adds a final touch.

Avemarie alla Langhirano
Rosary Beads the Langhirano Way

In the area around Parma they devised this exquisite dish combining Parma ham, the tender jewel-like insides of broad beans, and *avemarie* – the tiny pasta, shaped like rosary beads, usually cooked in broth and vegetable soups. This makes a first course for 8–10, but reheats well.

600g (1 lb 5 oz) avemarie or
    cannolichiette
500g (18 oz) fresh or frozen
    shelled broad beans
1 shallot or very small onion
150g (5 oz) Parma ham
    (prosciutto) off cuts

125g (4½ oz) unsalted butter
a little chicken broth
80–100g (3–3½ oz) good
    Parmesan cheese, grated
1 tablespoon sunflower oil
    (optional)

Parboil fresh beans for 10 minutes, thaw frozen ones. Remove the grey-green leathery jacket from each bean by cutting a nick in one end and squeezing the other end, so that the brilliant green 'kernel' pops out. You need to end up with 300g (10½ oz) of beans out of their skin. Then chop the shallot finely and chop the ham coarsely.

Gently soften the shallot in two-thirds of the butter in a large pan adding a tablespoon of sunflower oil if necessary. Stir in the chopped ham and the bean 'kernels'. Season, and add 2 ladlefuls of broth (or water and a fragment of chicken bouillon cube). Simmer until the beans are tender – 20–40 minutes depending on their size and whether they are fresh or frozen. If the broth cooks away add a little more, but the beans shouldn't be swimming in liquid, just nicely moist. When the beans are ready, taste and adjust the seasoning, then cover and keep warm.

Have ready a large pan of boiling salted water. Cook the pasta *al dente* and drain. Add to the beans the remaining butter cut in pieces, half the Parmesan, and then the pasta. Mix well together, transfer to a warm bowl and serve, passing round the remaining Parmesan and a pepper mill at table.

> *Under those archways, shops one after another were overflowing like horns of plenty with salamis, meats, cheeses, cakes, all shining as though varnished, but above all with yellow and green tagliatelle, in such profusion it seemed these tagliatelle and tortellini were not on show as food but as ornamental flowers.*
>
> *Italian Caprice*, Giovanni Comisso

Tortellini are one of the great specialities of this region. They were probably created to use up the leftovers from the banqueting tables of the nobility, for their thin pasta encloses all kinds of titbits. The filling varies slightly from town to town and household to household, and experienced cooks may adjust the quantities according to what they have to hand.

Some say tortellini are fashioned like the tummy buttons of the well-rounded women of Bologna, others that they imitate the navel of Venus herself. For legend has it that an innkeeper once peeped through the keyhole when Venus visited the inn with her lover, and then immortalized her navel in this pasta as a tribute to love.

In Italy the best way to eat tortellini is hotly debated: in broth, or drained and eaten with *ragù*, or with cream. Whatever you prefer, the Bologna tortellini, cooked in good chicken broth, are excellent. Their filling uses two of the delicacies of the area – prosciutto, the delectable raw smoked ham from Parma; and mortadella, the large sausage larded with little cubes of fat which has probably been made in Bologna since Roman times: early woodcuts show monks pounding meat in a mortar while fat sausages hang above them.

Like all filled pasta they take time to make, but their cutting and shaping is a restful occupation for a Sunday afternoon.

Tortellini alla bolognese
Tortellini Bologna Style

Although these excellent little tortellini, with their local mortadella sausage and Parma ham, are typical of Bologna, they are now made in pasta shops all over Italy and in many parts they are a Christmas speciality. It is hard to say whether this recipe or the next is the better – you may like to compare the two and decide for yourself.

This quantity makes about 100 little 'tummy buttons'. How many that serves depends on whether you are eating them in broth or with a sauce. In Italy they calculate 20–25 per person in broth and 40 with sauce: less doughty eaters may need only half as many. If you make more filling or tortellini than you need, either will freeze well – in a box.

egg pasta made with 300g (10½ oz) plain flour, see pages 17–22

Filling
50g (1¾ oz) lean pork
75g (2½ oz) chicken or turkey
  breast
a 'walnut' of unsalted
  butter
1 dessertspoon olive oil
25g (1 oz) prosciutto

25g (1 oz) mortadella
25g (1 oz) good Parmesan
  cheese, grated
nutmeg, grated
1 egg
1 litre (2 pints) chicken stock
  (optional)

93

Gently fry the pork and chicken or turkey in a little butter and oil until cooked but not brown. Mince or chop them finely with the prosciutto and mortadella. Add the Parmesan, season to taste with salt, pepper and nutmeg, then mix in the egg.

Roll the pasta very thinly – here they say it must be as round as a full moon and as light as a caress – cut in rounds 5cm (2 in) wide. Place a little filling on each, fold into a half moon, and press the damp edges well together. Flick up the edge, then curve, and press together the two points, to make your model tummy button.

Let them dry for several hours on a tray sprinkled with semolina. To cook, boil them in chicken broth until the pasta just tastes done – the timing depends on the thinness of the pasta, so keep testing them. If you have no broth, and will be serving them with a sauce, cook them in lightly salted water – but avoid bouillon cube broth for it overwhelms them with its saltiness.

A dessertspoon of Lambrusco, the Modenese wine suited to all this region's dishes, is often added to each plate of tortellini in broth before the Parmesan is sprinkled over – you can, of course, drink the rest. On Christmas Day they are always served in broth, but they are good with just butter and Parmesan, and excellent with the cream sauce on page 90.

Shaping tortellini and tortelloni

Methods and ingredients which may be unfamiliar are explained on pages 26–38.

Tortellini di Luisa
Luisa's Tortellini

Though simpler than the previous recipe, these tortellini are almost better. This quantity makes about 100 – a light dish for 3–5.

egg pasta made with 400g (14 oz) plain flour, see pages 17–22

Filling

70g (2½ oz) bone marrow	60g (2 oz) prosciutto
25g (1 oz) unsalted butter	60g (2 oz) mortadella
5 tablespoons good Parmesan cheese, grated	nutmeg, freshly grated
	2–3 egg yolks

Cream the bone marrow with the butter, in a bowl over hot water. Mix in the Parmesan and very finely chopped meat. Season to taste adding grated nutmeg, then mix in the egg yolks. Make, cook and serve the tortellini as in the previous recipe.

Unlike Christmas lunch, when such tortellini or cappelletti in broth are followed by splendid dishes of roast capon, the dinner on Christmas Eve contains no meat. To start the meal, people in Emilia-Romagna serve large cheese-filled tortellini – called tortelloni – and these are followed by excellent fish.

Tortelloni da vigilia
Christmas Eve Tortelloni

A light first course for 6 and, though parsley is traditional, these tortelloni are also excellent made with a little basil.

egg pasta made with 300g (10 oz) plain flour, see pages 17–22

Filling

300g (10 oz) ricotta cheese	2 tablespoons finely chopped
40g (1½ oz) good Parmesan	parsley
cheese, grated	nutmeg, freshly grated

Cream the ricotta, mix in the Parmesan and parsley, and season to taste adding grated nutmeg. Roll the pasta thinly. Cut in discs, 7cm (3 in) across, with the rim of a glass, and place a heap of filling on each. Fold into half-moons, close the moistened edges, flick up the rim and curve to press the points well together. Leave them to dry slightly on a tray dusted with semolina. Cook in boiling salted water until the pasta tastes cooked. Drain and serve with melted butter and grated Parmesan.

In this region stuffed pastas are truly appreciated. Every plateful may be compared with those which have gone before; especially when such pasta is traditional at certain festivals.

'Oh yes, very good – but I remember eating a dish of tortellini twenty years ago that was really something to talk about . . .' someone will often say, and a debate begins.

Caplétt
Little Hats

In Romagna these 'little hats' are often eaten at New Year, with the filling made from leftover Christmas turkey. An idea worth copying for their delicate lemony flavour is just what one needs after rich Christmas fare. A first course or light lunch for 6.

egg pasta made with 400g (14 oz) plain flour, see pages 17–22

Filling

90g (3 oz) cooked turkey or	1 egg (and 1 optional yolk)
chicken	nutmeg, freshly grated
200g (7 oz) ricotta cheese	grated lemon zest
30g (1 oz) good grated	
Parmesan cheese	

Choose moist pieces of the meat and chop them very finely. Then combine with the other ingredients of the filling, mix to a smooth paste and season to taste. (Only add the extra yolk if the mixture is too dry.)

Roll the pasta thinly and cut into 4cm (1½ in) squares. Place a little filling on each, fold into a triangle, press the edges well together (moistening if necessary), flick up the point, then curl until the two corners can be pressed together to form *cappelletti* – little hats. Place on a tray dusted with semolina to dry a little before cooking.

To cook, boil them in good broth (not bouillon cube broth), or boiling salted water, until a corner tastes ready. They can either be eaten in the broth or lifted out and served with good grated Parmesan and melted unsalted butter.

It is always difficult to judge the amount of filling needed for stuffed pastas; so leftover filling is often mixed with dried breadcrumbs, shaped into tiny balls and cooked in the broth without its pasta coat, and if a few break up it simply makes the soup even better.

Shaping caplétt

The next recipe is the practical Romagnan way of using up filled pasta which has already been cooked. As tortellini and cappelletti are traditional on New Year's Eve, this dish is supposed to bring good luck to all who eat it – and the more you eat the better your luck will be! Of course, it doesn't have to be made with leftovers.

Pastèzz ed caplétt
Little Hat Pie

Simple and good, but not a pie despite its name, it can easily be adapted to larger or smaller amounts of cappelletti, or surplus sauce can be eaten with other pasta. A light main dish for 4.

about 120 cappelletti or
  tortellini which have
  been cooked in broth
4 shallots or 2 smallish
  onions
1 carrot
1 garlic clove
1 small handful parsley

1 tablespoon olive oil
100g (3½ oz) ham fat,
  chopped
1 tumbler red or rosé wine
1kg (2¼ lb) fresh or tinned
  tomatoes, skinned and
  chopped

Chop the shallots, carrot, garlic and parsley. Sauté them in the oil with the ham fat until they begin to turn golden. Add the wine and let it bubble until almost evaporated, then add the tomatoes, season with salt and freshly ground black pepper and simmer for 1 hour, occasionally adding a little of the broth the cappelletti were cooked in.

The *pastèzz* is made by layering the cooked cappelletti and sauce in a deep oven dish and putting it in a really hot oven for about 8 minutes, until the cappelletti are just hot.

Timballo di maccheroni alla romagnola

Romagna's Macaroni Pie

One of the best pasta pies – hearty Romagna cooking which, in the land of its origin, is accompanied by heady Sangiovese wine. A main course for 4, and most of the cooking can be done well in advance.

Pastry
125g (4½ oz) plain flour
60g (2 oz) butter, or margarine
and lard

1 egg yolk
water

Filling
250g (9 oz) long macaroni,
or bucatini, or small penne
100g (4 oz) veal or lamb
sweatbreads
100g (4 oz) veal mince
1 very small carrot
¼ medium-sized onion
a finger-length celery
60g (2 oz) ham
45g (1½ oz) unsalted butter

1 pigeon, cut in 4
1½ teaspoons plain flour
2 tablespoons Marsala or port
poultry broth or water
3 tablespoons cooked peas
1 handful button mushrooms
1 handful good Parmesan
cheese, grated
1 beaten egg

Prepare the sweatbreads, pages 36–7. Season the mince and make meat balls the size of a hazelnut. Finely chop the carrot, onion, celery and ham and sauté briefly in a little of the butter in a small casserole before adding the pigeon and browning it. Season, stir the flour into the pan juices and cook a moment, then add the Marsala or port and evaporate a little before topping up with enough broth to just cover the bird. Cook slowly for 30–45 minutes, until the bird is tender and the sauce has thickened.

Meanwhile, make the pastry as usual, see page 33, slice the sweatbreads, and sauté them in a little butter till golden, then mix with the peas and season. Rinse, slice and briefly sauté the mushrooms. When the bird is cooked remove it from the sauce (don't bone the pigeon – it is eaten in the fingers), put in the meatballs and simmer them for 5 minutes. Add the mushrooms. Remove the pan from the heat and cover.

Have ready a pan of boiling salted water, break the pasta in thirds and cook so it is really *al dente*. Drain, and mix it with the sauce, Parmesan and remaining butter. Grease a pie dish, distribute all the ingredients in it nicely. Cover with the pastry. Make a hole in the centre to let the steam out. Brush with beaten egg and bake in a hot oven for ½ hour or until golden.

Lasagne verdi alla modenese
Green Lasagne the Modenese Way

Italian mothers go to great lengths to prepare delicious meals, and one of their great skills is producing two totally different dishes out of one lot of cooking. This classic lasagne uses the sauce from a pot roast or surplus Bolognese sauce. A main course for 4–6.

lasagne, made with egg pasta from 150g (5 oz) cooked spinach, well drained and very finely chopped, 300g (11 oz) plain flour and a pinch of salt, and 1 egg: or 350g (12 oz) packet spinach lasagne

Filling

2 cups Bolognese sauce or sauce from round pot roast beef	70g (2½ oz) plain flour
	¾ litre (1½ pint) milk
	a handful good Parmesan
70g (2½ oz) unsalted butter	cheese, grated

Make and cook the lasagne as usual, page 23. Then make the white sauce, page 37, and heat the meat sauce.

Butter a rectangular oven dish. Place in it a layer of lasagne, covered with spoonfuls of meat sauce. Scatter on some of the

Parmesan, then spoonfuls of white sauce. Continue these layers until everything is used up, ending with pasta, white sauce and Parmesan. Dot with a little butter and place in a moderate oven for 20 minutes, until the surface is golden.

Chicken livers, chopped and sautéed in butter, are sometimes added to the meat sauce, and they are an excellent addition.

6 LIGURIA

Roses and roses. They were so thick
at the roadsides
leading down to the sea
in my Liguria! From wall and espalier,
from hedge and pergola,
they split onto shores and rocks,
jingling with scent.

Tralci, Adriano Grande

 Liguria *is* sea and flowers: Italy's Riviera, a tiny region, tucked around the Bay of Genoa between the Alps and the sea. The mountains, dropping to form the rocky picturesque coast with its pastel-coloured towns, protect Liguria from cold winds; palms wave on promenades where old men sit playing cards and women hang their washing on lemon trees in pots. San Remo's flowers have spread everywhere – to balconies, streets, shop windows, gardens, railings, even railway stations. Pinks, crimsons, yellows in thousands contrast with the gentle backcloth of terrace vines, and the brilliant blue of the sea, with its spattering of white sails.

On every windowsill is a pot of basil – Genoa's herb *par excellence*, giving off the scent that, married to the tang of sea breezes, dominates Liguria's cooking. No exotic spices, no cloves or nutmeg here, for Genoa was a great port for the spice trade, and the sailors, after months aboard ships heavy with the pervasive clinging smell of spices had no desire for them in their food. So, in Liguria, the freshest of all pasta sauces was created, emerald green pesto made with basil, pesto with all sorts of pasta, and in minestrone; a perfect introduction to the seafoods and mixed salads which follow.

The whole region is swathed in it, as by sea foam. It's a bold, rousing smell that tells of discoveries and sea adventures to those ashore . . . a scent announcing 'homeland' to those returning from the high seas, whose noses twitch with its smell even before their eyes catch sight of the mountain ranges, still lost in the grey of the horizon. It's the smell of pesto.

The Wandering Glutton, Paolo Monelli

Pesto

Liguria's famous sauce is probably of very ancient origin, coming from *moretum*, a preparation described by Lucio in Roman times. Then it was made of oil, garlic, celery, cheese, vinegar, and a bitter herb few people would care to use today – rue.

Over the years the ingredients changed and the making of pesto became a domestic ritual, almost an art, woven deep into the lives of the Genoese. Everything is collected together to start with: white marble mortar, wooden pestle, sea salt crystals, golden and white cheese, fresh-picked basil leaves, garlic, pine kernels, and fine pale green olive oil from the first pressing.

Then the pounding begins, all five senses participating, until the ingredients are transformed, from a varied delight to eye and nose, into one singular taste.

Slowly, surely, the Genoese women pounded away while waiting for their men to return from the sea, but you can make it very well in a food processor, adjusting the ingredients to your own taste. Though, if you ever find yourself waiting for someone to come home, delayed by the traffic jams and strikes of modern life, you may like to try the traditional method, easing your waiting with the gentle ritual of preparation as the women of Genoa used to do, and offer the most fragrant uplifting scent to the man, woman or child who opens the front door.

You can use any of the following versions of pesto on narrow, ribbon-shaped, non-egg pasta such as linguine. It can also be eaten on plain lasagne sheets broken roughly into 8cm (3 in) squares, on cheese or spinach ravioli or agnolotti, and as the finishing touch to minestrone.

Don't worry if the pesto tastes very strong on its own, it will be just right when it melts over the pasta. And though tradition has it that pesto should be freshly made just before the meal – and the flavour is spoilt on keeping – it will sometimes keep a day or so in the fridge, if well covered.

I

The classic pesto. For 6 helpings of pasta.

*a large handful of fresh basil
    leaves*
1–2 cloves garlic
*100g (3½ oz) grated pecorino
    sardo cheese – or ½ pecorino:
    ½ Parmesan*

50g (1¾ oz) pine kernels
4–6 tablespoons best olive oil

TRADITIONAL METHOD

Chop the basil finely with the garlic and a pinch of salt. Put them in a mortar and pound well, adding the cheese and pine kernels

Methods and ingredients which may be unfamiliar are explained on pages 26–38.

little by little. Then add the olive oil dribble by dribble, while you continue pounding to work it into the mixture until it is smooth and creamy – though it will never be as smooth as mayonnaise.

MODERN METHOD

Put everything except the oil in an electric blender. Chop thoroughly, and continue blending as you very gradually add the oil. A tablespoon of tepid water can be added near the end if it becomes too thick to mix.

II

A milder, more modern pesto, particularly suited to electric blenders. For 6.

a handful fresh basil leaves
2 cloves garlic
1 tablespoon water
5 tablespoons best olive oil
50g (2 oz) grated pecorino
  sardo or romano cheese

50g (2 oz) good Parmesan
  cheese, grated
1–2 tablespoons unsalted
  butter

Put the basil leaves, garlic, water, and half the oil in the blender. Mix well. Then gradually blend in the remaining oil, cheeses and butter.

The butter softens the taste of garlic and sometimes – to the horror of purists – modern Italians use milk for this purpose. If it is still too strong for your taste a delicate and rather different version may be made by omitting garlic altogether.

III

A pleasant variation on the previous recipe is to substitute young spinach for a third of the basil.

Trenette col pesto alla genovese
Trenette with Genoese Pesto

A unique Genoese combination of pasta and potatoes which makes an unusual first course for 6, or a lunch for 4.

500g (18 oz) trenette, bavette or linguine
pesto: version I or II (pages 104–5)
250g (9 oz) waxy potatoes

2 tablespoons grated Parmesan, or pecorino sardo or romano cheese, or a mixture

Having made the pesto, peel the potatoes and slice as thickly as two matchsticks. Throw them into a large pan of boiling salted water, and when it returns to the boil add the pasta and cook together – they must be ready at the same time, so if the bavette are very thin cut the potatoes into thinner slices. When cooked, drain – but not too dry – and place in a warm dish, sprinkle with the cheese, and top with the pesto. Serve, mixing lightly at table.

Though ready-made pesto lacks the vigour of homemade pesto the better brands, such as Tigullio, are quite good with a dish like this.

Pesto is not the only sauce the Ligurians put on pasta. The range of sauces isn't great but some are most original, delicately coloured and softly flavoured. They are utterly different from those of Liguria's neighbour Piedmont.

Tagliatelle verdi alla genovese
Genoa's Special Green Tagliatelle

These are probably the most delicious homemade tagliatelle of all, and particularly easy to make with a food processor. They are excellent with just melted butter and good Parmesan cheese, but in Liguria they sometimes use a meat sauce or the mushroom sauce given for *Tagliatelle verdi ai funghi*, see below. For 6.

200–300g (7–10 oz) veal
   sweetbreads
100g (4 oz) good meaty
   sausages
2 tablespoons sunflower oil
¼ onion, finely chopped
1 clove garlic, chopped
a good pinch nutmeg or mixed
   spice

1 handful cooked spinach
1 handful cooked borage
   (optional)
600g (1 lb 5 oz) plain white
   flour
4 eggs, or less
2 tablespoons good Parmesan
   cheese, grated

Cleanse and blanch the sweetbreads as usual, page 36–7, then chop them. Skin and chop the sausages and cook them gently in the oil with the onion, garlic, and sweetbreads, stirring repeatedly for about 10 minutes. Season with salt, pepper and nutmeg and add the spinach and borage, both *very* well drained and finely chopped. Cook another 5 minutes to evaporate as much of the liquid as possible.

Chop on a board – or in a food processor – until the mixture is almost a purée. Combine with the flour and cheese, and continue as for egg pasta, pages 17–19, cut into tagliatelle, pages 19–20, and cook them in plenty of boiling salted water until they taste ready. Drain and serve with the sauce of your choice.

Tagliatelle verdi ai funghi
Green Tagliatelle with Mushrooms

In Italy porcini mushrooms are used for this generous mushroom sauce but, though they give a quite different flavour, button mushrooms are also very good. A delicious first course for 5–6.

600g (1 lb 5 oz) fresh green
  tagliatelle, or 500g
  (18 oz) packet tagliatelle
600g (1 lb 5 oz) mushrooms
1 small onion, finely chopped
1 clove garlic (optional)
1 tablespoon olive oil
100g (3½ oz) unsalted butter

1 tumbler dry white wine
600g (1 lb 5 oz) fresh or tinned
  tomatoes, skinned and
  chopped
freshly grated nutmeg
125g (4½ oz) grated Parmesan
  cheese

Rinse the mushrooms and slice them finely. Sauté the onion and crushed garlic, in a heavy pan, in the oil and half the butter. When they begin to take colour add the mushrooms, season, and sauté briefly, then add the wine. Let it bubble, and almost completely evaporate, before stirring in the tomatoes. Add a grating of nutmeg, taste, adjust the seasoning and cook for 15 minutes over a low heat, stirring occasionally to stop it sticking.

When the sauce is almost ready cook the pasta *al dente* in plenty of boiling salted water. Drain and transfer to a warm pasta bowl. Top with the rest of the butter in little flakes, half the sauce, and a handful of cheese. Mix lightly and serve. The remaining sauce and cheese are passed round at table in bowls.

Nuts are almost as important to Liguria's culinary tradition as basil – pine nuts for pesto from the woods near the coast, while on the slopes of the mountains which embrace the great arc of coastline there are chestnuts to be turned into marrons glacés and walnuts for subtle sauces like this next recipe which they prepare when the walnuts have just been collected and the new wine is transferred to its barrels. It is very good despite the simplicity of its ingredients, particularly with green tagliatelle – though they are not traditional.

Methods and ingredients which may be unfamiliar are explained on pages 26–38.

Salsa di noci

Nut Sauce

A nut and ricotta sauce which makes an unusual start to a meal for 6–8. It can be used on all sorts of pasta – spaghetti, trenette, lasagnette or even ravioli. For 500g (18 oz) pasta you need:

50g (2 oz) pine kernels
3 tablespoons olive oil
100g (3½ oz) shelled walnuts
a small handful basil leaves

1 garlic clove
50g (2 oz) ricotta
grated pecorino sardo, or
Parmesan cheese

Toast the pine kernels light gold in the oven with a drop of oil. Pound the walnuts, pine kernels, basil and garlic in a mortar with a pinch of salt until they form a paste – you can use a blender but, for some indefinable reason, the mortar gives a better flavour.

Cream the ricotta with a very little water. Add it to the nut paste, plus a little of the oil and a tablespoon of pecorino. Mix well together, and transfer to a bowl. Gradually stir in the remaining oil until the sauce becomes smooth and creamy. Taste for salt and if you like a stronger taste add more grated cheese. Serve on pasta which is al dente but not too well drained. Extra cheese may be passed round at table.

Pansôti di Rapallo

Ravioli from Rapallo

In Rapallo, a charming seaside town near Portofino, they make these delicious ravioli, called *pansôti* in the local dialect, filled with spinach cheese and eggs and served with a simple nut sauce. A first course for 6.

egg pasta made with 400g (14 oz) plain flour, see pages 17–19

Filling
2 hardboiled eggs
2–3 tablespoons pecorino
 romano or Parmesan cheese,
 grated

200g (7 oz) spinach, cooked
 weight, well drained and
 finely chopped

Sauce
8 shelled walnuts, crushed or
 finely chopped

4 tablespoons best olive oil
freshly ground pepper

Chop the eggs well, mix them with the cheese and spinach, and season to taste. Roll the pasta into two very thin sheets. Place little heaps of filling, evenly spaced, on one, moisten the surface of the other and place it on top. Press the two sheets together around the filling and either cut into square ravioli or make round ones with a circular pasta cutter. Allow to dry for a few hours on a tray sprinkled with semolina. (See page 21.)

To serve them, warm the nuts very gently in a tiny pan for 10 minutes with the oil, 2 tablespoons water and a seasoning of salt and freshly ground pepper. Meanwhile, cook the *pansôti* in plenty of boiling salted water until the pasta tastes cooked. Drain, place them in a warm bowl, mix in the hot sauce and serve. The sauce looks far too little but it is enough for these delicate ravioli.

In Sardinia they make an identical stuffed pasta except that they omit the hardboiled eggs and include in the stuffing little pieces of a sheep's cheese which melt deliciously. These *culingiones*, as they are called, are served with a simple tomato sauce.

Ligurian olives are to be found nowhere outside this area. Very small, shiny, and jet black, with just a thin film of flesh between skin and stone, their flavour is unique. Grown on stony terraces, hewn over centuries out of the precipitous hills facing the sea,

Methods and ingredients which may be unfamiliar are explained on pages 26–38.

they ripen slowly – not before November – and are picked as they ripen, right through to the following spring, not all together as in other regions. This way they are always milled when fresh and the resulting oil is paler, lighter in flavour – and for Ligurians superior – perfect for pesto, nut sauces, and for cooking fish.

Spaghetti alla perasca
Spaghetti the Borgo Peri Way

Borgo Peri is the fishermen's quarter of Genoa, a maze of little alleys which, until not long ago, was permeated by wonderful smells wafting from street-vendors' stalls: fried fish, artichokes, pizza, fresh pies and heaps of jet-black olives. That feature of Genoa has unfortunately disappeared, but this delicate, pale pink fish sauce is still made by the fishermen's wives. A first course or a light lunch for 4–5.

500g (18 oz) spaghetti or linguine
1 garlic clove, chopped
1 handful chopped parsley
350g (12 oz) hound fish or cod slices
100g (4 oz) fresh or tinned tomatoes, skinned and chopped
4 tablespoons good olive oil
a few black olives (optional)

Put a large pan of salted water to boil for the pasta. Soften the garlic and parsley gently in the oil, add the fish and tomatoes. Season to taste and simmer, covered, for 8–10 minutes, until the fish is cooked.

Take from the heat, and remove all bones and skin from the fish. Sieve the fish with its sauce – or purée it in a blender – to make a smooth thick cream. Warm this in the pan, and adjust the seasoning, adding also a little water if it is too thick, while you cook the pasta. Drain the pasta when *al dente*, place it in a warm bowl and top with the sauce, a sprinkling of parsley, and a fine dribble of olive oil. Decorate with the olives and serve with extra pepper but no cheese.

7 LOMBARDY

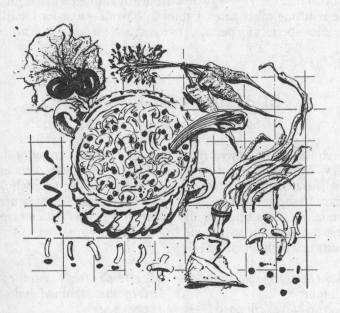

Lombardy lacks nothing, except a little sunshine. Its fields, backed by the Alps, and interspersed by birchwoods, are lush with water from the intricate network of canals. Large farms produce the butter and cheese which are such a feature of the region's cooking: mascarpone, Bel Paese, and most of all Gorgonzola, named after the town, but once called *stracchino*. For cows were driven down from the mountain pastures before the winter and arrived in the plain *stracche* – tired – and their thin milk was found to produce excellent cheese. Only with commercialization was the name Gorgonzola given to one of them.

Lombardy was not always so prosperous; a century ago meat was for weekends only. So, good use was made of offal, and of the onions, cabbages and potatoes which thrive here, combined with rice, polenta and wholemeal pasta. In rural areas dishes are still prepared from such ingredients, enriched with melted cheese. Here you find the simplest stuffed pastas, and also some of the most remarkable; with a sweet filling of amaretti, pumpkin and spiced fruit.

There is also another side to Lombardy: modern towns, satellites to commercial, industrial Milan; the richest city in Italy and one of the great centres of good food. Some of the best-known Italian dishes have their home here: minestrone in all its forms; Milanese risotto – the substantial rice dish, tinted with saffron; *osso bucco* – the succulent combination of veal and white wine; and *panettone* – the lightest, most irresistible of all Christmas cakes. And the region has some unique specialities: in Cremona they make *Mostarda di Cremona*, whole fruit in a mustard flavoured sugar syrup which, outlandish though it may sound, is exceedingly good with cold meat.

In Milan the pasta dishes are sophisticated. Milan's shops can provide delicacies from all over the world, and the Milanese have invented dishes to use these ingredients. Pasta sauces are no exception: spaghetti with caviar, or a pasta salad with palm hearts are conversation pieces at the dinner parties that the Milanese love to give. But some of the best, and most typical, dishes have their roots in rural cooking and are made with cheese, in particular with *Gorgonzola dolce*, the soft-flavoured Gorgonzola.

Penne al Gorgonzola
Penne with Gorgonzola

The softness of mild Gorgonzola mixed with cream makes this a beautiful sauce for 3–4, but it must be mild not ordinary Gorgonzola. Any short, not too chunky pasta can be used, and fusilli go especially well.

400g (14 oz) medium-sized
  penne
unsalted butter
150g (5 oz) Gorgonzola dolce
  or dolce latte cheese

250ml (½ pint) thick cream
a pinch of sugar

Cook the pasta in a large pan of boiling salted water. Meanwhile, melt 1 tablespoon of butter in a large shallow pan. Add the cheese cut in tiny pieces. Stir over the lowest heat. When it softens add a third of the cream. Cook gently for 5 minutes, add another third with a pinch of sugar and salt. Cook gently. Drain the pasta when really *al dente*. Toss it in the sauce, add the remaining cream and some white pepper, stir briefly together over gentle heat and serve quickly.

Lasagnette ricce alle noci e Gorgonzola

Narrow Wavy Lasagne with Nuts and Gorgonzola

The combination of blue cheese and nuts is unusual and excellent. A quick and easy first course for 4.

500g (18 oz) narrow, wavy-edged lasagne, or farfalle

200g (7 oz) Gorgonzola al mascarpone (a cheese with layers of each)

3–4 tablespoons Parmesan cheese

100g (3½ oz) shelled walnuts, well chopped

The sauce is made while the pasta cooks in plenty of boiling salted water. Cut the cheese into small pieces and place it in a warm pasta bowl with the Parmesan. Cream them together, adding a spoonful of pasta water, and mix in the nuts. Drain the pasta when *al dente*, leaving it a little damp, transfer it quickly to the sauce, mix delicately and serve at once, on warm plates.

Cheeses from all over Europe can be found in Lombardy's elegant shops and, inevitably, some find their way into pasta sauces.

Methods and ingredients which may be unfamiliar are explained on pages 26–38.

Maccheroncini ai quattro formaggi

Little Macaroni with Four Cheeses

A very good first course or light lunch for 6–8. The sauce requires any four of the following cheeses: provolone, fontina, Emmenthal, Gruyère, Edam, mozzarella. There are two versions of this recipe and they taste quite different.

I

600g (1 lb 5 oz) short macaroni or other short hollow pasta
4 cheeses totalling 350g (12 oz) – the proportions need not be equal

150g (5 oz) unsalted butter
100g (3½ oz) good Parmesan cheese, grated

Put a large pan of salted water to boil ready for the pasta. Cut the cheese into matchsticks. (Hard cheeses can be softened in a cup of milk for a while, if you wish.) Cook the pasta. Drain when *al dente*, leaving it a little moist. Mix it in an oven dish with the drained cheese, half the butter, and half the Parmesan. Cover with the remaining butter and Parmesan. Put briefly in a hot oven until the cheeses have *just* melted. Serve immediately on warm plates.

II

Prepare the four cheeses as above and cut up 40g (1½ oz) ham. Make a thin white sauce, see page 37, using a nut of butter, 2 teaspoons plain flour, 300ml (12 fl oz) milk, and seasoning to taste. The ham and strips of cheese – but not the Parmesan – are mixed into the well-cooked sauce and the mixture added to the drained pasta. If the heat of the sauce doesn't melt the cheese the dish can go in the oven for a moment. Pass round the Parmesan at table.

Bavette con le cipolle

Bavette with Onions

This melting onion sauce is one of Lombardy's classic recipes: a beautiful light lunch for 6, or first course for 8.

600g (1 lb 5 oz) bavette (or any long pasta, not too thick or thin)
4 large Spanish onions

150g (5¼ oz) unsalted butter
2 large eggs
good Parmesan cheese, grated

Slice the onions wafer thin. Cook them as slowly as possible in the butter, in a heavy casserole. They must not colour but simply melt to a transparent, deliciously scented mass, which may take half an hour. Stir frequently to prevent them sticking and, if necessary, add a tablespoon or so of water.

Then cook the bavette in plenty of boiling salted water. When they are almost ready beat the eggs and, off the heat, stir them quickly into the onions. Cover and set aside. Drain the pasta when *al dente*. Place in a warm pasta bowl, add the sauce and several spoonfuls of Parmesan, and mix well before serving. Parmesan and freshly ground pepper can be added to each helping.

Though no Lombard would countenance it, this is excellent with mature Cheddar instead of Parmesan – though it lacks the subtlety of the classic version. And the onions can be cooked in advance and gently reheated, provided the eggs have not been added.

Methods and ingredients which may be unfamiliar are explained on pages 26–38.

116

Tortelloni verdi al Gorgonzola

Green Tortelloni with Gorgonzola

If you like Gorgonzola this is a rather special sauce for green tortelloni, whether you buy them or make them. A first course for 6.

egg pasta made with 150g (5 oz) cooked spinach, very well drained and puréed, 300g (10½ oz) plain flour and 2 eggs, see pages 17–22

Filling

200g (7 oz) ricotta cheese
40g (1½ oz) good Parmesan
  cheese, grated

150g (5 oz) cooked spinach,
  well drained
nutmeg

Sauce

70g (2½ oz) unsalted butter
100g (3½ oz) Gorgonzola
  dolce or dolce latte cheese

a small handful best Parmesan
  cheese

Shaping tortelloni

117

For the filling, mix the ricotta with the Parmesan and finely chopped spinach, and season to taste, adding grated nutmeg.

Roll the pasta very thinly, and cut into rounds 7cm (3 in) across. Place some filling on each. Fold in half, press the moist edges well together and turn them up, before curving to press the points together. Spread out on a tray dusted with semolina until needed.

Cook the tortelloni in plenty of boiling salted water until the pasta tastes cooked. Meanwhile, heat the butter gently in a wide pan with the Gorgonzola cut into little pieces – they melt but stay slightly separate. When the tortelloni are done, drain and tip them into the creamy Gorgonzola. Mix briefly over the lowest heat, adding the Parmesan and a little pepper. Serve immediately on warm plates.

Casonsei di Bergamo
Bergamo's Ravioli

These large oblong ravioli from Bergamo are the least fiddly stuffed pastas to make but they require really good lean beef, not standard mince. They use so little that this is not an extravagant dish. A light main course for 6–10.

egg pasta made with 500g (18 oz) plain flour, see pags 17–22

Shaping casonsei

Filling

1 clove garlic, finely chopped	nutmeg
½ tablespoon parsley, finely chopped	2 tablespoons oven-baked breadcrumbs
30g (1 oz) unsalted butter	1 tablespoon good Parmesan cheese, grated
300g (11 oz) lean minced beef	1–2 eggs

Sauce

175g (6 oz) unsalted butter	good Parmesan cheese, freshly grated
7 fresh sage leaves	

Sauté the garlic and parsley in the butter until they soften. Add the mince and fry it gently for 10 minutes, to just cook it. Mix with the other ingredients for the filling. Season to taste adding grated nutmeg. Roll the pasta into thin sheets and cut into 9cm (3½ in) squares. Place some filling on each and fold in half pressing the moist edges of the rectangle well together. Place on a tray dusted with semolina. Cook in boiling salted water until a corner tastes done. Drain, place them in a warm dish and pour over a sauce made of the butter gently melted with the sage leaves. Add Parmesan at table.

In many country districts they serve both meat-filled pasta and plain spaghetti with *burro e salvia* – a butter and sage sauce like that. Not a luxury dish, but butter, sage and Parmesan are a surprisingly good combination, and beautifully quick.

Tortelli alla cremasca
Tortelli from the Town of Crema

These remarkable little stuffed pasta shapes date from the days when people were less fixed in their ideas about which courses should be sweet and which savoury. For, though eaten as a first course, and accompanied by Parmesan, they are essentially sweet. Outside Italy the only problem they present is when to eat them. But, as they are so surprisingly delicious, this is one problem it is a pleasure to solve. For 8–10.

egg pasta made with 500g (18 oz) plain flour, and 2–3 eggs, see pages 17–22

Filling
350g (12 oz) amaretti
80g (2½ oz) good Parmesan
  cheese, grated
2 egg yolks

a small brandy glass of brandy
  (or substitute whisky)
freshly grated nutmeg

Sauce
150g (5 oz) unsalted butter   good Parmesan cheese, grated

To make the filling, crush the amaretti finely, mix with the Parmesan, egg yolks, and brandy, and season to taste adding grated nutmeg. (Or mix everything in a blender.)

Cut thin sheets of pasta into circles 6cm (2½ in) across. Put some filling on each and fold in half, pressing the moist edges together. Leave them on a tray dusted with semolina until needed. Cook them in boiling salted water. Drain when the pasta tastes done – start testing after 5 minutes, but thicker pasta takes longer.

While they cook, carefully heat the butter to a light brown,

Shaping tortelli

120

and immediately remove it from the heat. Toss the drained tortelli in the butter, sprinkle with Parmesan and serve on warm plates.

'Zucche, le zucche!' – 'Pumpkins, the pumpkins!' – they say in Italy meaning – 'That's crazy!' And 'You've bumped your pumpkin,' they say, mockingly, meaning 'your head'. For in Italy the pumpkin, poor relation of courgettes and marrows, is the ass of the vegetable kingdom.

Nonetheless, pumpkins find a place with pasta. Their golden chunks are mixed with oil, garlic, and chillies as a pasta sauce in Campania, while in Lombardy they make golden creamy soups and unusual little tortellini.

Tortelli di zucca
Pasta Filled with Pumpkin

The *tortelli alla cremasca* are found only in Crema but, though far less common than they used to be, these pumpkin tortelli are still found in several country areas of Lombardy. A little less luxurious in flavour than the tortelli from Crema but still good. For 5.

egg pasta made with 200g (7 oz) plain flour, see pages 17–22

Filling

1kg (2 lb 3 oz) pumpkin	1 egg
60g (2 oz) Mostarda di Cremona	zest of ½ a lemon
	½ tablespoon sugar
60g (2 oz) amaretti, crushed to crumbs	1 tablespoon oven-baked breadcrumbs
1 tablespoon grated Parmesan cheese	2 tablespoons brandy
	freshly grated nutmeg

Sauce

60g (2 oz) good Parmesan cheese, grated	60g (2 oz) unsalted butter

121

Bake the seeded wedge of pumpkin covered with foil, in a moderate oven until the flesh is soft. Remove from the skin and sieve. Mix the pulp with the finely chopped preserved fruit from the *Mostarda di Cremona*, and with the other ingredients of the filling. Add grated nutmeg and salt to taste. Prepare, cook and serve as for *tortelli alla cremasca*, pages 120–1.

Surprisingly, industrial commercial Milan has excellent daily food markets, and special markets on Saturdays in various parts of the town. Here, southern Italians offer their wares: heaps of white goat's cheese, slabs of salt fish, dusty grey-green herbs and sacks of dried fruit and seeds. Beside them you'll find northern vegetables from Milan's allotments and fields: cabbages of every colour, knobbly dark-skinned pumpkins, piles of wine-red *treviso*, varied beans, edible thistles, potatoes, leeks – vegetables which, here in Milan, gave birth to the soup associated with Italian cooking the world over – minestrone.

Minestrone con cazzettini d'angeli
Vegetable Soup with Angels' Little Pricks

In Lombardy they usually put rice in minestrone, but a summery variation is made with pasta, which should be small, and not too thick. The favourite for this soup looks like little curved lengths of macaroni which earthy Italians call *cazzettini d'angeli* – angels' little pricks. They are given all sorts of other names, *diavolicchi* for instance. But if you ask for *diavolicchi* in a shop you are liable to be given a bunch of chillies, so it is best to stick to angels' pricks. Outside Italy the short lengths of quick-cooking macaroni are a good substitute. A hearty unsophisticated soup, or snack meal, for 6–8.

Methods and ingredients which may be unfamiliar are explained on pages 26–38.

100g (4 oz) cazzettini
  d'angeli or small quick-
  cooking macaroni
½ medium-sized aubergine
100g (4 oz) French beans
1 medium-sized courgette
½ carrot
½ celery stick
1 medium-sized potato
300g (11 oz) fresh haricot or
  frozen flageolet beans

250g (9 oz) fresh tomatoes
rosemary, parsley, basil
½ onion
½ garlic clove
25g (1 oz) fatty bacon
2 tablespoons olive oil
75g (2½ oz) button
  mushrooms
15g (½ oz) unsalted butter
grated Parmesan cheese

Wash the aubergine, and cut in small dice, sprinkle with salt and leave to drain for an hour.

Top and tail the French beans and cut in 2cm (1 in) lengths. Rinse, top and tail, then dice the courgettes. Clean the carrot and celery and cut into small pieces. Peel, rinse and dice the potatoes. Put all these, plus the haricot beans and the rinsed aubergine pieces, into a large pan and cover with water. Season with salt, bring to the boil and simmer gently, with the lid on, for about 2 hours.

Skin and chop the tomatoes. Then chop together some parsley, basil, a little sprig of rosemary, the onion, garlic and bacon. Sauté them gently in the oil until lightly golden. Add the tomatoes and simmer for 15 minutes. When the soup has cooked for 2 hours add this tomato mixture and simmer for 15 minutes more, so that the flavours combine. Meanwhile rinse and slice the mushrooms finely, and sauté them in a little butter. Taste the soup, adjust the seasoning, and make sure there is just enough liquid to cook the pasta – but don't add too much, for Italians like soups so crowded with vegetables and pasta they scarcely deserve the name soup, and adding liquid dilutes the flavour. Bring the soup to the boil, add the pasta and mushrooms and cook rapidly until the pasta is *al dente*. Then remove the pan from the heat and let it stand for a while before serving with grated cheese at table.

Minestrone is never served piping hot; to savour it at its best, serve warm in winter and tepid in summer.

In the villages of Valtellina, where Italy touches Switzerland, they like filling warming dishes. Meals get off to a good start with an antipasto of sliced *bresaola* and rye bread. Next may come *pizzoccheri*, a rustic dish made with brown buckwheat pasta. Then game casserole washed down with robust red wine.

Pizzoccheri della Valtellina
Valtellina's Buckwheat Tagliatelle

In Italy this is eaten alone as a hearty first course for 4–6, but it is also homely and comforting with grilled meat or sausages.

non-egg pasta made with 750g (1 lb 10 oz) buckwheat flour, and 250g (9 oz) plain flour (see pages 17–20) or 500g (18 oz) packet pizzoccheri or wholemeal tagliatelle

Sauce

2–3 medium-sized potatoes
½ medium-sized cabbage
200g (7 oz) fresh spinach
1 medium-sized onion, finely chopped
3–4 fresh sage leaves

100g (3½ oz) unsalted butter
100g (3½ oz) fontina cheese, thinly sliced
freshly ground black pepper
good Parmesan cheese, grated

Roll the pasta quite thinly and cut it into long ribbons ½cm (¼ in) wide (pizzoccheri).

Peel and dice the potatoes. Wash and shred the cabbage and spinach. Put the potatoes in plenty of boiling salted water. Bring the water back to the boil and put in the pizzoccheri, then add the cabbage and spinach. (Though not traditional, those who prefer crisp cabbage can add it slightly later.) While they cook gently, sauté the onion and sage leaves in the butter.

When the pasta is *al dente*, and the potatoes cooked, drain the mixture. Immediately place forkfuls of it in a warm casserole, alternately with slices of fontina, grated Parmesan, the oniony butter, and freshly ground black pepper. Cover and take to the table. The warmth of the casserole and the pasta should melt the cheese deliciously.

Quadrotti Duca di Mantova
The Duke of Mantova's Pasta Squares

A willow-green winter sauce which dresses the squares of pasta with the subtle flavour of leeks in butter. A first course for 4.

egg pasta made with 400g (14 oz) plain flour, rolled to the thickness of lasagne, and cut into 6cm (2½ in) squares (see lasagne, pages 17–20) or 400g (14 oz) packet lasagne cut in squares, or pappardelle

1kg (2¼ lb) leeks
90g (3 oz) unsalted butter
a little good broth

4 tablespoons grated Parmesan cheese

Remove the root and any spoiled or very dark green parts of the leeks. Cut into finger-lengths then, down the length, into quarters. Rinse the strips of leek well to remove all dirt.

Drop the leeks into boiling salted water for 2 minutes, drain quickly. Melt half the butter in a heavy pan and cook the leeks very very gently, adding a spoonful of broth from time to time. (If necessary, use a good broth cube.) When tender add half the Parmesan, season to taste, cover, and keep warm.

Cook the pasta in a large pan of boiling salted water, with a drop of oil to stop the squares sticking together. Meanwhile melt the remaining butter. Drain the pasta when *al dente*, place it in a warm bowl, pour on the melted butter, add the remaining Parmesan, stir lightly, top with the leeks, and serve.

Elegant Milan holds some gastronomic surprises; both in her excellent, and expensive, restaurants and in her food shops. Whether in the grey tram-lined streets of the older parts of town, or in exclusive Montenapoleone, the shops are irresistible. The windows, arranged with extraordinary artistry, show off every imaginable delicacy – eggs plump with caviar, rosy salmon, crab and lobster lying in state on silver trays – while among these international specialities familiar pasta is transformed into monumental mosaics, smothered in golden mayonnaise and studded with vegetable gems, for pasta salads often feature in buffets at the parties which the Milanese love to give.

Tagliolini marinari
Seaside Tagliolini

A very special salad which makes a light meal for 4, a first course for 6, or an excellent addition to a buffet.

350g (12 oz) tagliolini or tagliatelline
4 tablespoons best olive oil
zest of ½ small orange or lemon
200g (7 oz) tinned salmon
250g (9 oz) tinned palm hearts

a handful stoned black olives
100g (3½ oz) frozen shrimps or prawns, shelled
lemon juice
½ orange or sweet grapefruit

Cook the pasta *al dente* in plenty of boiling water – these thin egg pastas take only a couple of minutes, and it's essential not to overcook them. Drain, place on a large oval dish and dress immediately with the oil, mixing delicately.

Cut the zest into very fine strips and drop it in boiling water for 1 minute, then drain. Flake the salmon, and slice the palm hearts finely. Add these to the tagliolini, plus the olives and thawed, drained shrimps – reserving a little of each, to decorate. Season with white pepper and lemon juice to taste and toss lightly. Decorate with the reserved ingredients and the skinless segments of orange or grapefruit. Serve cold, but not chilled.

Methods and ingredients which may be unfamiliar are explained on pages 26–38.

Maccheroncelli
in insalata

Little Macaroni in Salad

A good salad to include in a buffet, or a light lunch for 4–6.

250g (9 oz) maccheroncelli,
  shells, or lumache
1 sweet red or green pimento
100g (3½ oz) cold tongue
100g (3½ oz) Italian salami,
  thinly sliced
5 thin slices Emmenthal
a small finger-length pickled
  gherkin
100g (3½ oz) frozen petits pois,
  cooked

1 small onion, finely chopped
4 tablespoons milk
10 tablespoons mayonnaise,
  homemade or good bought
about 1 tablespoon lemon
  juice
cayenne pepper
parsley
2 hardboiled eggs
3 firm tomatoes

Put a large pan of salted water to boil for the pasta. Wipe the pimento clean, remove the stalk and seeds and cut in fine strips. Cut the meat and cheese in small strips as well. Chop the gherkin. Put them all in a large salad bowl with the peas and onion.

Cook the pasta while you make the dressing by gradually mixing the milk into the mayonnaise and adding lemon juice, salt, pepper and cayenne pepper to taste. Drain the pasta when *al dente*, add it to the salad, and mix in the dressing. Cover and leave in a refrigerator for at least an hour. Serve decorated with parsley sprigs and wedges of egg and tomato.

Bavette in insalata
Bavette in Salad

An excellent salad for a buffet, or a light lunch for 4.

250g (9 oz) bavette, or
spaghetti
175g (6 oz) thinly sliced cold
tongue
150g (5 oz) thinly sliced cold
roast pork
½ cucumber
4 tablespoons olive oil

1–2 tablespoons wine vinegar
a good pinch sweet paprika
a dash Tabasco sauce
1 small onion, finely chopped
225g (8 oz) salad tomatoes, in
segments
2 tablespoons chopped parsley

Cut the meat into matchsticks. Cut the cucumber in half lengthwise, and slice thinly. Cook the pasta in plenty of boiling salted water while you mix together the oil, vinegar, paprika, Tabasco, and onion, in a salad bowl. Drain the pasta when *al dente*, and mix with the dressing. Add the other ingredients, toss, cover, and refrigerate for at least 30 minutes. Decorate with parsley, and serve cold but not chilled.

Tagliatelle al caviale
Tagliatelle with Caviar

With fresh tagliatelle this is simple yet excellent, a perfect way to eat mock caviar. A first course for 4.

500g (18 oz) fresh tagliatelle
or 400g (14 oz) packet
tagliatelle

120g (4 oz) unsalted butter
100g (3½ oz) jar lumpfish roe
(Danish caviar)

Soften the butter in a bowl of tepid water for 2 hours. Cook the pasta in plenty of boiling salted water. Meanwhile, put the drained butter in the pasta bowl in a warm place – it should not melt but you may cream it slightly. Drain the pasta when *al dente*, transfer it to the bowl, mix delicately and take to the table, with the roe in a little side dish. A gleaming spoonful of caviar tops each helping. Some people like to add a sprinkling of cayenne pepper and even a squeeze of lemon.

Scaloppine di animella alla milanese con fettuccine al burro

*Veal Sweetbreads with Buttery Fettuccine
the Milanese Way*

A sophisticated main course for 6 such as you might find in a smart Milan restaurant. The first half of the preparation can be done well in advance.

600g (1 lb 5 oz) fettuccine
900g (2 lb) veal sweetbreads
plain flour
1 large egg
*fresh breadcrumbs baked
    golden in the oven and
    finely crushed*

*90–100g (3–3½ oz) grated
    Parmesan cheese*
200g (7 oz) unsalted butter
olive oil
lemon wedges
parsley

Cleanse and blanch the sweetbreads as usual, see pages 36–37. Wrap them in a cloth and place under a well-weighted plate for 1 hour. Cut them in slices like escalopes of veal, dust with seasoned flour, dip in the beaten egg and then in several tablespoons of the crumbs mixed with 2 tablespoons of the Parmesan.

Put a large pan of salted water to boil for the pasta. Gently fry the sweetbreads in 45g (1½ oz) of the butter and a touch of oil, until golden on both sides. Drain on kitchen paper and keep warm. Cook the fettuccine while you warm a large flat dish. Put the remaining butter on the dish in flakes. Drain the fettuccine when *al dente* and toss them in the butter with the remaining

Parmesan. Heap them nicely, arrange the slices of sweetbread round the edge of the plate, with the lemon wedges to squeeze on the sweetbreads, and sprigs of parsley, and serve at once.

Lasagne alla naviglia
Lasagne the Naviglio Way

Milan was once a maze of waterways; most have now been covered over, but the Naviglio Grande remains, slipping through the oldest part of the town, under ancient bridges, and out to the fields beyond. Beside it a rustic restaurant makes a simple and unusual lasagne, flavoured with salami and courgettes, very much like this. A light main course for 6–8.

400g (14 oz) lasagne
100g (3½ oz) sliced Italian salami
2 carrots
1 medium-sized onion
2 sticks celery
4 tablespoons olive oil
850g (1 lb 14 oz) fresh or tinned tomatoes, skinned and chopped

1 tumbler dry white wine
800g (1 lb 12 oz) courgettes
sunflower oil for frying
a tiny pinch of oregano (optional)
300g (10 oz) mozzarella, thinly sliced
70g (2½ oz) good Parmesan cheese, grated

Remove the rind and cut the salami in little strips. Finely chop the carrot, onion and celery, and soften in the oil. When they begin to turn golden add half the salami, the tomatoes and wine. Simmer for 45 minutes, stirring occasionally, and tasting and seasoning the sauce when half cooked.

Meanwhile, cook the lasagne as usual, page 23. Wash, top and tail the courgettes and cut them, lengthwise, in slices about ½cm (¼ in) thick, halving any very long slices. Fry them in sunflower oil until tender and golden, then drain on kitchen paper. Season with salt and oregano.

Rub a large oblong oven dish with butter. Place a layer of

lasagne in the bottom, add a thin layer of sauce, some slices of courgette and mozzarella, some of the remaining salami, and a sprinkling of Parmesan – the ingredients can be dotted about, they don't need to cover their layer – then more lasagne. Continue until everything is used up, ending with lasagne topped by mozzarella and Parmesan. Put in a hot oven for 20–30 minutes.

Timballo di cavolo e mozzarella

Lasagne Pie with Cabbage and Cheese

Cabbage is popular in Lombardy and in this dish parcels of cabbage, filled with melting cheese, top little parcels of lasagne. If you don't want to make lasagne parcels, layer it like normal lasagne, but the cabbage parcels are essential to this delicate and unusual dish. A light meal for 4.

200g (7 oz) wide lasagne rectangles

½ medium-sized onion, well chopped

2 tablespoons sunflower oil

150g (5 oz) good beef mince

3 tablespoons freshly puréed tomatoes

300g (11 oz) green cabbage (after trimming)

80g (2¾ oz) unsalted butter

4 tablespoons plain flour

400ml (¾ pint) milk

50g (2 oz) good Parmesan cheese, grated

100g (3½ oz) mozzarella

Sauté the onion in the oil until golden. Add the mince and brown it slightly before adding the tomato and several tablespoons of hot water. Simmer for 30 minutes.

Meanwhile, cook the lasagne as usual, see page 23, and cut it into approximately 10cm (4 in) squares. Set aside 4 nice cabbage leaves and slice the rest. Drop the whole cabbage leaves in boiling salted water and cook for 5 minutes. Lift them out and put in the sliced cabbage, and cook for 5 minutes. Drain. Chop the sliced cabbage very thoroughly and sauté it for 5 minutes in

25g (1 oz) of the butter, without browning. When the meat has finished simmering, mix in the chopped cabbage. Season to taste and set aside. Make a white sauce, page 37, with the flour, milk and remaining butter.

Put a spoonful of the meat mixture on each square of pasta and fold into a little parcel. Place a layer of parcels in a fairly deep buttered oven dish, add half the white sauce and a third of the Parmesan. Repeat, tucking any spare filling round the parcels before adding the white sauce. Cut the mozzarella into four, and fold 1 parboiled cabbage leaf round each, cutting away any hard stalk. Place these on the lasagne, sprinkle with Parmesan, and put the dish in a hot oven for about 20 minutes, until the top begins to colour.

8 LUCANIA

What is there left in Lucania? There are a few, thrifty dignified people. There's nature, friendly and hostile. There are old villages, old towns, old houses. There's kindness; there's still poverty. And philosophy.

The Land of Lucania, Leonardo Sinisgalli

 Lucania is one of the most dramatic but least-known areas of Italy, and has suffered greatly from isolation. It is a region of contrasts – summers are scorchingly hot, winters snowy and bitterly cold – of wild mountains, impressive gorges, and torrential rivers. Little of that water reaches the land and the unforgiving climate, poor stony ground, and tortuous roads have combined with the tragedies caused by earthquakes to make life hard, and many have emigrated.

Those that remain are deeply attached to the land: an eerie, deserted place where solitary oaks dominate postage-stamp fields, shrubby vines yield only one exceptional wine, and corn is still threshed as it was in biblical times. Traditions die hard and a few old peasants still foretell the coming year by examining the entrails of animals, on the night of the full moon, in the manner of the ancient Etruscans.

The cooking here is extremely simple, contrived from whatever the countryside offers: herbs, snails, wild fennel, and leafy vegetables for salads. Their only luxury is the family pig. Few dishes are unique to Lucania but they sometimes eat pasta in a way unknown elsewhere – with fresh horseradish grated over the top in place of cheese. A good addition if, like the Lucanians, you like your food really hot, for here the strongest chilli recipes are found and chillies are eaten raw with bread, as the Sicilians eat onions.

Bucatini e peperoncini
Bucatini with Chillies

This is in a different league from the other recipes with these ingredients – a dish for fanatics, for chilli addicts who, like the people of Lucania, venerate the little flaming fruit like a pagan fire god. You need fresh chillies for this recipe, dried ones burn too easily. A first course for 4.

450g (1 lb) bucatini or spaghetti
7 tablespoons good olive oil
4 garlic cloves, peeled
6 medium-sized fresh red chillies
parsley (optional)

Have a large pan of boiling salted water ready for the pasta. Put 3 tablespoons of oil in a small pan with 3 whole garlic cloves and the chillies. Cook very gently. When soft, but not brown, remove the pan from the heat and pound the garlic and chillies well into the oil.

While the pasta cooks, warm the rest of the oil in a wide

Methods and ingredients which may be unfamiliar are explained on pages 26–38.

shallow pan with 1 clove finely chopped garlic. When it begins to colour add the pounded mixture, and the sauce is ready. Drain the pasta when *al dente*, toss in the sauce and serve. No cheese is needed, but a little chopped parsley can be used to garnish.

In Lucania bread, baked in every shape and size imaginable, is important, and, according to folklore, flat loaves were once decorated and offered as gifts to the pagan gods. White, brown or sand yellow, made from durum wheat, it is baked in coils, twists, rounds or rings, sometimes enriched with pork beastings or flavoured with peppers. Nothing is ever wasted in the south, and the bits from the breadboard are saved, baked golden in the oven, and rolled with a bottle into crumbs to give the finishing touch to one of the quickest and easiest of all pasta sauces, which is equally popular in Sicily and Calabria.

Pasta ammuddicata

Pasta with Crumbs

A 'poor' recipe, but with a really unusual texture and exciting taste – a favourite with those who like both chilli and anchovy. It makes an interesting first course for 4–6, but check if guests like chillies or they may refuse the crumbs, and without them it is not *pasta ammuddicata*. On no account try to use packet breadcrumbs, they would ruin the dish.

500g (18 oz) bucatini or
   spaghetti
8–10 anchovy fillets, *drained*
   and chopped

6 tablespoons *good olive oil*
1 handful *oven-baked*
   breadcrumbs
chilli powder, *to taste*

Put a large pan of salted water to boil for the pasta. Gently melt the chopped anchovies in the oil. Cover and keep this warm while you cook the pasta *al dente*. Meanwhile, lightly brown the very finely crushed breadcrumbs and chilli powder in 1 teaspoon of oil, without burning them. Drain the pasta, place in a warm bowl, pour over the anchovy oil, and toss. Serve, with the crumbs in a separate bowl. Each person sprinkles the peppery crumbs on their pasta. No cheese is added.

In such a poor area pork is vitally important. Even now, many families have only one pig and the pig-killing is a most important event, followed by a feast unequalled by any except that on a wedding day. Every part of the beast is used; the best meat is made into hams, pork rind and beastings are preserved in suet in large earthenware pots to provide fat for cooking and flavour for simple sauces, and the off cuts go into a special sausage called *lucanica*, or *luganega* when sold in Lombardy. Praised since Roman times for its succulence, and highly seasoned with every sort of pepper, it is slimmer than ordinary sausage and untied; so it goes on and on in one long rope and is coiled in spirals on shop shelves. Dried, it is eaten sliced like salami; fresh, it is cooked in a sauce like the following.

Fusilli con lucanica
Fusilli with Sausage

This sauce is unusual in having quite a lot of onion, and it needs good continental sausages (page 36). An easy light main course for 4, or first course for 6.

600g (1 lb 5 oz) fusilli, shells, or farfalle
2 red or yellow pimentos
200g (7 oz) really meaty peppery Italian sausages
500g (18 oz) finely sliced onions
4–6 tablespoons olive oil
600g (1 lb 5 oz) fresh or tinned tomatoes, skinned and chopped
1 handful grated pecorino cheese

Methods and ingredients which may be unfamiliar are explained on pages 26–38.

Remove the stalk and seeds from the pimentos and cut them into slim strips. Skin and chop the sausages. Gently soften the onions and peppers in the oil in a wide pan. Add the sausage pieces and sauté until cooked. Then put in the tomatoes, and season with salt. (If the sausage is peppery it will lend its fire to the sauce, if it isn't add a little chilli or chilli powder.) Cover, and simmer gently for 40 minutes, stirring occasionally and adding a touch of water if necessary. Taste, and adjust the seasoning.

Cook the pasta *al dente* in plenty of boiling salted water. Drain, place it in a warm bowl, pour on the sauce, add a handful of pecorino, and serve.

Timballo di maccheroni
Oven Macaroni

This recipe may seem rather fiddly to make but it's not difficult and the odd way of using the tomatoes does make a difference. Fresh tomatoes are always used in Italy, but where they are less ripe and red, tinned may be better. A light lunch or supper for 6–8.

350g (12 oz) long macaroni, or penne
600g (1 lb 5 oz) aubergines, sliced lengthwise
700g (1½ lb) tomatoes
1 clove garlic, sliced
4 tablespoons olive oil
1 chilli (optional)
corn or sunflower oil for frying
60g (2 oz) caciocavallo cheese, pecorino sardo, or provolone and pecorino mixed
a little fresh basil, chopped

Sprinkle the aubergines with salt and leave to drain for 1 hour. Skin and chop the tomatoes, place them in a colander and let their water drip into a bowl – to be used later.

Cook the garlic gently in the olive oil till golden. Add the tomato pulp, then the liquid from the bowl underneath, *but do not stir or mix them together*. Season with salt, and pepper or chilli if you wish, and cook rapidly for 4 minutes. The tomato water and oil should mix together into a light emulsion, and the pieces of tomato stay intact. Remove from the heat and keep warm.

Put a large pan of salted water to boil for the pasta. Rinse and dry the aubergines and fry them in hot oil until golden and tender. Drain them on kitchen paper and sprinkle with salt. Cook the pasta *al dente*, drain, place it in a bowl and tip in the liquid part of the sauce and a few pieces of tomato. Mix well. Place one-third in an oven dish, cover with a third of the aubergine, and sprinkle on a third of the cheese and a little basil. Continue these layers covering the top layer of aubergine with the cooked tomato pieces and then the cheese. Put in a hot oven for 10 minutes and serve.

Fusilli e involtini di Emilia
Emilia's Fusilli with Meat Rolls

An unusual and excellent way to eat pasta, with a taste all of its own, and the little rolls of stuffed beef look splendid sitting on top of the glistening twists of pasta. Mixed green and white fusilli look particularly attractive, but use the same brand or they may take different times to cook. A good lunch or an informal supper for 6.

600g (1 lb 5 oz) fusilli
300g (11 oz) thinly sliced lean
   roasting beef (at least 12
   slices)
1 large carrot
1 celery stalk
30g (1 oz) unsmoked bacon
thyme
plain flour
½ small onion, finely
   chopped
½ clove garlic, finely
   chopped

4 tablespoons olive oil
¾ tumbler red wine
   (optional)
1kg (2 lb 3 oz) fresh or tinned
   tomatoes, skinned and
   chopped
a piece of chilli
grated Parmesan and pecorino
   cheese
fresh horseradish root
   (optional)

Use meat from a round of meat, such as topside – not boned and rolled meat which will fall apart. Have it cut in the thinnest possible slices and beat them out to about 10×15cm (4×6 in). Clean the carrot and celery and chop a quarter of each very finely, for the sauce. Then cut the remainder of each into 10cm (4 in) matchstick strips, and the bacon in thin strips. Lay a mixture of these across each slice of beef. Season the meat, adding a little thyme, roll up tightly round the vegetables, dust with flour, and fasten with a wooden cocktail stick if necessary.

Soften the onion, garlic, chopped carrot and celery in the oil in a heavy casserole. Then add the meat rolls and brown nicely all over. Add the wine, tomatoes, and a little piece of chilli. Season with salt, cover, and simmer gently for about 1½ hours. Taste, adjust the seasoning, and remove any cocktail sticks.

Have ready a large pan of boiling salted water for the pasta. Cook the pasta *al dente*. Drain, put in a warm bowl, add a handful of cheese, and pour over the sauce. Mix lightly, so the meat rolls remain nicely on top, and serve. Extra cheese can be handed round at table, though in Lucania they often add freshly grated horseradish root instead.

Among Lucanians superstition is very strong, even today, and compliments are thought to tempt the devil. On entering a home in Lucania where pasta is being prepared, a visitor may say, '*che bella pasta*' – 'what lovely pasta' – but, traditionally, will quickly add 'Saint Martina bless you' to prove he is not a bringer of bad luck.

Lasagne con la ricotta
Lasagne with Ricotta

One of the few lasagne which even non-Italians would consider a first course. The essence of this dish is that fresh basil scents the ricotta lightly and deliciously: it cannot be made without it. To serve 4–5.

350g (12 oz) lasagne
60g (2 oz) unsalted butter
2 rounded tablespoons flour
about 500ml (1 pint) milk
1 tablespoon chopped fresh
  basil

100g (3½ oz) ricotta cheese
50g (2 oz) good Parmesan
  cheese, or pecorino sardo or
  50:50, grated
a few whole basil leaves

Cook the lasagne as usual, see page 23. Make a white sauce, page 37, with the butter, flour and milk and simmer gently until it tastes cooked. Stir in the chopped basil, ricotta and half the other cheese, and season carefully to taste. If it seems too thick add a little hot milk, for it should pour like thick cream.

Rub an oven dish with butter and arrange in it a layer of lasagne. Cover with a thin layer of sauce, some grated cheese, and a few pieces of basil leaf. Continue like this, finishing with a layer of sauce, grated cheese and basil. Put in a hot oven for a few minutes just to heat through – it doesn't need to brown. Serve at once.

9 THE MARCHES

 Tucked inconspicuously on the calf of Italy, the Marches were once a 'Mark' – a frontier province of Charlemagne's Empire. Despite a turbulent history, this is a peaceful region of gentle hills patchworked with fields of wheat and sugar beet, where roadside poplars rustle in the constant breeze from the Adriatic. This tranquillity is expressed in the cooking; not as flamboyant as in other regions, there is a quiet excellence and richness of flavour, and the influence of her neighbour Emilia-Romagna is seen in buttery oven dishes, their sauces scented with truffles of this region.

The aquamarine waters of the Adriatic provide some of the best fish in Italy, including delicacies such as scallops and plaice, seldom found in other regions. In the harbour towns that dot the long beige beaches, the speciality is *brodetto*, a superb fish soup: made from as many as twelve varieties of fish and shellfish, flavoured with wine, garlic and wild saffron, it rivals the great bouillabaisse of Marseille. As an antipasto, large green olives are served in a unique way; cut round the stone in a spiral, stuffed with a forcemeat of chicken and sausage, breadcrumbed, and fried. A perfect partner to the delicately perfumed wine of the region.

Around Loreto, where the Black Madonna is enshrined, game and mushrooms are found, and pasta sauces are like those of Tuscany; but the pasta itself is unique. Campofilone are probably the lightest, finest tagliatelle in all Italy. Made of eggs and flour, their indefinable delicacy can only depend on the wheat, the water and the skill of the women who make them. They are equally good with delicate fish sauces or rich *ragùs* of meat and wine.

Maccheroncini
di Campofilone
Finest Macaroni of Campofilone

This dish is unusual in combining two different pasta sauces. It makes an excellent main course for 5–6. Any good tomato paste can be used, but strengths vary with different brands. These quantities are for the standard paste made by Cirio.

egg pasta from 500g (18 oz) plain flour, see pages 17–20, made into very fine tagliatelle or 500g (18 oz) finest tagliatelle

First sauce

1½ medium-sized onions	3 tablespoons olive oil
½ carrot	250g (9 oz) tomato paste
½ celery stick	500g (18 oz) beef bone from
a touch of chilli	middle of shin bone, sawn in
basil leaves	5cm (2 in) lengths
marjoram	½ clove
25g (1 oz) unsalted butter	

Methods and ingredients which may be unfamiliar are explained on pages 26–38.

Ragù

1.5kg (3 lb 4 oz) tinned tomatoes, sieved	*1 fresh or dried chilli*
	basil, marjoram, a clove
250g (9 oz) lean minced beef	*100g (3½ oz) grated pecorino*
½ small onion, chopped	*sardo cheese*

For the first sauce, sauté the finely chopped onion, carrot, celery and chilli in the butter and oil for 10 minutes, with a pinch of each herb. Add the tomato paste, diluted in 250ml (½ pint) water, clove and marrow bones, and simmer uncovered for 1 hour, stirring occasionally. Strain the sauce. Scoop the marrow out of the bones and add it to the liquid.

While the first sauce cooks make the *ragù* by putting all the ingredients, except the cheese, into a casserole and simmering for 40 minutes, stirring and breaking up the meat as it cooks.

Have ready a large pan of boiling salted water for the pasta. Cook it *al dente* – very fine tagliatelle may be ready when their water returns to the boil. Drain, and mix with the first sauce until the pasta glistens. Add a handful of pecorino, transfer to a warm serving dish and top with the *ragù*. Add more pecorino and serve.

Chitarrelli
alla marchigiana
Chitarra Spaghetti in the Style of the Marches

This dish with its unusual, slightly piquant sauce, comes from near the border with Abruzzi. It is one of the few outside that region to use *maccheroni alla chitarra*. The great thing about this sauce is the way the richness of the bacon is complemented by the pungency of sage leaves and the refreshing hint of vinegar. It serves 6–7 as a first course, or 4–5 for a very light lunch.

500g (18 oz) chitarra
spaghetti, or long
macaroni
100g (3½ oz) bacon in slim
short strips
25g (1 oz) unsalted butter
500g (18 oz) fresh or tinned
tomatoes, skinned and finely
chopped

a little broth
50g (1¾ oz) capers
4 fresh, not dried, sage leaves
1 tablespoon vinegar
grated pecorino cheese

Put a large pan of salted water to boil for the pasta. Cook the bacon gently in the melted butter in a wide shallow pan for 5 minutes. Stir in the tomatoes, season lightly and simmer for 15 minutes, adding a tablespoon or two of broth when it thickens. Lower the heat and simmer very gently while you cook the pasta *al dente*.

When the pasta is almost ready add the capers, sage leaves and vinegar to the sauce. Taste and adjust the seasoning. Drain the pasta and toss it in the pan with the sauce for a few seconds. Serve immediately adding a little grated cheese to each plateful.

Rotolo di pasta e spinaci

Pasta and Spinach Roll

This spinach roll is a completely novel way of using pasta; an attractive and economical dish which serves 6. It can be made with a piece of pasta left over from making ravioli or lasagne, and most of the preparation can be done in advance. The meat sauce can be from round any of the pot roasts, or even be Bolognese.

a sheet of egg pasta made with 100g (3½ oz) plain flour, see pages 17–19

1kg (2 lb 3 oz) fresh or
frozen spinach
90g (3 oz) good ham,
chopped

1½ cups meat or tomato
sauce
good Parmesan cheese,
grated

Wash the fresh spinach thoroughly, discarding any coarse stalks and damaged leaves. Cook it gently in a covered pan with a touch of salt but no water. (Cook frozen spinach according to its instructions.) Drain the cooked spinach, press out the water, chop it very well, and season to taste.

Roll the pasta thinly into a rectangle. Spread the spinach evenly on it, sprinkle on the ham, and roll up like a swiss roll. Wrap it firmly in a piece of butter muslin – or other clean thin cloth – and tie the ends like a Christmas cracker. Place in a large pan of boiling salted water and boil steadily for 20 minutes or so.

Remove it from the pan, place on a long shallow oven dish, take off the cloth carefully, and slice, arranging the slices attractively. Spoon on the hot meat or tomato sauce and put in the oven for a few minutes to heat the slices thoroughly. Add Parmesan at table.

Lasagne al forno
Oven Lasagne

The combination of different types of meat, which have been finely chopped not minced, makes an unusually good lasagne for 6–8.

fresh lasagne sheets made with egg pasta from 400g (14 oz) plain flour, see pages 17–20, or 400g (14 oz) bought lasagne

Sauce
½ onion
40g (1½ oz) bacon or ham fat
1 tablespoon olive oil
70g (2½ oz) unsalted butter
200g (7 oz) lean pork mince
1 chicken breast
300g (11 oz) lean stewing beef

100g (3½ oz) prosciutto off cuts or ham, in strips
600g (1 lb 5 oz) fresh or tinned tomatoes, skinned and chopped
120g (4 oz) good Parmesan cheese, grated

White sauce

½ tablespoon finely chopped onion	*½ litre (1 pint) milk, or more freshly grated nutmeg*
100g (3½ oz) unsalted butter	*½ bay leaf*
5 level tablespoons plain flour	

For the meat sauce, sauté the finely chopped onion and ham fat in a heavy pan with the oil and three-quarters of the butter. When the onion turns golden stir in the pork, and very finely chopped chicken breast and beef. Brown the meat over moderate heat before adding the prosciutto or ham, and the tomatoes. Season, remembering the ham may add some saltiness, and simmer for about 1½ hours, stirring occasionally and adding a little broth or water if it gets too dry. Taste and adjust the seasoning.

Cook the lasagne as usual, see page 23, and make the white sauce, see page 37, adding a pinch of nutmeg and the bay leaf. When cooked remove the bay leaf.

When the meat sauce is cooked, rub a large oblong oven dish with the remaining butter. Place in it a layer of lasagne, then a thin layer of meat sauce, some spoonfuls of white sauce, and a little Parmesan. Continue these layers ending with pasta topped by white sauce and Parmesan. Put the dish in a hot oven for about 20 minutes, until pale golden and bubbling. Or assemble it in advance and heat it for twice as long.

Legend has it that the next dish was created by the cook of Prince Windisch Gratz, an Austrian general who visited the Marches in 1799 during the Napoleonic wars; but the recipe has been found in an earlier pamphlet, the creation of Antonio Nebbia from Macerata. Despite that, it still bears the general's name: the German Windisch Gratz corrupted to *vincisgrassi*.

Methods and ingredients which may be unfamiliar are explained on pages 26–38.

Vincisgrassi

Extravagant, elaborate, and very time consuming, this is one of the great classic dishes of the region. A dish for special occasions, seldom served in restaurants more than once a week – and then usually to order. It must be prepared the day before you need it. A main course for 8.

sheets of lasagne made like normal egg pasta, see pages 17–20, but with the following ingredients

500g (18 oz) plain flour
300g (10 oz) semolina
50g (1¾ oz) unsalted butter, softened

5 eggs
2–3 tablespoons Marsala or sherry (optional)

Sauce
a handful dried porcini mushrooms
1 medium-sized onion, finely chopped
100g (3½ oz) unsalted butter
a little chicken broth

1 tablespoon tomato paste
powdered cinnamon
200g (7 oz) lamb's sweetbreads
150g (5 oz) chicken livers, chopped

White sauces
150g (5 oz) unsalted butter
5 tablespoons plain flour
800ml (1½ pint) milk

good Parmesan cheese, grated
a truffle (optional)

Put the dried mushrooms to soak, in a little tepid water, for 1–2 hours. Soak and cleanse the sweetbreads, see pages 36–7. Cook the lasagne as usual, see page 23.

For the sauce: let the onion turn transparent in most of the butter over a very low heat. Add the soaked mushrooms, their liquid strained through a muslin, and 1–2 tablespoons of broth. Simmer for 5 minutes, then add the tomato paste, a pinch of cinnamon, and a little more broth. Season to taste, and continue simmering while you prepare the rest of the sauce. Put the sweetbreads in cold water, bring to the boil, drain, and chop. Sauté the chicken livers in a little butter until just cooked.

Make a thick white sauce as usual (see page 37) using 50g (1¾ oz) butter, 2 tablespoons flour, and just under 250ml (½ pint) milk. When cooked, mix with the onion and mushroom mixture and remove from the heat.

Rub a large oven dish with butter. Place a layer of pasta in the bottom. Scatter in some of the liver and sweetbreads, cover with a thin layer of sauce, then plenty of Parmesan, a couple of slices of truffle and tiny pieces of butter. Continue in layers like this, until all the ingredients are used up, ending with a layer of pasta, then cover and refrigerate for 6 hours.

Make a second white sauce with remaining 100g (3½ oz) butter, 3 tablespoons flour, and ½ litre (1 pint) milk. Pour over the *vincisgrassi*, spread to the edges, slice the truffle on top (if you have it) and place in a hot oven for 30 minutes or till the top is golden.

What a lovely smell of simmering you breathe in this town. Such country sunshine, such peace. On warm spring afternoons the churches smell of incense and, what with the glorious crowing of cocks and cackling of hens, one finds in these Marches towns the dust of days gone by.
Sky Over the Cities, Vincenzo Cardarelli

Just such a smell comes from this next old-fashioned recipe from Ancona: slowly simmered beef and rustic pasta. To save time you can use any short packet pasta, or long pasta which is not too slim – bucatini for example, or rigatoni.

Pincinelle all'anconetana
Pincinelle of Ancona

Pincinelle are the Marchese version of the cord-like pasta called *pici* in Tuscany. An easy and very filling rustic pasta often served

Methods and ingredients which may be unfamiliar are explained on pages 26–38.

with this satisfying sauce of braised beef. In Italy the beef itself is then served as a second course, so two courses are created from one lot of cooking, but it can be served with the pasta if you prefer. For 6–8.

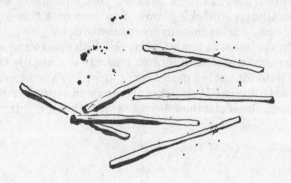

egg pasta made from 600g (1 lb 5 oz) durum flour, but with only 1 egg and ½ tablespoon oil, see pages 17–19

1kg (2 lb 3 oz) joint rolled braising beef
60g (2 oz) ham fat
1 handful parsley
2 tablespoons olive oil
90g (3 oz) unsmoked bacon
3 medium-sized onions
2 cloves garlic

1 tumbler red wine
800g (1 lb 12 oz) fresh or tinned tomatoes, skinned and chopped
30g (1 oz) unsalted butter
good Parmesan cheese, grated

The beef should be larded with the ham fat, rolled in pepper and chopped parsley. The lazy way is simply to unroll your joint, sprinkle it with chopped ham fat, some parsley and pepper, then roll it up again, and tie it with strong white cotton string or thread.

Brown the beef all over in the oil in a heavy casserole, with the well-chopped bacon, onions, garlic and parsley. Pour in the wine, evaporate a little, then add the tomatoes. Season, cover, and simmer for at least 2½ hours until the meat is really tender.

149

Or cook in a low oven for at least 3 hours. Stir it from time to time and add a spoonful of water if it threatens to stick. Taste and adjust the seasoning.

While it cooks, roll the pasta out in a fairly thick sheet. Cut it in strands and roll each, between your hands, to make long cords as slim as a drinking straw. Put them on a tray sprinkled with durum flour or semolina to stop them sticking.

When the meat is almost ready, cook the pasta in plenty of boiling salted water until it tastes cooked – this usually takes far longer than for packet pasta. Serve topped by the sauce which surrounds the meat, little flakes of butter and a sprinkling of good Parmesan. The beef is then sliced and served as a second course.

10 PIEDMONT

 In one of his letters from Italy Tobias Smollett wrote 'Beef, pork and capon imported from Piedmont are excellent and a good price.'

The same is true today. Piedmont borders France and its dishes have the charm of the region coupled with more than a touch of French finesse. Food is elegantly presented, and cooking is concerned with making the best use of butter, good meat, and the excellent wines of the region – which are little exported, for Italians like to keep their best wine, and women, for themselves: the local toast is '*Al piacere!*' – 'To pleasure!'

At one time true Italian cooking was only favoured among the peasant farmers, while the upper classes ate the French way. Here, as in most parts, the food is less rich than it was once. Then broth was only considered good broth if covered with 'swimming eyes' – little golden drops of fat – whereas nowadays fat is carefully removed. Rice is preferred to pasta; indeed pasta has only been in general use for the last hundred years and old people still think of it as something imported from the south. So pasta dishes are mainly cooked for special occasions.

Stuffed pastas are a speciality of this region – delicate parcels filled with meat and northern vegetables are served with melted butter and cheese. Tagliatelle and lasagne are eaten with the juices from a fine pot roast, or rich with melted mountain cheese, or with the exquisite local mushrooms, or with Piedmont's prized white truffles.

Many tales have grown up round the truffle: it used to be said that it grew only where thunder and lightning shook the earth, or that it was found under the trees where witches rested – and just why it grows where it does is still a mystery. In Piedmont the great area for truffles is round Alba. There licensed truffle hunters and their dogs search out white truffles, with their greeny yellow casing and hazel-coloured flesh, at the foot of willows, oaks and poplars.

In Italy the precious truffle is prized by gastronomes and Casanovas alike for it is still believed to be an aphrodisiac – which is why, at one time, it was strictly forbidden to the clergy. A curious idea for such an unseductive specimen: drab coloured and lumpy in shape, but with an irresistible scent the *Tuber ipogeus* is the culinary version of the frog waiting to be transformed into a prince. Despite its carbuncular skin even the smallest wafers of its firm cream flesh lend a remarkable flavour to any dish, and make a wonderful addition to pasta.

Tajarin are traditionally eaten with truffles, and were known in the Langhe area long before other pasta arrived from neighbouring regions. They are thin tagliatelle, like their famous sisters in Emilia. Never overcooked, as sometimes happens to pasta in the north, they are full flavoured and firm, to hold meat sauces enriched with porcini mushrooms or slices of white truffle.

Methods and ingredients which may be unfamiliar are explained on pages 26–38.

Tajarin con tartufi

Piedmontese Tagliatelle with White Truffles

If you are fortunate enough to have a fresh truffle it is well worth making this exquisite dish. Sadly the flavour of tinned truffles is no more than a faint gesture in the right direction, but it is still very good with no truffles at all. A first course or light lunch for 4.

egg pasta made with 400g (14 oz) plain flour and 1 tablespoon best Parmesan cheese, grated, but only 2–3 eggs, see pages 17–20

a white truffle
100g (3½) unsalted butter
3–4 tablespoons good chicken broth

100g (3½ oz) best Parmesan cheese, grated
grated nutmeg

Roll the pasta thinly and cut in tagliatelle ½cm (¼ in) wide.

Clean the fresh truffle and peel off the outer skin. Cook the tagliatelle in plenty of boiling salted water. Meanwhile, in a little pan, melt the butter very gently with the broth. Add the Parmesan, stir, remove from the heat and season with grated nutmeg and white pepper. Drain the pasta when *al dente*, transfer it to a warm bowl, pour over the butter mixture, mix lightly and cover with little slices of truffle. Serve at once.

In Piedmont anyone can obtain a licence to look for truffles, and they belong to the finder, no matter whose land they are on. So, in the truffle season young and old join the hunt for the crock of gold under the trees; and people flock to attend fairs where great mounds of truffles change hands for extraordinary sums and streets and squares are heavily perfumed with their unique aroma. Many of those truffles end up in Turin's elegant restaurants to be served in dishes like the following.

Lasagnette alla Cavour

Cavour's Ribbon Lasagne

This is very good, even without the truffle and quickly made, for the narrow lasagne are used like pappardelle, not arranged in layers. A light main dish for 4.

450g (1 lb) lasagnette or
   pappardelle
2 shallots (or a small onion)
70g (2½ oz) unsalted butter
3 tablespoons olive oil
450g (1 lb) mixed chicken
   livers and hearts (or just
   chicken livers)

6 tablespoons brandy
1 tumbler good poultry broth
60g (2 oz) good Parmesan
   cheese, grated
1 fresh white truffle or a fresh
   bay leaf and 2 sage leaves

Cook the very finely chopped shallots gently in the oil and most of the butter until they soften. Add the chopped livers and hearts, increase the heat slightly and sauté until well coloured. Pour in the brandy and let it bubble to reduce by half. Season to taste (adding a bay leaf and sage leaves if you have no truffle), add the broth, and simmer for 15 minutes.

Have ready a large pan of boiling salted water and cook the lasagne while you warm a large pasta bowl with a nut of butter in it. When *al dente*, drain the pasta, place it in the bowl, pour over the sauce and add little slices of truffle. Serve, passing round the Parmesan.

Tagliatelle all'albese

Tagliatelle Alba Style

In Piedmont chicken livers often give pasta sauces extra richness. Here they are combined with mushrooms to make a simple, and particularly good, light main course for 5–6.

Methods and ingredients which may be unfamiliar are explained on pages 26–38.

500g (18 oz) tagliatelle
1 medium-sized onion
3 tablespoons sunflower oil
45g (1½ oz) unsalted butter
225g (8 oz) chicken livers
110g (4 oz) button
mushrooms

1 scant tablespoon flour
1 tumbler dry white wine
110g (4 oz) good Parmesan
cheese, grated
parsley

Sauté the finely chopped onion gently in the oil and butter until soft. Add the rinsed and finely sliced livers and mushrooms. Cook them together for a few minutes, then stir in the flour. When it has blended stir in the wine. Season to taste and cook gently for 15 minutes, stirring occasionally and adding more liquid if it needs it.

When the sauce is almost ready cook the tagliatelle in plenty of boiling salted water. Drain when *al dente*, put in a warm bowl, add the sauce and Parmesan and mix lightly. Serve decorated with chopped parsley.

Tagliatelle alla biellese
Tagliatelle Biella Style

In Biella they use the very narrow cream-coloured tagliatelle for this dish, but it is almost better with green ones. A simple but surprisingly good first course for 4–5.

500g (18 oz) really good
tagliatelle
150g (5 oz) unsalted butter
3–4 tablespoons hot milk

freshly grated nutmeg
150g (5 oz) good Parmesan
cheese, grated

Cook the pasta in plenty of boiling salted water. Meanwhile, gently melt the butter in a little pan. Add the hot milk and season to taste with salt, white pepper and nutmeg. Remove from the heat and add the Parmesan. When the pasta is *al dente* drain it, but leave a little water clinging to the strands. Place it in a warm bowl, pour on the sauce, mix lightly, and serve at once.

Piedmont's cooking is at its best in autumn when prized porcini mushrooms appear; to be cooked in butter and garlic, like a steak, or thickly sliced and added to meat sauces. Though humbler, chanterelle mushrooms also make excellent pasta sauces. Their golden flesh must be well wiped with a damp cloth to remove any earth before they are used in a delicious sauce like the following.

Tagliatelle e gallinacci
Tagliatelle and Chanterelle Mushrooms

In Piedmont they use various wild mushrooms for this light dish for 4–5, but button mushrooms will do instead.

500g (18 oz) fresh tagliatelle	*nutmeg*
1 garlic clove, finely chopped	*1 brandy glass of brandy*
80g (2¾ oz) unsalted butter	*60g (2 oz) fontina cheese,*
250g (9 oz) chanterelle or	*thinly sliced*
button mushrooms	*3 tablespoons good Parmesan*
150g (5 oz) thickly cut ham,	*cheese, grated*
diced	

Sauté the garlic in the melted butter until golden, add the cleaned and sliced mushrooms and cook for 10 minutes. Add the ham and season to taste, adding a hint of nutmeg. Pour in the brandy and cook very gently for 15–20 minutes.

Have ready a large pan of boiling salted water. Cook the tagliatelle. Drain when *al dente*, mix briefly in the mushroom sauce over very low heat. Place in a warm pasta bowl with the Parmesan and fontina, toss, and serve quickly.

Every cook in Piedmont has a favourite way of making agnolotti: square and slightly larger than ravioli, they can be made with ordinary egg pasta – 1 egg to every 100g (3½ oz) flour, or with half as much egg and a little water. Most contain beef and a winter vegetable, such as cabbage or spinach, but the filling varies because it is made with leftovers. They are lengthy to make but they can be made the day before, or well in advance and frozen – but use a box so they don't break.

Agnolotti di spinaci

Spinach Agnolotti

This recipe is a useful home for beef left over from a pot roast such as *tagliatelle alla piemontese* – page 161. A first course for 5–7.

egg pasta made from 400g (14 oz) plain flour, see pages 17–22

40g (1½ oz) uncooked rice
1 tumbler milk
200g (7 oz) cooked beef
200g (7 oz) cooked spinach
1 egg and 1 yolk

100g (3½ oz) good Parmesan
  cheese, grated
125g (4½ oz) unsalted butter
5 fresh sage leaves (optional)
freshly ground black pepper

Cook the rice in the milk with a pinch of salt, draining while still slightly hard. Chop or mince the beef with the rice and well-drained spinach. Mix with the egg and yolk, and 2 tablespoons Parmesan, seasoning to taste and adding grated nutmeg.

Roll the pasta in two thin sheets. Place little heaps of the stuffing evenly on one sheet. Brush the other with the leftover egg white, beaten with a little water, place it over the first sheet (egg side downwards), and press them together round the heaps of filling before cutting in little squares. Put on a tray dusted with semolina until needed. (See page 21.)

They can be cooked in plenty of boiling salted water and served with the butter melted with the sage leaves, or be served with plain melted butter and grated Parmesan, or with the sauce from round a pot roast. Alternatively, such agnolotti can be cooked and served in good broth with Parmesan on top.

Agnolotti di Angelino
Angelino's Agnolotti

Angelino can barely reach up to the counter of his little bar in Clavière, and with his ruddy cheeks and bushy beard he could be taken for a character from Snow White. His speciality is cooked agnolotti heated in the oven in a meltingly rich mixture made from fontina, mushrooms and tomatoes. The recipe is his secret but to make something similar let a very little finely chopped unsmoked bacon, onion and celery turn golden in butter. Then lightly sauté a good handful of thinly sliced mushrooms with them, add a pinch of fresh thyme, some skinned and chopped tomatoes, season to taste and cook for about 15 minutes, until a sauce forms. The cooked meat-filled agnolotti are then layered in an oven dish with this sauce and thin slices of fontina, and put in a hot oven until the cheese melts into the sauce.

Piedmont's wine is her pride and glory and adds much to her cooking, for, ideally, only good wine should enter the kitchen; not necessarily the most expensive, but sound and genuine. Whenever a dash of wine is added to a sauce at the end of cooking, as in the following recipe, it is called *ubriaco* – 'tipsy'.

Methods and ingredients which may be unfamiliar are explained on pages 26–38.

Maccheroncelli ubriachi

Tipsy Little Macaroni

Good wine and good sausages make this a surprisingly tasty dish for 3–4.

400g (14 oz) penne, rigatoni or other short pasta
1 carrot
1 celery stalk
200g (7 oz) Italian sausages, skinned and chopped
60g (2 oz) unsalted butter
150ml (¼ pint) thick cream
about 1½ tablespoons tomato paste
1 tumbler rosé wine
a little brandy
good Parmesan cheese, grated

Clean the carrot and celery and chop them finely. Sauté gently, with the sausages, in a wide pan with a small lump of the butter until the meat loses its pinkness. Add the cream and stir in the tomato paste a little at a time, tasting as you go – some tomato pastes are much stronger than others and you only want a hint of tomato, not a tomato sauce. Stir in most of the wine, season to taste, and cook very slowly until it thickens. Then cover and keep warm, but be careful not to put it anywhere too hot.

Cook the pasta in plenty of boiling salted water. Meanwhile, melt the remaining butter in a wide pan. Drain the pasta when *al dente* and transfer it to the melted butter. Stir well, sprinkle with the brandy and remaining wine and evaporate over a very low flame. Then add a handful of grated Parmesan, give it a quick stir and serve in a pasta bowl topped by the rich sausage and wine sauce.

Tagliatelle al
sugo di arrosto
Tagliatelle with Roast Meat Juices

So typically Italian to find an excellent use for the juices which run from a roast joint. A very good instant meal for 4–5.

500g (18 oz) tagliatelle
1 large tea cup roast meat
  juices
1–2 tablespoons grated
  Parmesan cheese

90g (3 oz) fontina cheese,
  thinly sliced

Cook the pasta in plenty of boiling salted water until *al dente*. Drain, and place in an oven dish rubbed with butter. Add the meat juices, without their fat, and the Parmesan, toss lightly and cover with the fontina. Put in a hot oven for 5 minutes – or just long enough to melt the cheese. Serve immediately.

Spaghetti al forno
con la fontina
Spaghetti in the Oven with Fontina Cheese

When there are no meat juices to hand, the Piedmontese make a similar dish with just butter and more cheese. The extra cheese makes it very good.

In a sense, this is the lazy man's macaroni cheese, and you can substitute long macaroni broken in thirds if you wish. For 6.

600g (1 lb 5 oz) spaghetti
150g (5 oz) unsalted butter
150g (5 oz) good Parmesan
  cheese, grated

300g (11 oz) fontina cheese in
  small strips

Methods and ingredients which may be unfamiliar are explained on pages 26–38.

Cook the pasta *al dente* in plenty of boiling salted water. Drain. Immediately mix it in a bowl with three-quarters of the butter, cut into pieces, and Parmesan. Rub an oven dish with butter. Put in a layer of spaghetti, then scatter with fontina. Continue until the ingredients are used up. Top with the remaining Parmesan and the butter, in little flakes. Put in a hot oven for just 10 minutes so the cheese becomes melting and golden.

In the Val d'Aosta, the alpine region bordering Switzerland where fontina is made, there are few pasta meals – polenta and gnocchi are considered better food for the mountains – and the classic dish is *fonduta*, fondue, made from melted cheese as it is in Switzerland but with fontina. And to start a meal you can sometimes find delicious little ravioli, filled with fonduta and served with melted butter and sage leaves.

Tagliatelle alla piemontese
Tagliatelle Piedmont Style

This substantial and excellent family dish serves 4–5 as a main course, and in Italy the meat is often cooked the day before. This makes a fair amount but some of the meat can go into *agnolotti di spinaci* and the extra sauce can form the basis of *lasagne pasticciate*, and if you don't want to make these follow-on dishes straight away, both the cooked meat and sauce will freeze until they are needed.

161

egg pasta made with 450g (1 lb) plain flour, plus 25g (1 oz) good
Parmesan, grated, see pages 17–20, or 500g (1 lb) packet
tagliatelle

Sauce

1–2 tablespoons dried porcini
  mushrooms (optional)
1 slice unsmoked streaky
  bacon
2 small carrots
1kg (2¼ lb) joint lean stewing
  beef
a piece pork rind (optional)
40g (1½ oz) ham fat,
  chopped
½ calf's foot (optional)
a clove
250g (9 oz) piece boneless shin
  of veal

1 medium-sized onion,
  chopped
a clove garlic, chopped
a good stick of celery
2 tablespoons plain flour
thyme, bay leaf, marjoram
1½–3 tumblers red wine
100g (3½ oz) fresh or tinned
  tomatoes, well chopped
70g (2½ oz) unsalted butter
90g (3 oz) good Parmesan
  cheese, grated
a truffle (optional)

Soak the dried mushrooms in a little warm water for 1 hour.

Cut the bacon and 1 carrot in matchsticks. Unroll the joint,
season, and lay these on it. Re-roll and tie with white cotton
string. Parboil the pork rind for 5 minutes and drain. Place with
the ham fat in the bottom of a heavy casserole. Add the joint,
calf's foot (singed if any hairs remain), clove, veal, onion, garlic,
and chopped celery and remaining carrot. Season, and cook over
a moderate heat, turning till the meat starts to brown – the ham
fat and pork rind provide all the fat that is needed.

When the meat has browned, stir in the flour, add a bouquet
garni of the herbs, and the wine. Let it bubble fiercely to
evaporate most of it. Add the tomatoes, the porcini, and almost
all their liquid – strained through a muslin – and boiling water
to nearly cover the joint. Bring to the boil, cover, and transfer
to a slow oven (gas mark 2, 150°C, 300°F) for 4 hours. Taste and
adjust the seasoning during cooking. The meat should be really
tender and the sauce rich and full flavoured.

Roll the pasta thinly and cut into tagliatelle ½–1cm (¼–½ in)
wide. Set aside the meat and a little of the sauce (so it can be

reheated in the reserved sauce for another meal). Sieve the rest and cook to reduce if it is too thin – but it must not be too thick. Cook the pasta in plenty of boiling salted water. Drain, transfer to a warm dish, add the butter in little flakes, half the Parmesan, freshly ground pepper, and grated nutmeg. Decorate with slices of truffle and serve. Pass round the hot sauce and remaining Parmesan in separate bowls.

11 ROME AND LAZIO

 In Italy all roads really do lead to Rome and the dishes of surrounding Lazio have, over the centuries, crossed the Roman *campagna* and become part of Rome's cooking. So one need look no further to find all the pasta of the region.

Romans are robust, and so is their pasta: for most of them it is as much part of the daily ritual as waking up, and Romans stay willingly at table. Their dishes are rich and satisfying: you need a good stomach and no weight problems for this pasta – but what Roman has ever worried about his paunch?

The sauces draw their ingredients from rich Lazio and the surrounding regions – hams, bacon, eggs, meat, chicken, a variety of local cheeses, and excellent fish from both lake and sea. Traditional Roman cooking is the cooking of its artisans, the people of Trastevere – across the Tiber – and of the marketeers who bring their wares in from the countryside. You see this in the names 'poor man's pasta', 'marketeer's pasta', 'charcoal burner's pasta' – and, appropriately for the city of love, even 'harlot's pasta'. These are the dishes which have survived the years – genuine Roman cooking.

In Rome, as in the countryside, dishes come and go with the seasons, in a way forgotten in most modern cities, as their ingredients appear in the colourful open markets: Easter brings artichokes, then come peas for delicate pasta sauces and golden courgette flowers for stuffing as an antipasto, and in summer peppers and aubergines in shining heaps.

In the trattorias of Rome's seven hills, surrounded by family and friends, the Roman is on his throne – at table – drinking golden frascati, of which it was said, 'This wine is peed by angels', and awaiting this next, most Roman of dishes.

Fettuccine con rigaglie
Fettuccine with Chicken Livers

This typically Roman dish makes a cheap, easy, and extremely good light main course for 4–6.

600g (1 lb 5 oz) fettuccine
1 medium-sized onion
1 medium-sized carrot
1 small stick celery
50g (2 oz) unsalted butter
500g (18 oz) chopped chicken or turkey livers (and hearts, optional)
2 teaspoons plain flour

1 tumbler red or white wine (optional)
800g (1 lb 12 oz) fresh or tinned tomatoes, skinned and well chopped
1 bay leaf
1 handful good Parmesan cheese, grated

Sauté the finely chopped onion, carrot and celery gently in most of the butter, stirring until golden. Add the well-chopped chicken livers, and sauté for 1–2 minutes. Stir in the flour for a minute or two, then add the wine and let it bubble a little before putting in the tomatoes and bay leaf. Season to taste and simmer gently for 1½ hours, adding a little water if it gets dry. Then cook the fettuccine in plenty of boiling salted water, drain when *al dente*, place in a warm bowl, and dress with the sauce and a few pats of butter. Serve with extra Parmesan at table.

This dish can also be made by adding sautéed onion and chicken livers to an existing Bolognese sauce.

Another very popular Roman dish is *Spaghetti alla carbonara*. *Carbonara* comes from charcoal burners, who, not far from Rome, used to make charcoal in primitive cone-shaped furnaces from branches covered with earth and coal dust. All the ingredients of this sauce would keep for the time a charcoal burner spent in the woods.

Nowadays, *Spaghetti alla carbonara* is one of the most classic and most controversial of all Roman dishes. Both at family meals and at dinner parties there are heated discussions as to whether or not cream should be added. It is even rumoured that husbands and wives have come to blows over this issue. Originally, of course, cream wasn't included – the dish being one for simple charcoal burners – but recipes change with time. So, to save anyone coming to blows, here is the original recipe and two of its variations – one of them with cream. Bucatini or a short, not too chunky, pasta may be used instead of spaghetti. Not too thick, not too thin, is the rule for pasta with these bacon-based sauces, and beware of using salty bacon for it will spoil the dish.

Spaghetti alla carbonara
Charcoal Burner's Spaghetti

This serves 4 as a first course or a light main course. In Italy this quantity of sauce is eaten with 600g (1 lb 5 oz) pasta, but outside Italy, where this may be eaten as a main course, the following proportions may be better.

Methods and ingredients which may be unfamiliar are explained on pages 26–38.

400g (14 oz) good spaghetti
150g (5 oz) from a thick slice
 unsmoked bacon
4 medium-sized eggs

50g (2 oz) good Parmesan
 cheese, grated
1 tablespoon oil or butter

Put a large pan of water to boil for the pasta. Dice the bacon. Beat the eggs lightly, and mix in the Parmesan and a good grind of black pepper. Cook the pasta while you lightly brown the bacon, in the fat, in a wide casserole. When the pasta is *al dente* drain it – but not too thoroughly – and quickly put it in the casserole with the bacon, over the very lowest heat. Stir, remove from the heat, add the cheese and egg mixture, and mix well together. The drops of water clinging to the pasta should blend with the eggs and fat to make a creamy sauce. The warmth of the pan should just heat it, but you don't want scrambled eggs so make sure it is off the heat.

I

An excellent variation uses a little onion, white wine and parsley. A small onion is finely sliced, and cooked gently with the diced bacon. When both are golden half a glass of wine is poured in and allowed to bubble until it evaporates a little, and the finely chopped parsley is added to the egg and cheese. Otherwise the method is the same as in the recipe above.

II

Those who like to add cream should follow the first recipe but beat 2 tablespoons rich cream in with the eggs – that is all – which just goes to show that it is not only the French who mind passionately about the details of their cooking.

Scarlet, salted mountain ham and black figs; spaghetti all'amatriciana . . . served with a sauce of garlic, pepper, fresh tomatoes – but above all with guanciale and grated pecorino. To follow these, chicken pieces scented with wine and marjoram, Abruzzi cheeses, cake, and peaches from Castelgandolfo – smooth as a parson's cheek.

A Feast at Frascati, Paolo Monelli

Sadly tastes have changed and *guanciale*, the tasty, fatty bacon with a unique flavour, made from the pig's cheeks, is often replaced by *pancetta*. But *guanciale* may still be found in the oldest parts of Rome. In the great open market of Piazza Vittorio, among the multicoloured stalls, it hangs like giant mittens, its skin dusty brown with pepper, with cheese, skirts, lentils, salt anchovies, pots, pans and live chickens all around. There is no real substitute, and recipes in which it was once used are the poorer without it, though even with factory-made unsmoked bacon they are still good.

Bucatini all'amatriciana
Bucatini the Amatrice Way

Nothing complicated or expensive, just the excellent simplicity typical of Italian cooking. It was originally made with *guanciale* so use fatty bacon. A light lunch or supper for 4, and, though the Romans don't eat it that way, very good with wholemeal spaghetti.

500g (18 oz) bucatini or spaghetti
100g (4 oz) thick unsmoked bacon, diced
1 medium-sized onion, finely chopped

part of a chilli
500g (18 oz) skinned fresh or tinned tomatoes, chopped
50g (2 oz) grated pecorino romano cheese
1 tablespoon olive oil

Put a large pan of water to boil for the pasta. Fry the bacon in the oil. When nicely browned and crisp remove it from the oil, cover, and keep warm. Soften the onion in the oil with a little chilli – how much is up to you, but Roman dishes are not usually as fiery as southern ones. Don't overdo it at this stage, you can always add more during cooking. Add the tomatoes and simmer for only 6–7 minutes. They must not become a smooth sauce but be, as they say in Rome, *mortificate* – mortified – humbled and softened a little, and in Rome they sometimes add fewer tomatoes, so the sauce is only a little red.

While the tomatoes 'mortify', cook the pasta. Drain when al dente. Place it in a warm bowl, add the cheese, then the sauce, and garnish with the diced bacon. Mix at table, passing round more cheese.

Some insist that the real recipe of Amatrice, the little town where the dish originated, is quite different – but one must go back centuries to find it. Romans made the *amatriciana* their own – adding oil, onion and tomatoes in pure southern style. But sometimes *amatriciana* is served *in bianco* – white, without tomatoes – and it is close to the old recipe. In Amatrice they serve this sauce on homemade tagliolini.

'L'amatriciana' in bianco
Simple Amatriciana Sauce

An excellent quick winter lunch for 2–3, if the sausages are good, see page 36.

*300g (11 oz) thin tagliolini
  or spaghetti
200g (7 oz) Italian or
  bratwurst sausages
100g (4 oz) guanciale or
  thickly cut fatty unsmoked
  bacon, diced*

*a piece of chilli
plenty of grated pecorino
  romano cheese*

Put a large pan of salted water to boil ready for the pasta. Cut the skinned sausages in small pieces. Put them over a low heat with the bacon and a little chilli, but no other fat or oil, until the meat browns nicely and is cooked through. Cook the pasta *al dente*. Drain it, but not too well, put it in a warm bowl with the sauce and grate over enough pecorino to turn the pasta white, which is a fair amount, and serve at once.

The flavour of the sheep's cheese pecorino is important, but if it can't be found Caerphilly is surprisingly good instead.

Rigatoni con salsicce e uova

Rigatoni with Sausage and Eggs

A winter lunch for 4, rich tasting but cheap and easy, this is one of the few recipes in which the pasta is cooked in the sauce.

350–400g (12–14 oz) rigatoni, large penne, or bombolotti
4 really meaty Italian sausages, or German bratwurst
45g (1½ oz) good dripping
1 tablespoon olive oil
¾ litre (1½ pint) good beef or chicken broth
2 eggs
60g (2 oz) good Parmesan cheese, grated

Skin and break up the sausages. Cook them gently in 1 tablespoon dripping and the oil, in a large casserole, occasionally adding a little broth. Meanwhile, half cook the rigatoni in plenty of boiling salted water, drain while still fairly hard and add them to the sausage mixture. Mix well, add a little more broth, cover, and cook slowly, adding more broth if it is needed. When the pasta is *al dente*, and a little liquid is left, stir in the remaining dripping and the grated cheese and season to taste. Pour the beaten eggs over the mixture and stir together to *lightly* cook the eggs – the sauce should be creamy not scrambled. Serve immediately, passing round a pepper mill.

For plain basic food with a minimum of effort Romans make *bucatini con le salsicce* – bucatini and sausages. Full-flavoured meaty Italian sausages are simply put in a casserole, with skinned and chopped tomatoes, then cooked in a moderate oven for 1½ hours and mixed with the cooked pasta. For 4 you need 500g (18 oz) pasta, 8–10 sausages and 1kg (2¼ lb) tomatoes. This makes an easy meal, but it will only be as good as the sausages you use.

Methods and ingredients which may be unfamiliar are explained on pages 26–38.

Spaghetti a 'cacio e pepe'
Spaghetti with Cheese and Pepper

This is the simplest, 'poorest' of all pasta dishes – spaghetti with cheese and pepper. In Rome they use the strongest sheep's cheese of all, *pecorino romano*. Don't despise the simplicity of this dish; if you like cheese and pepper it is surprisingly good and, in moderation, slimming.

For each person you need:

125g (4½ oz) spaghetti
a handful grated pecorino
  romano cheese

freshly ground black pepper

Cook the pasta *al dente* in plenty of boiling salted water. Drain, leaving it a little wet, and save some of the water. Place in a warm bowl, cover with the grated cheese and plenty of pepper, and mix well. The spaghetti must slip through the fork. If it sticks, add some of its water. The secret of this dish is that the water melts the cheese and blends it with the spaghetti. Add more cheese at table if you want. Wholemeal pasta is particularly good eaten this way.

Penne all'uovo e ricotta
Penne with Egg and Ricotta

A subtle sauce with a lovely texture. A first course for 3.

250g (9 oz) medium-sized
  penne or similar pasta
1 egg yolk
125g (4½ oz) ricotta cheese
75ml (3 fl oz) thick cream

3–4 tablespoons good
  Parmesan cheese, grated
25g (1 oz) unsalted butter
freshly ground black pepper

Cook the pasta in plenty of boiling salted water. Meanwhile, beat the egg yolk in a pasta bowl, and mix in the ricotta. Warm the cream, remove from the heat, stir in the Parmesan, and season to taste. Drain the pasta when *al dente*, put it with the ricotta. Add the butter in little flakes, a grind of black pepper, then the warm cream. Mix, taste, adjust the seasoning, and serve at once.

They say that in Rome fettuccine are not twiddled deftly round the fork, as are the vermicelli of Naples, nor popped neatly in the mouth as are Bologna's tagliatelle, but are simply 'dug into, shovelled in and sucked up'. However they are eaten, this is a northerner's impression of how Romans enjoy them on the August festival of Ferragosto.

There were forkfuls, spillings, avalanches of steaming yellow noodles glistening and moistened by frequent additions of butter. Mouths bent over the tangled golden pasta, tongues and palates savoured never-ending delights that rose incessantly to befuddled, foolish, brains. They experienced shivers of joy on tasting the fat and the pasta and the stinging, tingling bite of the cheese. If they happened across a slippery morsel of butter, as yet unmelted, they experienced a sort of cool voluptuousness such as one feels on kissing a pure maiden.

Giovanni Faldella
(correspondent for the *Piedmont Gazette*, 1880)

Such noodles are the great speciality of Alfredo's, a famous restaurant in Rome, where their lightning tossing and twirling with a golden spoon and fork has been made into a virtuoso performance. The exact recipe is a secret – but here is a way of making them which is hard to beat.

Methods and ingredients which may be unfamiliar are explained on pages 26–38.

Fettuccine al triplo burro

Fettuccine with Triple the Butter

One of the most effortless first courses imaginable, yet good enough for a dinner party, if you make sure the food afterwards is not too rich. The secret is in the quality of the ingredients. You need the best butter, freshly grated Italian Parmesan, not Parmesan from a packet, and the best fettuccine you can make or buy. A first course for 6.

500–600g (1 lb 2 oz–1 lb 5 oz) fresh fettuccine
200g (7 oz) best unsalted butter

200g (7 oz) best Parmesan cheese, grated

Put the butter in a basin of cool water to soften for a few hours without melting it. Warm a pasta bowl, and put the fettuccine to cook in plenty of boiling water. Cut the butter in small pieces and grate the Parmesan. Drain the pasta when *al dente*. Place immediately in the warm bowl, add the Parmesan and butter. Mix well, and serve as quickly as possible.

Fettuccine alla squarciarella

Cut Throat's Fettuccine

Despite its alarming name this is a smooth comforting sauce. A lovely first course or light lunch for 4.

400g (14 oz) fettuccine
100g (3½ oz) unsalted butter
½ medium-sized onion, finely chopped
150g (5 oz) good diced ham

4 eggs
2–3 tablespoons thick cream
80g (2¾ oz) good Parmesan cheese, grated

Put a large pan of salted water to boil for the pasta. Gently melt ½ tablespoon of butter in a small pan and let the onion and ham turn golden in it. Remove the pan from the heat.

Cook the fettuccine while you gently melt the remaining butter in a wide casserole and beat the eggs well. When the fettuccine are almost ready, put the eggs, cream, Parmesan, and cooked ham and onions (without the fat they cooked in) into the melted butter. Season to taste and stir a moment, over the lowest possible heat, to thicken very slightly. Drain the fettuccine when *al dente*, toss them in the sauce, and serve with freshly ground pepper at table.

Fettuccine, the Roman tagliatelle, are the pasta most typical of this city; called fettuccine because of their width, the width of a seamstress's tape and straight as a Roman road. In fact there is a road called La Fettuccia leading south from Rome.

Fettuccine alla papalina
Pope's Cap Fettuccine

Goodness knows how it got the name, but this delicate buttery sauce is fit for any pope, and very easy. A light main course for 4, or an attractive first course for a supper party.

500g (18 oz) fresh fettuccine, or 400g (14 oz) packet fettuccine	a little chicken broth
	120g (4 oz) slice ham, diced
1 small onion, finely chopped	2 eggs
100g (3½ oz) unsalted butter	80g (3 oz) good Parmesan cheee, grated
300g (11 oz) fresh shelled young peas or frozen petits pois	

Soften the onion gently in the butter in a wide pan without browning. Add the peas and cook them slowly, adding a tablespoon or so of broth, until tender. Add the diced ham, season to taste, and keep warm.

Cook the pasta in a large pan of boiling salted water. Meanwhile, beat the eggs in a large serving bowl with half the Parmesan, and put the bowl in a warm place (not hot). Drain the fettuccine when *al dente*, but leave them rather moist, and toss them immediately in the bowl with the eggs and quickly mix in the hot ham and pea sauce. Serve, passing round the remaining Parmesan and a black pepper mill at table.

A good variation uses the yolks of 3 eggs, instead of whole eggs, and adds a handful of sliced button mushrooms to the onion.

One of the many dishes which Rome has taken as her own is *maccheroni alla Ciociara*. The women in the farming region of Ciociara – which takes its name from *ciocie*, the classic Roman thong sandal – are famous for their special pasta. The buxom Ciociarans (who until recently went to Rome as wet nurses) mix their egg pasta with wine instead of water, roll it to transparent thinness, and cut it into little rectangles which are shaped round a finger into macaroni. But there is no need to make the pasta, for the simple sauce is very good with fettuccine and other egg pasta.

Sometimes in Ciociara they put a pasta board in the middle of the table and use it for a serving dish instead of a bowl, mixing the pasta, Parmesan, bacon and peas right there on the table.

Maccheroni alla Ciociara
Ciociaran Pasta

The rosy bacon and tiny green peas make this delicate sauce both pretty and surprisingly delicious, if the ingredients are good. For 5–6.

500g (18 oz) fettuccine, or
   other egg pasta
120g (4¼ oz) unsmoked bacon
   or Parma ham (prosciutto)
90g (3 oz) unsalted butter
400g (14 oz) fresh shelled
   young peas or good frozen
   petits pois

2–3 tablespoons good chicken
   broth
several spoonfuls good
   Parmesan or pecorino
   romano cheese, grated

Set a large pan of salted water to boil for the pasta. Chop the bacon or ham in small pieces. Gently melt the butter, without browning. Add the peas, bacon or ham, and season. Stir together over a low heat to cook a little, then add the broth and simmer gently. The sauce is ready when the peas are cooked. Cook the pasta. Drain when *al dente*, put it in a warm bowl, add some of the cheese and top with the sauce. Serve, passing round the extra cheese.

The hills round Lake Bolsena, in the north of Lazio, are clothed with olives, and with sweet white grapes that are made into the curiously named wine, *Est, Est, Est*. Tradition has it that it got its name when a German bishop, and great lover of Italian wines, was on his way to visit the pope in the thirteenth century. His servant went ahead to discover the best wine cellars and chalk on their doors the word 'Est' – Latin for 'is' or 'this is it'. On arriving at Montefiascone, overlooking Lake Bolsena, the servant became so enthusiastic about the wine he chalked up 'Est, Est, Est'. The bishop, it is said, was equally keen and drank so much that he died. That wine is no longer so highly rated, but the food is still excellent. The next dish is from that area.

Methods and ingredients which may be unfamiliar are explained on pages 26–38.

Penne d'oro

Golden Penne

The flavour of artichokes seems to permeate the pasta in this dish and make it almost addictive to artichoke lovers. When tender young artichokes are hard to obtain, a passable dish can be made with tinned artichokes in brine or frozen artichoke hearts; but the best substitute is tinned artichoke hearts in oil, sometimes called *carciofini alla giudia*. They are quite different from those in jars, which were steeped in vinegar before being preserved in oil and would ruin the dish, and different also from the fried artichokes of the same name. This dish makes a light lunch for 4, or first course for 6.

500g (1 lb 2 oz) penne
2–3 medium-sized leaf artichokes, or 225g (½ lb) tinned artichokes
200g (7 oz) button mushrooms
10 tablespoons petits pois, fresh or frozen
4 tablespoons best olive oil

2 garlic cloves
½ chilli, just to give 'pep' to the dish
3–4 tablespoons white wine (optional)
500g (18 oz) fresh or tinned tomatoes, skinned and chopped
good Parmesan cheese, grated

Prepare the fresh artichokes, as on page 26, or parboil the frozen artichokes for 5 minutes. Slice the artichokes finely. Rinse the mushrooms and slice them finely. Parboil and drain the fresh peas. Put a large pan of salted water on to boil for the pasta.

Gently heat the olive oil in a large casserole, add the finely sliced garlic and the chilli. When slightly golden add the sliced artichoke hearts and cook, turning gently until they begin to take colour. Add the mushrooms and sauté briefly, then sprinkle on the wine (a few tears, as they say in Italy). After a minute add the tomato and peas, and season to taste with salt. Simmer gently, uncovered, for 10 minutes or until the artichokes are cooked. Cover and keep warm while the pasta cooks.

Cook the penne *al dente*, drain, and mix them with the sauce. Add as much grated Parmesan as you like, and serve.

A Roman saying, in dialect, goes:

> *O de paja o de fieno*
> *Abbasta ch'er corpo sii pieno!*

> Be they hay be they straw
> Fill the stomach with pasta galore!

It refers, of course, to the mixed yellow and green tagliatelle called *paglia e fieno* – straw and hay.

Paglia e fieno con i carciofi
Straw and Hay with Artichokes

This is a most attractive first or light main course for 4–5.

500g (18 oz) mixed yellow and green tagliatelle, or ordinary tagliatelle

4 small artichokes

100g (3½ oz) unsmoked thick streaky bacon, or prosciutto off cuts, chopped

½ medium-sized onion, finely chopped

2 tablespoons olive oil

90g (3 oz) unsalted butter

½ tumbler dry white wine

½ tumbler good chicken broth

70g (2½ oz) good Parmesan cheese, grated

Prepare the artichokes as on page 26. Sauté the bacon and onion in the oil and half the butter. When they turn golden add the drained artichoke slices, stir a little, and sprinkle on the wine. When the wine evaporates add the broth and cook gently for 30 minutes or until the artichokes are tender. A few extra spoonfuls of wine can be added near the end and bubbled a little if you wish.

Cook the pasta *al dente* in plenty of boiling salted water. Drain, put in a warm bowl with the remaining butter in flakes, toss, add the sauce and Parmesan. Serve at once.

Spaghetti alla puttanesca

Harlot's Spaghetti

It's typical of the Romans to let the harlot give her name to one of the region's recipes and so take her place among the ladies of Lazio. Spicy, colourful, and tasty, this dish does her justice. A first course for 4–5.

450g (1 lb) spaghetti
5 tablespoons olive oil
3 garlic cloves
a piece of fresh chilli
8 anchovy fillets, drained of oil
150g (5 oz) big black olives, sliced

1 tablespoon capers
200g (7 oz) fresh or tinned tomatoes, skinned and chopped
1 teaspoon tomato paste
fresh oregano
1 tablespoon chopped parsley

Gently heat the oil in a wide pan with the finely chopped garlic and a little piece of chilli (this dish should be just slightly peppery, so taste the chilli first). When the garlic begins to colour add the chopped anchovies and stir until they break up.

Have ready a large pan of boiling salted water, and put the spaghetti to cook. To finish the sauce, add the sliced olives, capers, tomatoes, tomato paste and a pinch of oregano. Heat them together, and by the time the spaghetti is *al dente* the sauce will be ready too. Drain the pasta, put it in a warmed pasta bowl, pour over the sauce, mix lightly and sprinkle with the chopped parsley.

Spaghetti 'er roscio'

Red-head Spaghetti

'Er roscio' is Roman slang for red-head. Julius Caesar would have been called *er roscio* behind his back if the Romans had spoken today's colourful Roman dialect. This full-flavoured dish, red in taste and colour, is a light lunch or substantial first course for 4–5.

500g (18 oz) spaghetti
1 medium-sized onion
80g (3 oz) celery
2 cloves garlic
a little chilli
¼ red pimento in strips
  (optional)
4–5 tablespoons olive oil
400g (14 oz) fresh or tinned
  tomatoes, skinned and
  sieved

160g (5½ oz) pimento-stuffed
  green olives
50g (2 oz) peppery salami,
  diced
4 tablespoons pecorino romano
  cheese, grated

Sauté the chopped onion, celery, garlic, chilli and pimento in the oil in a wide casserole. When softened add the tomato pulp, season with salt and simmer for 20–30 minutes. During the last 10 minutes add the sliced olives.

Cook the spaghetti *al dente* in plenty of boiling salted water. Drain, and toss it in the sauce, remove from the heat, top with the pecorino and salami.

If you dislike peppery food you may prefer a similar dish called *Occhi di lupo alla cappuccetto rosso* – Little Red Riding Hood's wolf's eyes. Bombolotti are used instead of spaghetti and the onion, chilli, pecorino and pimento are left out and the tomatoes increased to 600g (1 lb 5 oz). The method is the same, but instead of the salami use 100g (3½ oz) diced crisply cooked bacon.

Minestra di fave fresche alla romana
Roman Broad Bean Soup

Each pasta has its own character; cannolichi, small short pasta, are popular in soups and with beans – and used to be the pasta most often served in Rome's barracks and prisons, which shouldn't be considered a reflection on their qualities. A homely soup for early summer, to serve 6–7.

300g (11 oz) cannolichiette,
  or similar pasta
100g (3½ oz) guanciale, or
  unsmoked streaky bacon
1 celery stalk
1–2 spring onions
1 garlic clove
1 tablespoon chopped parsley
100g (3½ oz) fresh or tinned
  tomatoes, skinned and
  sieved

300g (11 oz) broad beans,
  shelled weight, or good
  frozen beans
2 litre (4 pints) good
  homemade broth
60g (2 oz) grated pecorino or
  Parmesan cheese
1 tablespoon olive oil
  (optional)

Chop the bacon, and cook it until the fat runs. Add the chopped onion, celery and garlic, and a little oil if needed. When they turn golden add the tomatoes and parsley. Season to taste and cook for 10 minutes before putting in the beans. Stir, pour in the broth, and boil gently until the beans are tender. Taste and adjust the seasoning, and add the pasta. When the pasta is cooked the soup is ready. Sprinkle in the cheese, let the flavours mingle a minute and serve.

Minestra di quadrucci e piselli
Soup with Little Pasta Squares and Peas

Making soup can be a slow affair but this delicate Roman soup is splendidly quick and easy. If you have pasta left over from making lasagne or ravioli it can be cut and dried ready for this soup. For 5–6.

300g (10 oz) little squares
  egg pasta
1 small onion
100g (3½ oz) guanciale or
  unsmoked bacon
1 garlic clove (optional)
2 tablespoons olive or
  sunflower oil

300g (10 oz) fresh young peas,
  shelled weight, or frozen
  petits pois
2 litre (4 pints) chicken or veal
  broth
Parmesan cheese, grated

Finely chop the onion, bacon and garlic. Sauté them in the oil until just golden. Add the peas (plus a pinch of sugar if they have lost their fresh sweetness), and half the broth. Season to taste, cover and cook gently until the peas are tender. Add the remaining broth, bring to the boil, add the pasta squares and serve as soon as they are cooked, passing round the Parmesan at table.

Minestrone alla borghese

Bourgeois Vegetable Soup

This soup was originally created by Luigi Carnacina, one of the great cooks of this century, and the recipe is adapted from that given in his book *La Grande Cucina*. The contrast between the golden peppers and the green courgettes makes this one of the prettiest soups, and quite stylish enough for a dinner for 6.

200g (7 oz) cannolichiette	*1 small celery heart*
50g (2 oz) good ham in a single piece	*1½–2 litre (3–4 pints) tasty chicken broth*
1 clove garlic	*4 small potatoes*
1 tablespoon finely chopped onion	*2 yellow pimentos*
50g (2 oz) unsalted butter	*4 courgettes*
100g (3½ oz) fresh or tinned tomatoes	*fresh basil or parsley*
	good Parmesan cheese, grated

Gently sauté the finely chopped ham, garlic and onion in the butter in a soup pan, until the onion begins to colour. Add the skinned and chopped tomatoes and simmer. Meanwhile, wash the celery and slice finely. Add the celery and stock to the soup 10 minutes after the tomatoes. As with all minestrone, the vegetables should not be swimming in liquid but just nicely surrounded by it, so add it cautiously; you can always add more

Methods and ingredients which may be unfamiliar are explained on pages 26–38.

later. Season to taste and continue simmering. After 15 minutes add the peeled and diced potatoes.

Wash and dice the courgettes. Skin the pimentos, see page 34, then cut in half, remove the stem and all the seeds, and slice into small strips. When the potatoes are half-cooked add the courgettes, pimentos and pasta, and more boiling broth if necessary, taste, adjust the seasoning and continue cooking until the pasta is *al dente*, stir in the chopped parsley or basil. Serve, passing round grated cheese at table.

During his travels in Italy in 1845 Humphreys wrote of ricotta:

> *In appearance and consistency it is something similar to fresh cream cheese sold in London as York cheese; but instead of being pressed between rushes, as that one is, it is turned out of small wicker baskets. . . . It has a deliciously sweet creamy fragrance and is made of sheep's milk, and when placed on a good slice of genuine brown bread I know of nothing that I could better enjoy . . . especially if it is accompanied by a flask of Orvieto, the Roman's champagne, that costs sixpence a flask and is their most expensive wine.*

Though Orvieto is, sadly, no longer sixpence a flask, and today's ricotta is turned out of little plastic containers, which only imitate wicker baskets, the subtle pleasure of ricotta on good fresh bread is still savoured and many of its lovely recipes were certainly being eaten in Humphreys' time.

Rigatoni con la ricotta
Rigatoni with Ricotta

A very old, very unusual dish, a sweet pasta once served as a first course; though, to any Anglo-Saxon with a penchant for milky puddings, it makes a delightful and unexpected dessert. Being filling, this much may serve 4 or more.

200g (7 oz) small rigatoni, or
   other short pasta
100g (3½ oz) ricotta cheese
2 rounded teaspoons castor
   sugar

¼ teaspoon powdered
   cinnamon
warm milk

Cook the pasta in plenty of boiling salted water. Meanwhile cream the ricotta with the sugar and cinnamon, adding enough warm milk to make a smooth creamy sauce. Drain the pasta when *al dente*, mix it with the cheese, sugar and spice, and serve at once, adding more cinnamon if you wish.

12 SARDINIA

*When God finished creating the world he found left in his
hand little pieces of all the things created – a patch of sky,
a wave, a clump of forest trees, a mountain top, and so on.
Not knowing what to do with the remnants he threw them
down from the heavens, stamped on them with his foot –
and made Sardinia.*

So goes the children's story, and from the air that
is how it seems. Sardinia is nothing like Sicily and
mainland Italy with their romantic scenery. The
second largest Italian island, it sits in the
Mediterranean buffeted by the four winds. Rocky,
arid, yet extremely beautiful, it possesses a primordial quality,
a spaciousness – mountains, marshes, dunes, a bare wild
coastline and beyond, a sea so blue it seems never to have been
crossed. Man is alone here: the isolated shepherd, the solitary
huntsman, the outlaw hiding in the mountains are as much part
of the present as of the past.

In remote villages traditional costumes are still worn and though Sardinians seem less flamboyant than other Italians, they have the same love of festivals, carnivals and music – and of the good food that goes with them. The traditional dish is *porceddu* – roast piglet on a spit, a custom left over from the days of nomadic shepherds. Roasting often takes place outside on a wood fire where burning myrtle and olive branches lend their perfume to the roasting meat.

Pasta is not a special feature of Sardinian cooking for, as the Italians say, 'one learns to cook, but one is born a roaster'. And Sardinians are roasters. But the original sauces they do have make good use of tangy salami, leftover meat, and local cheese. The sheep which graze the low hills provide milk for a variety of cheeses – young, they can be soft table cheeses; mature they become hard grating cheese for pasta sauces all over Italy. The island also has a unique speciality – little ochre-coloured gnocchetti of durum wheat tinted with saffron, not to be confused with the large potato gnocchi sold in some shops.

Malloreddus

Sardinian Gnocchetti with Salami

These gnocchetti are hard to make well but the very easy, strongly flavoured sauce is equally good with bought pasta. A tasty lunch for 4–6.

non-egg pasta made from 400g (14 oz) durum wheat flour, pages 17–19, plus a pinch of powdered saffron, or 600g (1 lb 5 oz) bought gnocchetti or other small pasta

Sauce

1–2 garlic cloves, chopped
2 tablespoons olive oil
1kg (2 lb 3 oz) fresh or tinned
   tomatoes, skinned and
   chopped

300g (10 oz) peppery Italian
   salami
60g (2 oz) pecorino sardo
   cheese

Roll pieces of the pasta into pencil-thick cords. Cut these into 2cm (¾ in) lengths, shape each into an oval bead, and dent deeply down the length with a fork. Place on a tray dusted with semolina till cooking time.

Sauté the garlic in the oil until golden. Add the tomatoes and finely diced salami, and season. Simmer for 40 minutes, stirring occasionally. Taste and adjust the seasoning. Have ready a large pan of boiling salted water and boil the pasta until it tastes cooked. Drain, place in a warm bowl, top with a handful of pecorino then the sauce. More pecorino may be added at table.

The meat was really lovely, red with white fat, as though just cut from the beast; but the macaroni was pushed aside with such indignation by the mistress of the household that it fell into the hearth.

– 'When there's flour in the house and women with strong arms there's no need to buy bread or pasta from shops. Get up, lazy bones' –

Patiently Mikedda picked up the broken pieces of macaroni, and Annarosa slipped out to fetch some flour so they could make it at home, and together they mixed it and began to knead the pasta with all their might on the kitchen table, talking softly, so as not to be overheard by Granny.

Fire in the Olive Grove, Grazia Deledda

Such was once the attitude towards pasta making.

Ciciones

In Sassari, a town in the north of Sardinia, they make gnocchi like those for *malloreddus* (pages 186–7) but add 2 tablespoons of olive oil to 600g (1 lb 5 oz) of durum wheat flour, to give a slightly smoother pasta with an individual flavour. Their sauce is equally good with packet pasta. A light main dish for 5–6, in which the characteristic flavour of pecorino cheese plays a big part.

600g (1 lb 5 oz) homemade gnocchetti, or 500g (18 oz) packet gnocchetti or shells
150g (5 oz) lardo, or ham fat or unsmoked bacon
2 tablespoons olive oil
1 medium-sized onion
½ medium-sized green pimento
a little chilli

350g (12 oz) lean minced pork, cooked or raw
1kg (2 lb 3 oz) fresh or tinned tomatoes, skinned and chopped
fresh or dried parsley, sage and basil
125g (4½ oz) pecorino sardo cheese, grated

Chop the lardo, or other fat, very finely and gently soften it in the oil with the chopped onion, pimento and some chilli. When they take colour add the meat. Brown it slightly before adding the tomatoes, and a little of each of the herbs. Season and simmer 1½ hours.

Cook the pasta in plenty of boiling salted water. Drain when *al dente*, place in a warm bowl, add all the cheese, mix in the sauce and serve.

Maccarones con la ricotta
Macaroni with Pork and Ricotta Sauce

A good way to use a cheap cut of pork, but being a milder sauce than its beef-based cousins it needs the flavour of good pasta. For 5–6.

600g (1 lb 5 oz) homemade
   macaroni, pages 68–9, or
   good short pasta
1kg (2 lb 3 oz) cheap pork joint
   – more if it has a large
   bone
2 tablespoons olive oil
1 carrot
1 celery stick
1 small onion

1 garlic clove
1 tablespoon chopped parsley
1 tumbler dry red or white
   wine
1.5kg (3 lb 5 oz) fresh or tinned
   tomatoes, skinned and
   chopped
225g (8 oz) ricotta cheese
100g (3½ oz) grated pecorino
   sardo cheese

Brown the meat gently all over in the fat or oil with the finely chopped carrot, celery, onion, garlic and parsley. Pour in the wine and reduce a little, then add the tomatoes and water to come to the top of the meat. Cover and cook gently for 2 hours on top of the stove or in a low oven (gas mark 2, 300°F, 150°C).

Cook the pasta in plenty of boiling salted water. Meanwhile, cream the ricotta in a pasta bowl with a spoonful or two of pasta water. Set aside the meat and a little sauce: the remaining sauce may be sieved or left as it is. Drain the pasta when *al dente*, put it with the ricotta, add the pecorino, and mix lightly before adding the sauce. The meat is eaten as a second course, or for another meal.

The following recipe comes from the tiny island of San Pietro at the south-west tip of Sardinia – one of those incredibly simple dishes which never fail to satisfy real pasta lovers. It proves how good a really easy sauce can be.

Spaghetti aglio, olio, pecorino
Spaghetti with Garlic, Oil and Pecorino Cheese

The oldest version of this leaves out the pine kernels but they give a special nutty flavour. Use any long thin pasta – spaghetti, spaghettini, vermicelli or linguine. A first course for 4–5 but, with a green salad, it makes a very good light lunch.

500g (1 lb 2 oz) spaghetti	*1–2 garlic cloves*
6 tablespoons olive oil	*3 handfuls grated pecorino*
2 handfuls pine kernels	*sardo cheese*

Cook the spaghetti in plenty of boiling well-salted water. Meanwhile, cook the pine nuts and chopped garlic in the warm oil in a wide casserole, until they begin to turn golden, then set aside. When the pasta is *al dente* drain it, but not too well, tip into the oil and garlic, toss a moment or two over a very low flame, remove from the heat, sprinkle on a handful or so of cheese and serve. More cheese is passed round at table.

The particular flavour of the Sardinian pecorino is very much part of this dish but it's worth experimenting with other hard cheeses (see page 33).

I ravioli di Sant'Antioco
Ravioli from Sant'Antioco

Off Sardinia's southern tip lies the island of Sant'Antioco where they make ravioli subtly flavoured with mountain ham, and sauced with pistachio nuts. An interesting combination served for feast days and family parties. A first course or light lunch for 4.

egg pasta made with 250g (9 oz) plain flour, plus ½ teaspoon olive oil, see pages 17–20.

Filling
½ lamb's brain	*1½ tablespoons pecorino sardo*
125g (4½ oz) mountain ham	*cheese, grated*
off cuts or 150g (5 oz)	*½ tablespoon unsalted butter*
prosciutto off cuts	*1 egg*
150g (5 oz) beef bone	*freshly grated nutmeg*
marrow	

Methods and ingredients which may be unfamiliar are explained on pages 26–38.

Sauce
70g (2½ oz) unsalted butter
40g (1½ oz) chopped pistachio
 nuts, shelled weight

70g (2½ oz) pecorino sardo
 cheese, grated

Cleanse and prepare the lamb's brains, as on pages 27–8. Dry, and chop them finely with the ham and bone marrow. Mix well with the cheese, butter and raw egg. Add seasoning and a hint of nutmeg.

Roll the pasta thinly. Cut it into little circles with a biscuit cutter, put a tiny heap of filling on each, fold in half and press the moist edges to seal, flick up the edge, then curl and press the two points together. Place on a tray dusted with semolina until cooking time.

Cook the ravioli in boiling salted water until a corner tastes ready. Meanwhile, gently melt the butter for the sauce until it *just* browns, without burning. Drain the cooked ravioli, transfer to a warm serving dish, add half the pecorino, pour over the butter, sprinkle with chopped pistachio nuts and serve, passing round the remaining cheese at table.

Shaping ravioli from Sant'Antioco

13 SICILY

The lemons hang pale and innumerable in the thick lemon groves. Lemon trees, like Italians, seem to be happiest when they are touching each other all around. Solid forests of not very tall lemon trees lie between the steep mountains and the sea, on the strip of plain . . . lemons, lemons innumerable, speckled like innumerable tiny stars in the green firmament of leaves. So many lemons! Think of all the lemonade crystals they will be reduced to. Think of America drinking them up next summer.

So wrote D. H. Lawrence, in *Sea and Sardinia* after a visit to Sicily, but his view of Palermo also reflects another side to the island.

. . . piles of white and green fennel, like celery, and great sheaves of young purplish sea-dust-coloured artichokes, nodding their buds, piles of big radishes, scarlet and bluey

purple, carrots, long strings of dried figs, mountains of big oranges, scarlet large peppers, a last slice of pumpkin, a great mass of colours and vegetable freshness.

 Curiously, one of the vegetables he leaves out is the one most loved in Sicily and one of the glories of their cooking – the aubergine. Introduced long ago by the Arabs, it is only one of the aspects of their food to reveal how much this island has been influenced by its invaders – Greeks, Carthaginians, Arabs, Normans and Spaniards have all contributed to its architecture, customs, and cooking.

Sicily's hot climate calls for dishes which are stimulating, peppery, sour or sweet, to overcome the enervating effect of the heat. Throughout the long Sicilian summer they sip cool, thirst-quenching syrups, sorbets and ices made from the famous oranges and lemons. Birthplace of cassata and marzipan, Sicily's cakes rival those of Greece for sweetness; but it is pasta which is most important of all to Sicilians, maybe more important here than in Rome, or even Naples. A plate of pasta must start every meal, be it lunch, dinner or even an outing. A meal is not a meal without it. Which explains why Felix Lope de Vega, Spain's seventeenth-century playwright, was convinced that every Sicilian dreamed of a Sicily made out of macaroni, with Etna a mountain of grated cheese and the lighthouse of Messina brimming with muscadel wine.

Around Catania, on the east cost, dishes similar to traditional Italian cooking are presented in an original Sicilian way. While round Palermo, to the west, the Arab influence remains: food is spicy, fiery and sweet. Here one finds the most extraordinary dish of all, the pride of Sicilian pasta.

Pasta con le sarde
Pasta with Pilchards

The pilchards must be really fresh for this unique and beautifully tinted pasta sauce. Wild mountain fennel is needed too, but you can use the young shoots of the cultivated herb. The extraordinary combination of flavours makes an excellent dish. An acquired taste maybe, but, for many, a lifelong favourite. It is not a light dish: if eaten for lunch you will only need a light salad – and a long siesta – to follow. For 6 or more.

*750g (1 lb 11 oz) long
   macaroni*
250g (9 oz) wild fennel
*450g (1 lb) very fresh raw
   pilchards, or large sardines*
*1 handful blanched and
   toasted almonds*
6 tablespoons olive oil

*2 medium-sized onions, finely
   chopped*
10 anchovies, drained of oil
1 handful pine kernels
1 handful sultanas
a pinch saffron powder

Rinse the fennel and boil it in lightly salted water until really tender. Drain it, keeping the water, and chop it to a mist. Gut the fish, discard the heads, remove the spines and open them flat. Slice the almonds finely.

Sauté the onion in the oil until golden. Add the anchovies and just over half the pilchards. Cook gently, stirring and squashing the ingredients for several minutes. Add the pine kernels, sultanas and fennel. Season, adding a good pinch of saffron. Cook for about 20 minutes, adding a little fennel water occasionally, until it becomes thick and creamy. Taste and adjust the seasoning.

Add enough water to the remaining fennel water to cook the pasta, bring to the boil and put in the pasta broken in thirds. Oil an oven dish. While the pasta cooks fry the remaining fish in hot oil until nicely done, then sprinkle with salt. Drain the pasta when very much *al dente*. Put a layer in the oven dish, cover with some of the sauce, and continue the layers of pasta and sauce until both are used up. Arrange the fried fish on top, sprinkle with toasted almonds and bake in a moderate oven (gas mark 4, 350°F, 180°C) for 15 minutes.

Methods and ingredients which may be unfamiliar are explained on pages 26–38.

Tuna fish are caught in the waters near Trapani on the west coast of Sicily and the following recipe uses fresh tuna fish and the aromatic little capers that grow profusely on the volcanic rock of the wild and beautiful island of Pantelleria, a hundred kilometres from Sicily, near the coast of Africa.

Vermicelli della tonnara
Vermicelli of the Tuna Fishing Grounds

Fresh tuna fish is so delicious, with its beautiful bacon-pink flesh and meaty texture, that it is well worth searching for it. This makes a light main course for 5.

*500g (18 oz) vermicelli or
   spaghetti
500g (18 oz) fresh tuna fish
5–6 tablespoons olive oil
2 garlic cloves
a handful of parsley*

*a piece of chilli
½ tumbler dry white wine
3 fresh tomatoes, skinned and
   chopped
50–60g (1¾–2 oz) capers*

Skin and bone the fish and cut it in strips about half the length and width of your little finger. Sauté the finely sliced garlic, chopped parsley, and as much chilli as you like, in the oil in a wide shallow pan. When slightly golden put in the fish, season with salt, and cook gently for about 10 minutes, turning it so that it cooks all over. Add the wine and let it bubble and evaporate a little over the heat before putting in the tomatoes. Taste the sauce and add more salt and chilli if it needs it. Cook slowly for 15–20 minutes, adding a spoonful or two of water if it gets too dry. Add the capers during the last few minutes.

Have ready a large pan of boiling salted water for the pasta. Cook it *al dente*, drain, transfer it to a warm bowl, add the sauce, and garnish with chopped parsley. Serve, mixing lightly at table.

If you have to make do with tinned tuna fish the next recipe, which combines it with the green olives for which Sicily is famous, is an excellent way to use it.

Spaghetti all'isolana
Island Spaghetti

One of the lovely things about this dish is the way the wine seems to permeate the pasta. Pimento-stuffed olives are not traditional in this dish but they are excellent and easier to slice than those with stones. It serves 4–5 as a substantial first course or a light lunch.

500g (18 oz) spaghetti	4 tablespoons good olive oil
160g (5½ oz) large green olives	1 garlic clove, finely chopped
	a handful of parsley, chopped
170g (6 oz) tinned tuna, in oil	1½ tumblers dry white wine

Slice the olives, flake the drained tuna, and put a large pan of salted water to boil for the pasta.

Heat the oil in a wide casserole and let the garlic begin to turn golden in it. Put in the olives and cook gently for 5 minutes. Add the drained tuna fish and half the parsley and cook another 5 minutes. Now add the wine and let three-quarters of it cook away over a fairly brisk heat. Season to taste then cover and keep warm.

Cook the pasta *al dente*. Drain it – but don't shake off all the water – tip it into the sauce and toss lightly together over the lowest heat for a moment or two. Sprinkle with the remaining parsley and serve straight from the pan.

Spaghetti col tonno
Spaghetti with Tuna

This foolproof, quick and surprisingly good light main dish needs no recipe. Make a basic tomato sauce (see page 73) and add flaked tinned tuna fish, drained of its oil, for just long enough to heat it. It is even better when a few anchovy fillets are softened in the oil at the start of the tomato sauce. For 5 you need 1kg (2 lb) sauce and 125g (4½ oz) tuna, and 6 anchovy fillets. It should be garnished with chopped parsley.

On Mount Etna's fertile slopes, to the east of Sicily, grow almonds, hazels, pistachio nuts, and also grapes which are turned into strong, full-bodied, amber-coloured wine, while below them are oranges and lemons in profusion. This area came greatly under the influence of Greece, which accounts for certain dishes of sweet pasta. A dish called *la scuma* used to be made by deep-frying the pasta in oil. It was then lifted out with forks and arranged in little heaps, sauced with melted butter, egg yolk, cheese and hot honey. Unfortunately the tradition has quite died out, but what has survived is the love of onion, and here sauces use more onion than in most other regions.

Maccheroncelli con cavolfiore

Slim Macaroni with Cauliflower

A curious and delectable combination of flavours makes this a good prelude to any main course. It serves 5–6.

600g (1 lb 5 oz) long slim macaroni or bucatini
1 medium cauliflower
90–100g (3–3½ oz) pine kernels

1 largish onion, finely sliced
8–9 tablespoons good olive oil
6 anchovy fillets, in oil
a pinch saffron powder

Break the cauliflower into florets and cut each into much smaller sprigs. Rinse them well in salted water, then cook in boiling water for 5–10 minutes and drain while slightly crisp. Meanwhile, toast the pine kernels in the oven until they just turn gold – which happens rapidly. Then put a large pan of salted water to boil for the pasta.

Gently sauté the onion in the olive oil, in a wide casserole, until soft and golden. Add the drained chopped anchovies, the cauliflower and the saffron, and cook them together for a few minutes, to heat thoroughly. Add a little ground pepper, and taste before adding salt (the anchovies may make it salty enough). Cook the pasta *al dente* and drain, leaving a little water clinging to it. Transfer it to the sauce, stir briefly over a moderate heat to mix, top with the pine nuts, and serve directly from the pan. No cheese is needed.

Vermicelli alla siciliana
Sicilian Vermicelli

A rich dish with a most distinctive taste, typical of Sicilian cooking. Lunch for 4–5 or a hearty first course.

500g (18 oz) vermicelli, or spaghetti	2–3 yellow pimentos
1 large aubergine	a handful of black olives, stoned
2 cloves garlic, chopped	2 tablespoons capers
½ tumbler olive oil	6 anchovy fillets, in oil
12 really ripe, fresh or tinned tomatoes, skinned and chopped	1 tablespoon chopped fresh basil or parsley

Cut the aubergine in small cubes, sprinkle with salt and leave to drain for 1–2 hours.

Sauté the garlic in the oil until golden. Remove it and add the tomatoes and the rinsed and dried aubergine. Simmer gently. Meanwhile, skin the pimentos (see page 34), remove the seeds, cut them into slim strips. Put a large pan of salted water to boil for the pasta.

When the aubergine is tender add the olives, capers, pimento, chopped anchovy fillets, and the parsley or basil. Cover and cook for 5 minutes more. Cook the pasta. Drain when *al dente* and place in a warm bowl. Top with the sauce, and a good pinch of black or red pepper, if you wish.

Pasta a 'picchi-pacchi'

Of all aubergine sauces this is perhaps the most subtle and seductive. Rich but not heavy, it suits many types of pasta and serves 4 or 5 as a first course or light lunch.

500g (18 oz) spaghetti or
  other long pasta
300g (11 oz) aubergine
sunflower oil for frying
2 medium onions, thinly
  sliced
6 tablespoons olive oil

175g (6 oz) fresh or tinned
  tomatoes, skinned and
  chopped
1 clove garlic, crushed
a little fresh basil (optional)
6–8 anchovy fillets, drained of
  oil

Cut the aubergines in thinnish slices, sprinkle with salt and leave for 1–2 hours.

Rinse, dry, and fry the aubergine slices until golden on both sides. Drain on kitchen paper. In a fresh pan cook the onions gently to a pale gold in the olive oil. Add the tomatoes, garlic and basil, and season – but do not over-salt. Cover and cook very gently, for about 20 minutes, to a smooth thick sauce, stirring frequently and adding a spoonful of water if it threatens to stick. Now add the aubergines and continue cooking until they almost dissolve in the sauce – which takes 30 minutes or so.

Cook the pasta in a large pan of boiling salted water. Meanwhile, add the chopped anchovy fillets to the sauce. Taste, adjust the seasoning and simmer until the pasta is ready. Drain the pasta when *al dente*, put it in a warm bowl, and pour over the sauce. Mix lightly as you serve but do not hand round cheese.

The showiest of all Sicily's aubergine dishes is also one of the cheapest and simplest. It was created in honour of Vincenzo Bellini, the famous eighteenth-century musician born here in Catania, and named after his opera *Norma*. It is a speciality of his home town.

Spaghetti alla Norma
Spaghetti Norma Style

One of the most attractive of all pasta dishes; a lovely way to make very basic ingredients into a dish fit for an occasion. For 5–6.

600g (1 lb 5 oz) spaghetti
500g (18 oz) aubergines
3 sliced garlic cloves
4 tablespoons olive oil
1kg (2 lb 3 oz) fresh or tinned
  ripe red tomatoes, skinned
  and chopped

sunflower oil for frying
grated pecorino sardo, or
  Parmesan cheese
a little hard ricotta cheese
fresh basil or parsley

Slice the aubergines lengthwise, rather thinner than sliced bread, sprinkle with salt and leave in a colander to drain for 1–2 hours.

Make a tomato sauce by gently cooking the garlic in the olive oil until soft, adding the tomatoes, seasoning and cooking over moderate heat for 15–20 minutes to thicken slightly. Put a large pan of salted water to heat for the pasta. Rinse the aubergine slices, dry well, and fry until tender and nicely golden on each side. Place on kitchen paper, sprinkle lightly with salt and keep warm.

Cook the pasta *al dente* while you reheat the tomato sauce and arrange the aubergine slices, like petals, round the edge of a large flat serving dish which is well warmed. Drain the pasta, place it in the centre of the dish, add a handful of pecorino, and some hard ricotta too – if you can get it. Spoon a little of the sauce into the centre and the rest in a ring round the spaghetti. Decorate quickly with basil leaves or parsley sprigs and serve, passing round more cheese at table.

The cooking of the Benedictine monks was praised all over the town; their timballo of macaroni with its topping of shortcrust pastry, their rice balls big as melons, the stuffed

olives, and honey crêpes were dishes that no other cooks knew
how to make. At midday, when all were gathered in the
refectory under the frescoed dome, lit by the light from
twenty-four windows big as doorways, the rector climbed up
to the pulpit and at the first forkful of macaroni – after grace
– began to mumble . . . 'The thirty-fifth commandment: not
given to wine. The thirty-sixth commandment: not a great
eater . . .'

De Roberto describing the Benedictine monks of Catania

Timballo di bucatini
con melenzane
Bucatini and Aubergine Pie

Pasta pies are made all over Italy but this aubergine pie is
typically Sicilian. A main course for 3–4.

*shortcrust pastry made with 250g (9 oz) plain flour, 125g (4½ oz)
butter, 1 egg (see page 33)*

250g (9 oz) bucatini, or ziti
400g (14 oz) aubergines
sunflower oil, for frying
1 garlic clove, crushed
1½ tablespoons olive oil
250g (9 oz) tinned tomatoes,
  drained weight, chopped

25g (1 oz) unsalted butter
60g (2 oz) good Parmesan
  cheese, grated
1 tablespoon fresh basil or
  parsley, chopped

Peel the aubergines, slice them like bread, sprinkle with salt and
leave for 1–2 hours. Roll out the pastry, line a medium-sized
spring-sided cake tin with it, and weight it with beans and keep
in shape with crumpled foil. Cut and decorate a pastry lid and
place it on a baking sheet. Bake both in a fairly hot oven until
only just cooked.

Rinse, dry and fry the aubergines until just soft. Drain on
kitchen paper, and sprinkle with salt. Cook the garlic, until

golden, in the olive oil, add the tomatoes and cook rapidly for 5 minutes without stirring. Season and set aside.

Cook the pasta, broken in thirds, in a large pan of boiling salted water. Drain when still rather undercooked, mix with the tomato sauce, the flaked butter, half the Parmesan, and the basil or parsley. Put a third of the mixture in the pastry case, then a layer of aubergine, repeat until all the ingredients are finished. Cover with the lid, but don't worry if it doesn't fit exactly, and bake in a moderate oven for 15 minutes.

Pasta 'ncaciata

Mixed Up Pasta

One of the classic recipes of Sicily with its combination of aubergines, tomato and cheese. Any medium-width short pasta can be used – penne, shells, or even long macaroni broken in pieces. A light main course for 6.

600g (1 lb 5 oz) pasta
800g (1 lb 12 oz) aubergines
800g (1 lb 12 oz) fresh or tinned tomatoes, skinned, and sieved or liquidized
2 tablespoons olive oil
chilli powder
sunflower oil
2 hardboiled eggs

60g (2 oz) mozzarella or similar soft cheese
70g (2½ oz) peppery Italian salami
1 tablespoon chopped parsley
several torn leaves of fresh basil
good Parmesan cheese, grated

Slice the aubergines lengthwise, sprinkle with salt, and leave to drain for 1–2 hours.

Cook the tomatoes with the olive oil for 10 minutes to form a sauce, adding a little chilli powder if your salami isn't really peppery. Rinse the aubergines, dry well, and fry in hot oil until golden and tender on each side. Drain on kitchen paper. Have

Methods and ingredients which may be unfamiliar are explained on pages 26–38.

ready a large pan of boiling salted water and put the pasta to cook.

Place half the aubergine slices on the bottom of an oven dish. Roughly chop the eggs and mozzarella. Drain the pasta when really *al dente*. Mix with the tomato sauce, remaining aubergine slices, salami, sliced eggs, mozzarella, parsley and basil. Fill the aubergine-lined dish with this mixture, cover with Parmesan and cook in a moderate oven for 10–15 minutes until the cheese melts. Serve quickly.

This dish is especially popular in Messina where it is served in an original way. Meatballs, prepared as for *orecchiette del trullo* (page 56), are mixed in, and caciocavallo cheese is used instead of mozzarella. Each portion is then put in an individual earthenware pot before being baked in the oven – which makes sure everyone has a little of everything.

Glazed earthenware pots for a dish like this can be bought at stalls and supermarkets all over Italy: before using one for the first time it is traditional to rub it all over with a garlic clove. On gas they are ideal for many slowly cooked sauces provided a mat protects them from too much heat.

As the island's pastures are more suited to sheep and goats than to cattle, good meat is at a premium and this beef roll, with its lovely pink and white filling, is a traditional Sicilian method of making a small quantity go a long way. Each family has its own favourite way of preparing it, but here are two versions: the first is a substantial filling, the second a more economical one. For either you need a large thin slice of lean beef.

Farsumagru
Falsely Lean

The meat in this dish is usually made well in advance and served cold. The sauce is then heated and embellished to use on pasta. Each dish serves 5–6.

I

600g (1 lb 15 oz) tagliatelle	100g (3½ oz) salami, cut in
5 small eggs and 2 yolks	little strips
100g (3½ oz) fatty unsmoked	100g (3½ oz) caciocavallo or
bacon, in strips	provolone cheese, cut in
400g (14 oz) beef mince	strips
1 tablespoon chopped parsley	sunflower oil
2–3 tablespoons grated	2 finely sliced onions
pecorino romano cheese	1 tumbler red wine
a handful fresh breadcrumbs	½ litre (1 pint) tinned
a little milk or broth	tomatoes, puréed, seasoned
grated nutmeg	and cooked to a sauce
600g (1 lb 5 oz) lean beef in one	1–2 meaty sausages
slice	

To make the stuffing, hardboil 4 eggs, shell, and slice them. Cook the bacon in boiling water for 2 minutes and drain it. Mix together the beef mince, parsley, 2–3 tablespoons pecorino, 1 raw egg and 2 yolks, and the breadcrumbs soaked in a little milk or broth and squeezed out. Season well, adding nutmeg. Beat the beef slice out as thinly as possible, then spread it with the mince mixture. Cover this with the salami, bacon, sliced eggs and provolone. Roll the beef slice up like a swiss roll – if it splits open just sew it up with some strong thread – and tie it firmly with white cotton string.

Melt 2 tablespoons of vegetable oil or dripping in a casserole which will just take the meat. Put in the meat and onions, and brown the meat all over. Season, add the wine, cover and simmer for 2–3 hours, or cook in a moderate to low oven. Turn the meat once and add more wine, or even water, if necessary. Stir in the tomato sauce 15 minutes from the end, taste, and adjust the seasoning. When the *farsumagru* is cooked, remove it from the sauce and cool.

To make the pasta sauce cut the sausages in small pieces and simmer them in the sauce from round the meat, taste and adjust the seasoning. Then cook the pasta *al dente* in plenty of boiling salted water. Drain, place in a warmed pasta bowl, top with the sauce and a handful of grated pecorino, and served with extra cheese at table.

For the main course slice the *farsumagru* and arrange it on a dish. Serve it with a salad such as the Sicilian *caponata*, made with cooked aubergines, green olives, capers and raw celery, in a cold tomato sauce.

II

A cheaper and simpler filling for *farsumagru*. The method is exactly as above.

3 hardboiled eggs
1 raw egg and 1 yolk
150g (5 oz) mixed prosciutto and salami, cut in slim pieces
1 large grated carrot
2 small very finely chopped onions

1–2 celery stalks, finely chopped
100g (3½ oz) grated caciocavallo, provolone or Gruyère
2 tablespoons grated Parmesan cheese
1 tablespoon chopped parsley

At one time it was traditional in country districts for families to get together on Easter evening to eat tagliatelle in a way known only here and in Calabria. In the centre of the table was placed a large wooden board on top of which the tagliatelle were dropped, smothered in sauce – often from *farsumagru*. Everyone simply bent over the board, fork in hand, and pulled their share towards them on the communal platter, and it was a competition to see who could eat the most.

On a hazy summer's day the southern tip of Sicily seems timeless: asphodels with their pale ghostly blooms carpet the fields and the slopes are purple with thyme. While under the circles of shade from the carob trees rest copper-coloured oxen. Here, in Syracuse, Archimedes is reputed to have rushed naked into the street shouting 'Eureka' when he realized his body displaced its own volume of bathwater, and it is certainly a landscape he would recognize. Here, in Ragusa, they prepare a simple but very good lasagne for Sundays and special occasions.

Lasagne alla maniera di Ragusa

Lasagne the Ragusa Way

This needs cooked veal, so it's a good way to use up the leftovers from a pot roast like Abruzzi's *ragù per maccheroni carrati* (page 50). A main course for 8, but it can easily be halved.

400g (14 oz) packet lasagne, or
    500g (18 oz) fresh lasagne
½ medium-sized onion
1 carrot
a finger-length of celery
2 tablespoons parsley
3 tablespoons olive oil
1 tumbler red wine
1kg (2 lb 3 oz) fresh or tinned
    tomatoes, skinned and well
    chopped
1 clove

1 bay leaf
1 teacup broth (if needed)
500g (18 oz) cold veal from a
    roast
150g (5 oz) hard ricotta
    cheese, or 200g (7 oz) fresh
    ricotta and 60g (2 oz) feta
100g (3½ oz) pecorino sardo
    cheese, grated, or 50:50 with
    Parmesan
2 tablespoons dry oven-baked
    breadcrumbs

Cook the finely chopped onion, carrot, celery and parsley gently in the oil until just golden, add the wine, let it bubble fiercely to reduce a little, and add the tomatoes, clove and bay leaf. Season to taste, cover, and simmer gently for 30 minutes, stirring occasionally and adding a little broth if it gets too dry. Put in the finely chopped veal and cook for another 15 minutes.

Meanwhile cook the lasagne as usual, see page 23, and chop up the ricotta cheese, or ricotta and feta.

Brush a large oblong oven dish with oil. When the sauce is cooked lay a quarter of the lasagne in the dish, spoon on a quarter of the sauce, scatter with a quarter of the ricotta or ricotta and feta, then with a quarter of the pecorino. Continue these layers until the ingredients are used up, and top with the breadcrumbs. Add a dribble of oil and brown the top in a hot oven for 15 minutes.

Feta is, of course, Greek not Italian but fresh ricotta is too mild for this and feta adds some of the flavour hard ricotta would provide in Sicily.

14 THE THREE VENETIAS

 Venice, with its romantic associations, myriad canals, graceful bridges and elegant palaces is a city which grew rich on food: for the merchants of Venice made the city one of the great doorways to Europe for the vastly profitable spice and sugar trade of the sixteenth century. And it is the city which – pernicious luxury though it was considered – invented the fork. Today it is the focal point of the area called Veneto. But, unlike Rome and Naples, it does not encompass the cooking of the whole region, for within the Three Venetias come two other areas, so different they seem almost to belong to another country.

Trentino Upper Adige borders Austria: here Italy's stone houses yield place to chalets, and polenta and soups are preferred to pasta, so we include no typical recipes from there. Friuli-Venezia Giulia borders Yugoslavia and although, or perhaps

207

because, there is a distinctly Slav flavour to its cooking they have the most unusual filled pastas in all Italy, strongly flavoured with spices.

In Venice, and its tiny islands, the cooking is that of a seafaring people. Meals centre around fish, with a preference for rice as a first course: fish risottos studded with mussels, shellfish antipastos of superbly fried squid and scampi; and to follow, giant crabs or beautiful firm soles to equal any from the North Sea. But pasta is not completely forgotten and fish straight from the sea are expertly cooked, usually *in bianco* – without tomato – as a sauce for pasta. Delicious, but the recipes are the same as in other parts of Italy. An exception is *spaghetti in camicia nera* – blackshirt spaghetti – which takes its name from Mussolini's 'Blackshirts' and from the fact that the sauce uses the squid's jet-black ink. A strongly flavoured dish also very popular in Sicily, though not practical in countries such as Britain, where squid lose their ink bags on the way to the fishmonger.

Two other features of Venetian cooking are more unusual. In Venice – unlike the other great spice city, Genoa – the spices are still used. Not just nutmeg, which is found all over northern Italy but, distinctively, cinnamon: in bean soups, stuffed pastas and nut sauces. In Veneto they also have a unique pasta – bigoli. Deep golden brown, made of buckwheat flour, and shaped like spaghetti, it has a strong flavour unlike other pasta, and is served with sauces richly flavoured with duck or salty with anchovies. Indeed, so prized are these bigoli dishes that at one time the phrase 'to go for bigoli' meant to go for a good meal. Bigoli are little exported but good wholemeal spaghetti, though not the same, makes a reasonable substitute.

Bigoli con le noci
Bigoli with Walnuts

This Venetian version of pasta with nuts with its subtle hint of cinnamon makes a curiously good first course for 5–6 and is very easily made. Cinnamon loses its flavour with keeping, so you may need to adjust the quantity.

500g (18 oz) bigoli, or
   wholemeal spaghetti
100g (3½ oz) shelled walnuts
5 tablespoons olive oil
a pinch sugar

grated nutmeg
¼ teaspoon ground cinnamon
2 good tablespoons dry, oven-
   baked breadcrumbs
60g (2 oz) butter

Make the sauce while the pasta cooks in plenty of boiling salted water. Chop the walnuts quite well and put them in the oil, in a small pan, over a gentle heat. Season, adding the sugar, nutmeg and cinnamon. While the nuts warm, put the breadcrumbs in a little strainer over a cup, melt the butter, and pour the butter on the crumbs. When the pasta is *al dente* drain it – but leave it a little wet – place in a warm bowl, top with the nuts and buttery breadcrumbs. Mix lightly together and serve.

Think of Venice and you think of waterways, and of gondolas passing gracefully under delicate bridges, but it's easy to forget that where there is water there are likely to be ducks. This mundane fact isn't overlooked by the Venetians.

Bigoli con salsa d'anitra
Bigoli with Duck Sauce

This makes a main course for 6, but it's wise to cook the duck the day before you need it, then the fat can be removed from the broth before it's needed for the pasta.

700g (1 lb 9 oz) bigoli, or
   wholemeal spaghetti
2 small onions
2 carrots
2 celery stalks
6 black peppercorns
3 tablespoons good oil
1 duck, weighing about 1.5kg
   (3 lb 6 oz)

800g (1 lb 12 oz) fresh or tinned
   tomatoes, skinned and
   puréed
70g (2½ oz) unsalted butter
60g (2 oz) good Parmesan
   cheese, grated

Clean and trim the vegetables. Set aside the duck heart and liver. Place the duck in a large pan of boiling water with 1 stick celery, 1 carrot, and 1 onion, adding salt and the peppercorns. Simmer for 1 hour, or until tender. Lift out the duck and set the broth to chill while you remove the skin, and slice the breast and set aside. Remove all the other flesh, and cut it in slithers.

To make the sauce: finely chop enough onion, celery and carrot to make 2–3 tablespoons in all, and slice the liver and heart. Sauté the vegetables in the oil until golden, stir in the liver and heart and cook briefly. Add the tomatoes, season, and simmer for ½ hour.

Meanwhile, remove the fat from the broth, strain, and boil 3½ litre (7 pint) in a large pan. When the sauce is almost ready put the bigoli to cook in the broth and stir the chopped duck into the sauce to heat. You can either cut the breast in strips and add it with the other meat, or heat nice slices in a little broth, and use them to decorate the dish. When the bigoli are *al dente* put a colander over another large pan – to catch the broth – and drain them. Place them on a large warmed dish, add the butter in little flakes, half the Parmesan, and half the sauce. Serve, passing round the remaining sauce and the cheese. The broth can be used for the following soup another day.

Pappardelle e fegatini
Broth with Pappardelle and Chicken Livers

In Verona fresh pasta and chicken livers are used to give body to a basic broth. Any good broth can be used but it is an excellent way to embellish the broth left over from the recipe above, or made from the carcass of the Christmas turkey, especially if you can tuck the turkey liver in the freezer until you make the soup. For 4–6.

100g (3½ oz) pappardelle
1.2 litre (2½ pint) good broth
150g (5 oz) chicken livers

25g (1 oz) unsalted butter
Parmesan cheese, grated

Put the broth to heat. Fry the finely chopped chicken livers gently in the butter in a little pan. When they are no longer pink add them, with the pappardelle, to the boiling broth. The soup is ready to serve as soon as the pasta is al dente. At table, sprinkle a little cheese on each bowl, or they sometimes add a squeeze of pomegranate juice.

Saint Zen is Verona's patron saint and the Veronese expression which means 'God's in his heaven, and all's right with the world' is '*San Zen che ride e paparele calde*' – 'Saint Zen laughing and hot pappardelle'.

Spaghetti con salsa di quaglia
Spaghetti with Quail Sauce

Sadly, wild quails are increasingly rare, but those which now reach the shops have been bred for the table so this can be made with a clear conscience. A first course or light lunch for 4–5.

500g (18 oz) spaghetti or linguine
5 quails
100g (3½ oz) unsalted butter
1 tablespoon chopped fat from unsmoked bacon
8 small fresh sage leaves
6 juniper berries, crushed
1 tablespoon brandy
¼ litre (½ pint) light broth

Gently brown the seasoned quails in half the butter, cover, and cook slowly for 15 minutes, or until tender. Remove all the flesh from the bones and chop it finely on a board – don't be tempted to use a blender, it spoils the texture.

Put the bacon fat in the quail pan, add the chopped sage, and heat until the fat begins to run. Add the juniper berries, brandy, quail meat, and enough broth to moisten. Simmer slowly for 20 minutes. Cover and keep warm.

Cook the pasta in plenty of boiling salted water. Drain when al dente. Place in a warm bowl, add the remaining butter in flakes and the hot sauce. Mix lightly as you serve.

Cannelloni alla vicentina
Cannelloni the Vicenza Way

These unusual cannelloni aren't hard to make but it takes a little time, so it is worth making twice as many as you need and freezing half. A light main course for 6–8.

fresh lasagne made with egg pasta from 300g (11 oz) plain flour, see pages 17–24, or 250g (9 oz) wide oblongs of packet lasagne

500g (18 oz) fresh or tinned tomatoes, skinned and chopped
1½ bay leaves
1 clove garlic, finely chopped
2 chopped sage leaves
60g (2 oz) butter
½ tablespoon finely chopped onion
5 flat tablespoons plain flour
good ½ litre (1 pint) milk

100g (3½ oz) lean cooked pork
100g (3½ oz) cooked tongue
100g (3½ oz) roast veal
100g (3½ oz) cooked spinach (drained weight)
grated nutmeg
thyme
1 large or 2 small eggs
good Parmesan cheese, grated

Make a tomato sauce by putting the tomatoes in a pan with 1 bay leaf, the garlic, and sage, seasoning to taste and simmering till thick. Then remove the bay leaf.

Heat the milk, add a pinch of thyme and ½ a bay leaf and let it stand a while. Soften the onion in the butter, then add the flour and some of the strained milk to make a very thick white sauce in the usual way, see page 37.

Mince or chop all the meat finely, and combine with the very well-chopped spinach, the tomato sauce, a little nutmeg, a nut of butter, 1 tablespoon Parmesan, the beaten eggs and 2 tablespoons white sauce, and season to taste.

Cook the lasagne, as on page 23. Cut packet lasagne in half to make squares.

Use a loop whisk to mix the remaining milk smoothly into the remaining white sauce. Add half a bay leaf, a pinch of thyme and simmer until smooth and glossy. Rub a large, shallow oven dish with butter. Divide the filling between the rectangles and roll each one into a little log, overlapping the two edges and placing each cannelloni, edge side down, in the oven dish. Cover with white sauce, sprinkle with grated Parmesan, and put in a hot oven until the surface browns.

In farm kitchens in the old days, geese were roasted with herbs and then preserved in their own fat in great earthenware pots. During the winter a little meat and goose fat would be heated and served, with cheese, over homemade noodles: a simple old-fashioned dish which you may like to try if you have part of a roast goose, and its fat, left over from Christmas.

> . . . *the darkness was broken only by the sparkle of crackling red coals and greenish light from two tiny windows . . . there was dense swirling smoke and there was the eternal bubbling of beans in monstrous pots.*
> *Confessions of an Italian*, Ippolito Nievo

A little boy's impression of cooking in a Venetian villa in days gone by, but beans still bubble in less infernal kitchens, and they are often combined with pasta. Those of the Bellunese district, around Lamon on the Trentino border, are said to have the finest flavour, and in Venice they serve them cold, with cuttlefish, as an antipasto. But, all over Italy they are made into bean soups.

Pasta e fagioli
alla Veneta

Beans with Pasta the Venetian Way

The soup of Venetia is spiced with cinnamon and flavoured with a Parma ham bone, but an ordinary ham bone can replace it, or even off cuts of ham. The best beans to use are black-eyed beans, white with a black spot, or the speckled borlotti beans.

As this soup needs long cooking it is worth making extra to freeze. This gives about 10 large helpings. Set aside the amount you want to freeze before adding the pasta.

225g (8 oz) tagliatelle, broken into 5cm (2 in) lengths	*1 prosciutto, or other ham, bone*
500g (18 oz) black-eyed or borlotti beans	*1 onion, chopped*
	a pinch ground cinnamon
	1 tablespoon olive oil
250g (9 oz) pork rind	*Parmesan cheese (optional)*

Soak the beans overnight, rinse and drain them. Put the drained beans in plenty of cold water, bring them to the boil and cook rapidly for 15 minutes. Drain. Parboil the pork rind for 10 minutes, and drain it. Put all the other ingredients – except the pasta – in a large pan with a tight lid, season and cover with cold water. Bring to the boil, cover and simmer until the beans are well cooked and a few have begun to thicken the broth. Take out the bone, cut up any meat from it and return it to the pan. Bring the soup back to the boil, taste and adjust the seasoning, and add the pasta. When the pasta is cooked the soup is ready. Let it stand a moment before serving. Cheese can be added at table.

The Romans have an interesting version of this soup. In their *Pasta e fagioli* the quantities and method are the same but they leave out the cinnamon and flavour the soup with an onion, celery stalk, clove of garlic, and a handful of parsley, all finely chopped and softened in oil, then simmered for 10 minutes with

4 skinned and chopped tomatoes. This mixture is then added to the soup just before the pasta, and cannolicchi are used instead of tagliatelle.

The last area of Venetia is Friuli-Venezia Giulia, on the border of Yugoslavia. The Friuli cooking, even among the better off, has always been based on simple country dishes; they like to eat meat as meat, and vegetables as vegetables. In the sixteenth century, while much of Italy indulged in every delicious dish gluttony could invent, Friuli was on the verge of famine. The food has remained simple to this day: staple dishes are vegetable soup, broth with rice and, in the mountains, polenta.

The general use of pasta in this region is not very old; although it was mentioned in medieval convent books, it was reserved for the sick and it was only a century ago that it found its way into family kitchens. In general it is nothing like as light as the pasta of many other regions but there are some curious and interesting dishes.

Bauletti di carne
Little Trunks of Meat

Shaping bauletti

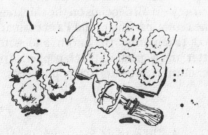

Of all the stuffed pastas, these little circles in broth are among the quickest to make. The stuffing is not really meat but ham. They use the cooked ham of Trieste which has a particularly

215

fine flavour, and this dish depends very much on the quality of the ham and the broth. You need the real thing, not plastic ham, nor a bouillon cube. For 3–5.

egg pasta made with 300g (10 oz) plain flour, see pages 17–22

30g (1 oz) good cooked ham
30g (1 oz) Parma ham
25g (1 oz) Gruyère cheese
150g (5 oz) ricotta cheese
1½ tablespoons finely chopped
  parsley

20g (¾ oz) Parmesan cheese
nutmeg
2 small eggs
1 litre (2 pints) good chicken
  broth

Finely chop the hams and Gruyère. Beat the ricotta to a cream, mix in the parsley, Gruyère, ham, Parmesan, and season to taste, adding grated nutmeg, then the eggs. (All this can be done as one process in a blender.)

Roll the pasta into two very thin sheets. On one, place little heaps of the filling, the size of a hazelnut. Moisten one side of the other, place it over the first sheet and press well down round each heap. Cut into little round 'pillows' about 4cm (1½ in) across with a round pasta cutter or a very small glass. Gather up and re-roll the pasta scraps to use any filling that is left. Put the bauletti on a tray dusted with semolina till needed.

To cook, drop them into boiling broth, and cook until a piece of the edge tastes done. Homemade pasta may take longer than the bought variety – it all depends on the thickness of the pasta.

Serve in the broth, passing round Parmesan at the table. They are also good taken from the broth and eaten with melted unsalted butter and a grind of black pepper. And in this part of Italy they sometimes use butter and poppy seeds.

While the Genoese like their food savoury the people of the Venetias like their food sweet. In the upper part of Veneto, they eat pasta in a fresh country style and often use ricotta in their

---

Methods and ingredients which may be unfamiliar are explained on pages 26–38.

sauces. Often it is creamed with the juices which have spilled from roast meat, but in spring they flavour it with sweet young peas and butter, and their recipe is very similar to an old Roman one, for it is sweetened with sugar and spiced with ground cinnamon. Such sauces have only a hint of sugar, but in Friuli they once made remarkable stuffed pastas which were really sweet: containing dried and candied fruits, and even chocolate. Today, only a few sweet pasta dishes remain.

Ciarscóns alla carniola

Ravioli the Carnia Way

These surprising little ravioli have only a hint of sweetness and are still made for celebrations. A first course for 6.

egg pasta made with 500g (18 oz) plain flour and 4 eggs, see pages 17–22

Filling
60g (2 oz) parsley
75g (2½ oz) sultanas or raisins
100g (3½ oz) ricotta cheese

40g (1½ oz) baked breadcrumbs
nutmeg
1 egg

Sauce
120g (4 oz) unsalted butter

100g (3½ oz) good Parmesan cheese

Ciarscóns

Chop the parsley and the sultanas or raisins thoroughly. Mix them with the ricotta and crumbs, and season to taste with salt and a little nutmeg. Add the lightly beaten egg. Roll the pasta into thin sheets. Place the filling in hazelnut-sized heaps, on one sheet, cover with another moistened sheet and press down round the filling before cutting into little square ravioli. Place on a tray dusted with semolina for an hour or so.

Cook them in plenty of boiling salted water. The cooking time depends on the thickness of the pasta, so keep tasting an edge. Drain, and serve them covered in melted butter, adding Parmesan at table.

The area round Trieste, close to the border with Yugoslavia, has a gentle almost Mediterranean climate, but the cooking is far from Mediterranean. For centuries men have come here from Yugoslavia looking for work, and you can detect the Slav influence in the food. They wrap pasta round plums and boil them like agnolotti, and lasagnette with poppy seeds was a very popular dish in Trieste at the turn of the century, and is still found in Austria.

Lasagnette ai semi di papavero
Wide Noodles with Poppy Seeds

This has all the childhood charm of butter and sugar eaten on white bread, fresh from the baker. It is difficult to believe it used to be eaten at the start of a meal, and for the nostalgic it makes an irresistible pudding either with the poppy seeds, as they eat it here, or without them. But you need really good tagliatelle made with their full quota of eggs. For 5–6.

500g (18 oz) fresh tagliatelle   *2 tablespoons poppy seeds*
100g (3½ oz) unsalted butter   *30g (1 oz) caster sugar*

Cook the pasta in plenty of boiling salted water. Meanwhile, melt the butter until it is almost turning brown – taking care not to burn it – add the poppy seeds and sugar, and keep warm. Drain the pasta when *al dente*, transfer to a warm bowl, pour over the poppy seed butter and serve at once.

Cialzóns di pianura
Agnolotti of the Plain

This delicious dessert has an interesting history: not so very long ago this part of Italy belonged to the Austrian Empire and these agnolotti differ only in shape from *zwetzken knoedelen*, Austria's renowned plum dumplings. In Austria they also make *marillen knoedelen*, apricot dumplings, and you may like to try this pasta with apricots when they are in season – or even juicy, dried apricots, well soaked. The lovely thing about this dish is the way the pasta captures all the juiciness and flavour of the hot fruit. It's hard to predict how many this will serve, so much depends on the thickness of the pasta, but about 4–6 on average.

Shaping cialzóns

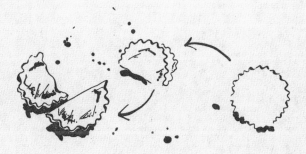

egg pasta made with 250g (9 oz) plain flour, 250g (9 oz) mashed potatoes, and only 1 egg, see pages 17–22

Filling
1–1.5kg (2–3 lb) small sweet plums, Switzen are ideal

To serve
100g (3½ oz) unsalted butter
2 tablespoons very fine oven-baked breadcrumbs

Peel and boil the potatoes, drain them the instant they are soft, return them to the pan and shake over a low flame to dry. Mash them thoroughly, then proceed as usual for egg pasta, though if the potatoes are overcooked you may need no egg at all, or may even need extra flour.

Rinse and stone the plums and cut them in sections if they are large. Roll the dough out thinly and cut it in circles large enough to enclose a plum, or part of one. Place a piece of plum in each, folding and pressing the moistened edges firmly together. Place them on a tray dusted with semolina, then cook them in plenty of boiling salted water until the pasta tastes done.

While they cook melt the butter, and slightly brown the breadcrumbs in it. Drain the cooked pasta and serve it with butter and breadcrumbs. Those with a sweet tooth may like to add sugar.

15 TUSCANY

 Tuscany is the part of Italy which most often captures the hearts of foreigners. Beloved of Keats and Shelley, it has a romantic quality: curving hills, peaceful cloisters, cypresses rising darkly against clear skies, and nightingales singing in box-scented parks. It seems gently painted in pastel colours: jade greens, soft silvers and old gold are found in convents, on the walls of palaces, and on the slopes of Fiesole near Florence.

Birthplace of the Renaissance, it cradled many of those who laid the foundation of today's civilization – and not least in cooking. For though Tuscany produced no da Vinci of the kitchen, sixteenth-century Florence had a sophisticated cuisine which neighbouring countries lacked. So when Catherine de Medici married the king of France, she took her Florentine cooks with her – and laid the foundation for French cooking as it is today. For the French – never slow to appreciate the good things of life – rapidly made the new cooking their own.

Today Tuscan cooking is among the best in Italy, not lavish but quietly excellent. Florentine steaks, grilled to perfection over log embers, are as famous as the chianti drunk with them, and produced from grapes grown on the Chianti hills between Florence and Siena. The pastas served before such a dish are delicious; the sauces are of game, duck and chicken, or richly flavoured with wild porcini mushrooms or golden chantrelles found in Garfagnano – near where the pure white marble for Michelangelo's sculptures was quarried. Probably the best known, best loved pasta in Tuscany is *Pappardelle con la lepre*.

Pappardelle con la lepre
Pappardelle with Hare Sauce

This dark sauce needs wide ribbons of pasta. If you can't get pappardelle choose the widest fettuccine; the sauce will be too heavy for anything narrower. A hare weighing over 1.75kg (3½ lb), carefully cut, should provide a saddle for roasting and enough meat for this dish as well. If you have some good game broth use it instead of broth from the hare; otherwise make the broth some hours before you need to cook the dish. A main course for 4, or luxurious first course for 6.

600g (1 lb 5 oz) pappardelle
a hare large enough to give 600g (18 oz) meat without skin or bone
1½ onions
1 carrot
a stick of celery
4 peppercorns
100g (3½ oz) unsmoked streaky bacon, chopped

½ tablespoon unsalted butter
1 tablespoon plain flour
1 tumbler dry full-bodied red wine
½ litre (1 pint) broth (see below)
good Parmesan cheese, grated
parsley (optional)

Methods and ingredients which may be unfamiliar are explained on pages 26–38.

If the hare is large enough set aside the saddle for another dish. Then strip all the meat from the bones and place it in the refrigerator. For the broth, put the bones in a large pan of cold water with an onion cleaned but unskinned and stuck with 1 clove, the sliced carrot, a finger-length of celery, 4 peppercorns, and a touch of salt. Bring slowly to the boil and simmer for at least 3 hours, topping up the water if necessary. Then strain the liquid, and boil it to reduce it to about ¾ litre (1½ pint) – or add more water if there is too little.

To make the sauce, cut the hare meat into very small pieces. Sauté the bacon, and a finely chopped finger-length of celery and half onion, in the butter in a wide casserole, till they take colour. Add the hare, and more butter if needed, and brown the meat nicely all over. Stir in the flour for a moment or two. Then mix in the wine, and evaporate by half before adding ½ litre (1 pint) broth. Season to taste, cover, and simmer very slowly until the hare is tender – at least 1½ hours. Stir it occasionally and add a spoonful or so of broth or wine if it gets dry.

Cook the pappardelle *al dente* in plenty of boiling salted water. Drain, place them on a large warm serving dish, sprinkle on a handful of cheese, pour over the hare sauce and, though Tuscans don't use it, a few sprigs of parsley give a finishing touch. Serve immediately.

Le penne del germano

Wild Duck Quills

Being a hunting area wild ducks are not the luxury they are in some other places, and they make a very satisfying pasta sauce typical of the region. But this might not be one's first choice of recipe if duck had to be bought expensively. A main course for 4–5.

500g (18 oz) penne, or
farfalle
1 medium onion
1 carrot
1 celery stick
4 tablespoons olive oil
1 wild duck, weighing about
1kg (2¼ lb), chopped in 4,
plus its giblets
2 fresh sage leaves
a sprig rosemary

2 fresh basil leaves (optional)
zest of ½ a lemon
½ stick cinnamon
1 tumbler red wine
5 ripe red fresh or tinned
tomatoes, peeled and
chopped
a little game or chicken
broth
a little unsalted butter

Sauté the finely chopped onion, carrot and celery in the oil till they begin to colour. Add the chopped duck liver and heart. When nicely brown add the duck, season, and add the herbs, lemon zest, and cinnamon. Brown the duck all over, pour in the wine, bubble to reduce it slightly, then add the tomatoes. Cover and simmer on the lowest possible heat for 2–3 hours, stirring occasionally, and adding a little broth if necessary.

Take out the duck when tender, slice and set aside the choicest pieces, and keep them warm. Remove the rest of its meat and chop it very thoroughly. Take the cinnamon and lemon zest out of the sauce, sieve it, and return it to the pan with the chopped meat. (For guests, all this can be done in advance.) Warm the sauce gently and adjust the seasoning.

Have ready a large pan of boiling salted water and cook the pasta *al dente*. Drain, mix it briefly with the sauce over a low heat, and place on a warm dish. Add a few flakes of butter and decorate it with the reserved meat.

Pappardelle alla cacciatora
Pappardelle the Hunter's Way

This popular Tuscan dish is an easy way to make a main course which needs no vegetables to go with it. If you can't get, or make, pappardelle, use fettuccine – green ones are particularly good with this sauce. It serves a main course for 6, and all it needs is a green salad to follow.

500g (1 lb) pappardelle
1 small onion, finely chopped
2 garlic cloves, lightly
  bruised
50g (2 oz) unsalted butter
3 tablespoons olive oil
1kg (2¼ lb) chicken, in 6
  pieces
100g (3½ oz) lean unsmoked
  bacon

½ tumbler Marsala
1kg (2¼ lb) fresh or tinned
  tomatoes, skinned and
  chopped
1 tablespoon chopped fresh
  basil and parsley
good Parmesan cheese,
  grated

Sauté the onion and garlic gently in the butter and oil in a large casserole, until soft but not brown. Season the chicken and cut the bacon in strips. Add both to the pan, raise the heat and brown the pieces all over. Remove the garlic. Pour in the Marsala, let it bubble and evaporate a little, then add the tomatoes. Cover and cook over a medium heat for 20–25 minutes stirring occasionally, to stop it catching, and adding a spoonful or so of water if it gets too dry.

Cook the pasta in a large pan of boiling salted water. When the pasta is almost ready remove the chicken from the sauce, taste and adjust the seasoning. Drain the pasta when *al dente*, place it on a warm oval dish, add the sauce, mix gently and arrange the chicken pieces on top. Sprinkle with the chopped basil and parsley, and serve, passing round the Parmesan at table.

In autumn Tuscany experiences a kind of mushroom fever. Since the edible varieties of the prized porcini are almost impossible to confuse with the poisonous ones, people set off for the woods as soon as word gets out that the first porcini have been sighted. Some years the mushrooms come up so thickly that the woods become riddled with pickers, cars parked in previously deserted lanes, just like outside a football stadium. The search starts at dawn, the pickers treading carefully as they search for the shiny brown dome, often its distinctive aroma being smelt before the mushroom is seen. Then porcini are sold at the roadside, from large baskets.

When gathering wild mushrooms in Britain one rarely finds many porcini in a day. So a pasta sauce is a good way to share a small quantity of these delicious mushrooms between several people – *but make sure they are porcini before you eat them.*

Tagliatelle ai funghi porcini
Tagliatelle with Wild Mushrooms

In Tuscany this is made with fresh porcini but, though it will not be quite so good, this excellent sauce can also be made with dried porcini. Use 20g (¾ oz) soaked in a very little tepid water for 2 hours. A first course for 2–3.

250g (9 oz) tagliatelle	*3 tablespoons best olive oil*
300g (11 oz) fresh porcini mushrooms	*a small handful chopped parsley*
½ garlic clove, chopped	*2 tablespoons unsalted butter*

Put a large pan of salted water to boil for the pasta. Remove all dirty and damaged parts from the mushrooms. Then them cut in chunks. Sauté the garlic in the oil and before it colours add the mushrooms and salt to taste. Stir until the mushrooms are cooked. Add the parsley and cover while you cook the pasta. Drain the pasta when *al dente*, toss quickly in the hot sauce, transfer to a warm serving dish, add the butter in flakes, a grind of white pepper and serve.

Spaghetti con salsa di funghi
Spaghetti with Mushroom Sauce

Cultivated mushrooms are also used to make excellent mushroom sauces, and although it may seem odd to put anchovies in this mushroom sauce, they don't make it taste of fish, but simply give it an indefinable richness. A light main course for 4, or first course for 6.

500g (18 oz) spaghetti, or linguine
2 garlic cloves
5–6 tablespoons olive oil
2 anchovy fillets, drained of oil
300g (11 oz) fresh or tinned tomatoes, skinned and chopped

300g (11 oz) button mushrooms, thinly sliced
a pinch of fresh thyme
a large handful chopped parsley

Sauté the lightly crushed garlic in the oil until golden. Remove it if you wish, then add the anchovies and stir them in the oil until they break up. Add the tomatoes and, after a few minutes, the mushrooms and thyme. Season to taste and simmer the sauce for 20 minutes. Adjust the seasoning.

Have ready a large pan of boiling salted water for the pasta. Cook it *al dente*. Drain it, but not too well. Place it on a warm serving dish, dress it with the hot sauce mixed with the parsley, and serve. Cheese is not added.

Cannelloni ripieni di carne
Meat-filled Cannelloni

Cannelloni are a classic Italian dish for a special occasion and the large proportion of mushrooms makes these some of the best of all, and worthy of any occasion. A first course for 4–5 or a light main course for 3.

227

8–10 sheets wide lasagne
250g (9 oz) button
  mushrooms
200g (7 oz) minced veal or
  pork
130g (4½ oz) unsalted butter
freshly grated nutmeg

110g (4 oz) Parmesan cheese,
  grated
60g (2 oz) plain flour
¼ litre (½ pint) milk
½ litre (1 pint) broth or a good
  stock cube

Put a large pan of well-salted water to boil for the pasta. Rinse the mushrooms and chop finely. Gently brown the meat in 30g (1½ oz) butter in a heavy pan, add the mushrooms and sauté for 5 minutes. Season to taste, adding a good grating of nutmeg. Remove from the heat and mix in 20g (1 oz) butter and 2–3 tablespoons of Parmesan.

Cook the lasagne, as on page 23. Cut in half to make large squares. Lasagne varies in how much it swells so you may not need all of them. Place a nice amount of stuffing on each square, roll up so that the edges overlap, and place a single layer in an oven dish rubbed with butter.

Make a white sauce, as on page 37, with the remaining butter, the flour, milk and broth. Season to taste and simmer till well cooked, before stirring in most of the Parmesan and pouring it over the cannelloni. Sprinkle on the remaining Parmesan and put in a hot oven for 15 minutes, until the surface is golden. If necessary finish the browning under the grill.

These can be made in advance, and even frozen, but the sauce is best added just before you cook them. If you need to keep the sauce standing, trickle a thin layer of milk on its surface to stop a skin forming, and stir the milk in before you use it. When heating them from cold, use a moderate oven and allow at least twice the time.

Methods and ingredients which may be unfamiliar are explained on pages 26–38.

Lasagne
di San Frediano

Lasagne of San Frediano

San Frediano is the poor district of Florence, but there is nothing poor about this dish, which Florentines make with excellent porcini mushrooms. It is also very good with ordinary mushrooms and makes a light main dish for 6–8. The quantities can be halved for a small family but it is worth making this much and dividing it between two small oven dishes to eat on different days.

400g (14 oz) lasagne sheets
200g (7 oz) veal or pork
  mince
60g (2 oz) unsalted butter
100g (3½ oz) good ham in
  small strips
500g (18 oz) mushrooms,
  porcini or button
1 smallish onion

1 garlic clove
2–3 tablespoons olive oil
½–1 tumbler dry white wine
1 tumbler broth
¾ litre (1½ pint) white sauce
nutmeg, grated
60g (2 oz) good Parmesan
  cheese, grated

Brown the meat in half the butter, add the ham, and cook briefly before setting aside.

Remove any dirty or damaged parts from the porcini and wipe clean, or simply rinse the button mushrooms, then slice finely. Sauté the finely chopped onion and garlic in the oil and remaining butter, till they colour slightly. Add the mushrooms and cook briskly, stirring, till just cooked. Season. Pour in the wine and let most of it evaporate before adding 4 tablespoons of broth. Cover and cook over moderate heat for about 10 minutes, adding more broth if it gets dry.

Combine the meat and mushroom mixtures and cook gently for another 15 minutes, stirring occasionally, and adding a little broth now and then as it thickens. When nearly done, season to taste. Meanwhile make the white sauce (page 37) flavoured with nutmeg.

Cook the lasagne as usual, see page 23. Oil an oven dish lightly, place a quarter of the lasagne in the bottom. Cover with a third of the mushroom sauce, sprinkle with Parmesan, continue these layers finishing with the remaining lasagne. Cover with white sauce and a good sprinkling of Parmesan. Put in a hot oven for 20–25 minutes until the top is golden and serve. Or it can be assembled in advance and heated up for longer.

If you have dried porcini mushrooms, a few can be used to boost the flavour of ordinary mushrooms. Just soak them in a ladle of tepid water for an hour or so and add them and their liquid, strained through a muslin, when you add the broth.

Cannelloni alla moda di Porsenna

Cannelloni Porsenna's Way

A light, but very good, first course for 6.

fresh lasagne made with egg pasta from 200g (7 oz) plain flour, 1 egg and 1 yolk, see pages 17–24, or 225g (8 oz) wide packet lasagne

Filling

70g (2½ oz) butter	2 tablespoons good Parmesan
50g (1¾ oz) plain flour	cheese, grated
¾ litre (1½ pint) milk	60g (2 oz) ham, in tiny dice
350g (12 oz) button	125g (4½ oz) fontina cheese,
mushrooms	in tiny dice

Cook the lasagne (page 23) and cut the bought lasagne in half to make large squares. Make a white sauce as usual (page 37) with 50g (1¾ oz) of the butter, flour, and ½ litre (1 pint) of the milk. Season to taste, and put two-thirds in a bowl to get cold. Trickle milk over the remainder to stop a skin forming.

Rinse the mushrooms, slice finely and sauté in the remaining butter. Add them to the cold white sauce. Mix in 1 tablespoon of Parmesan and the ham, and taste and adjust the seasoning, adding a touch of milk if the mixture is too thick. Place some of this filling on each pasta square, roll up overlapping the edges, and place in a single layer in a lightly buttered oven dish. Scatter on the ham and fontina, thin the remaining white sauce with the milk. Pour it over the cannelloni, sprinkle with the rest of the Parmesan and put in a moderate oven until pale golden – about 20 minutes.

In Montalcino a little restaurant, called Il Leccio – The Holm Oak, the holm oak being a magic tree to the Romans and Etruscans – serves spaghetti with a rich sauce in which the flavour of tomatoes is deliciously softened by egg yolk. A dish well worth remembering if you have yolks left over after making meringues.

Spaghetti alla vaccara
Cowherd's Spaghetti

This dish is based on the one served in Il Leccio. A main course for 4.

500g (18 oz) spaghetti, or tagliatelle
150g (5 oz) good ham, cut in strips
60g (2 oz) lean thick-cut bacon, diced
90g (3 oz) unsalted butter

800g (1 lb 12 oz) really ripe fresh or tinned tomatoes, peeled and chopped
4 egg yolks
60g (2 oz) best Parmesan cheese, grated

Sauté the ham and bacon lightly in most of the butter. Add the tomatoes, season to taste and simmer for 15–20 minutes. Put a large pan of salted water to boil for the pasta, and mix the yolks in a pasta bowl with the Parmesan.

When the sauce is ready cook the pasta *al dente* in plenty of boiling salted water. Drain, toss in the sauce, then mix, piping hot, with the egg mixture. Add the remaining butter and serve.

Pici

In Chiusi they serve steaming plates of their special pasta, pici: long cords, like thick spaghetti, served with rich sauces of meat and mushrooms. Needing no special equipment, they are one of the easiest pastas to make at home, and remarkably good basic food. For 4–6.

egg pasta made with 400g (14 oz) durum flour and 1 egg, see pages 17–18

Mix the pasta to a firm dough in the usual way. Then roll pieces of dough between your palms – like a child making plasticine worms – till they turn into a cord about the length and thickness of a drinking straw. Lay them on a tray dusted with semolina.

They are cooked in plenty of boiling salted water, and the timing depends very much on how thick you made them, so it's a matter of tasting till they seem done. They can then be served with any rich meat or tomato sauce, or with the mushroom sauces on pages 226 and 227.

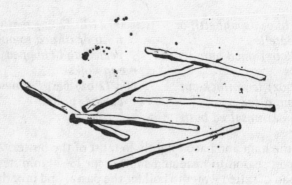

Penne all'arrabbiata

Angry Penne

They can be as angry as you like, for their temper is provided by the chilli, and you can use as much or as little as you – and your friends – please. This tasty unsophisticated dish is equally good for a family meal or simple entertaining. A light main course for 3–4, or a filling first course.

500g (1 lb 2 oz) penne
20g (1 oz) dried porcini, or 300g (10 oz) button mushrooms
150g (5 oz) lean unsmoked bacon, in a slice
100g (3½ oz) unsalted butter
2–3 tablespoons olive oil
2 cloves garlic, crushed

1 fresh or dried chilli
500g (18 oz) fresh or tinned tomatoes, skinned and chopped
6–7 fresh basil leaves, or parsley
80g (4 oz) Parmesan and pecorino cheese mixed

Soak the dried mushrooms in a very little water for 1 hour, if used. Sauté the diced bacon in the oil till golden. Lift out and keep warm. Rinse the button mushrooms and slice finely. Cook for a couple of minutes, then lift them out and keep warm. Sauté the garlic and chilli (whole and crushed if you want to take them out later, chopped if you know you love them). Let them colour slightly, then remove them if you wish. Add the tomatoes, and the torn basil leaves, or chopped parsley. Season with salt and simmer for 20–30 minutes. Taste and adjust the seasoning.

Have ready a large pan of boiling salted water for the pasta. When the sauce is ready cook the pasta *al dente*. Drain, place in a warm pasta bowl, add the sauce, the bacon, mushrooms, and the butter in flakes. Toss, top with grated cheese, and serve.

Penne alla toscana

Penne Tuscan Style

This is rich and good, a main course for an informal meal, and an excellent way to make 2 sausages feed 4 people, but you do need really meaty sausages (see page 36).

450g (1 lb) penne, or similar pasta
1 small onion, finely chopped
2 tablespoons olive oil
60g (2 oz) unsalted butter, cut into 3 pieces
250g (9 oz) fresh or tinned tomatoes, skinned and chopped

450g (1 lb) fresh or frozen spinach
2 meaty sausages, about 150g (5 oz)
1 tablespoon milk
50g (1¾ oz) good Parmesan cheese, grated

Sauté the onion in 1 tablespoon of oil and 1 piece of butter in a wide pan. When softened slightly add the tomatoes, season to taste and cook slowly until quite thick – about 30 minutes.

Meanwhile, wash the spinach well, remove any tough stalks, and cook gently in a large covered pan with a touch of salt but no water – enough stays on the leaves from the washing. (Or heat the frozen spinach.) Drain and chop well. Skin, and break the sausages into small pieces. Then cook thoroughly in 1 tablespoon oil, and add them to the tomato sauce. Melt another piece of butter in the pan and mix in the spinach and milk. Remove from the heat and add half the Parmesan cheese. Keep this and the tomato sauce warm, separately.

Cook the pasta in plenty of boiling salted water. Drain when *al dente*. Put in a warm pasta bowl, cover with the tomato sauce, then with the spinach. Sprinkle on the remaining cheese and top with the last portion of the butter. Toss together as you serve it.

This sauce can be made in advance and reheated, provided you don't add the Parmesan to the spinach till after the heating. A crisp green salad is perfect to follow this rich dish.

Methods and ingredients which may be unfamiliar are explained on pages 26–38.

The next recipe comes from the Island of Giglio – Lily Island – off the coast of Tuscany. It is a speciality of the restaurant in the castle at the top of the hill. Down in the port they serve pasta with fresh tomato sauce, shellfish, even lobster, but on the hill the cooking is based on game. For, in Italy, the cooking can even vary between a hill and the valley below.

Rigatoni all'erba magica
Rigatoni with Magic Herb Sauce

This sauce is meaty with a unique flavour. For some while the name of the 'magic herb' remained a mystery. Giglio is beautiful and thickly covered with herbs. As you approach it on the ferry, in the mellow sunshine of the late afternoon, the scents of thyme, lavender and oregano greet you on the breeze. So, for a time, it seemed it must be some such plant. In fact, it was mace. Mace from Saracen times because Giglio was invaded by the Saracens, and it was then that the islanders named this strange new flavour 'the magic herb'.

If no rigatoni can be found, simply use another large short pasta, but choose one with a hole into which the sauce can ooze if you want this dish at its best. A main course for 5–6.

500g (18 oz) rigatoni, or similar pasta
1 tablespoon chopped onion
1 small stick of celery
1 small carrot
1 tablespoon unsalted butter
1 tablespoon olive oil
1 small Spanish onion, stuck with a clove

200g (7 oz) good beef mince
a thumbnail-sized piece mace
1–2 really meaty sausages
500g (18 oz) fresh or tinned tomatoes, skinned and chopped
60g (2 oz) good Parmesan cheese, grated

Sauté the finely chopped onion, celery and carrot gently in the butter and oil until soft and golden. Add the Spanish onion, the mince, the mace, and the sausage – skinned and broken in pieces. Season. Stir and break up the meat as you cook it gently for 5 minutes. Stir in the tomatoes, cover, and cook slowly for at least 1 hour, stirring occasionally and adding a spoonful of water if it gets too dry. Taste, and adjust the seasoning.

When the sauce is almost ready cook the rigatoni, in plenty of boiling salted water. Drain when *al dente* and serve topped with the sauce and plenty of Parmesan cheese.

> *The marsh birds took flight . . . the swamps turned deep red in the sunset; trees, bare of underbrush, were stamped black and flat against the light like Chinese shadow pictures; horse and cowboy shot out suddenly, brushing past the traveller on his way, to vanish in a moment as though moving in another world.*
>
> *Journey in Italy*, Guido Piovene

The Maremma region, stretching flatly from the sea to the hills in southern Tuscany, is a region of wild horses, game, marshes and swirling mists where, early in this century, men still herded the cattle on horseback. This next recipe is for pasta as the cowboys used to cook it.

Bucatini alla maniera del buttero
Bucatini Cowboy Style

A simple, tasty supper for 4, and if pecorino cheese is hard to find, Cheddar can be substituted.

400g (14 oz) bucatini, or small penne
2–3 tablespoons olive oil
2 large potatoes, peeled and thinly sliced

1 medium onion, finely sliced (optional)
500g (18 oz) fresh or tinned tomatoes, skinned and chopped

a pinch of fresh oregano or
    marjoram
1 tablespoon chopped parsley
60g (2 oz) grated pecorino
    romano or sardo cheese

½ litre (1 pint) broth (a
    good bouillon cube
    will do)

Brush a medium-sized oven dish with oil. Break the bucatini in thirds, and place a layer in the oven dish, then some potato, some onion (if used), some tomato, salt, pepper, a touch of herbs, a trickle of oil, and some grated cheese. Continue these layers until everything is used up. Heat the broth and pour it, boiling hot, over the dish – don't worry if it comes above the top layer, it will cook away. Sprinkle on extra cheese and put the dish in a very hot oven for 15 minutes. Finish cooking it in a moderate oven, until both the pasta and the potatoes are cooked – 25–40 minutes.

Spaghetti alla viareggina

Spaghetti Viareggio Style

Shellfish are popular along Tuscany's silver coastline, and this is how they cook clams in the seaside town of Viareggio. A light main course for 4–5.

500g (18 oz) spaghetti
1kg (2 lb 3 oz) clams, or more
    if the shells are large
1 medium-sized onion, finely
    chopped
3 tablespoons olive oil
½ tumbler dry white wine

800g (1 lb 12 oz) fresh or tinned
    tomatoes, skinned and
    sieved
1 handful chopped parsley
1½ tablespoons unsalted butter
    (optional)
chilli powder (optional)

Prepare the clams as usual, see page 29. Put them in a heavy covered pan over medium heat, shaking occasionally for a few minutes until they open. Remove from their shells – except two or three for decoration – and cut up any very large ones. Strain the liquid through muslin or a coffee filter paper if it seems sandy.

Sauté the onion gently in the oil until golden. Stir in the clams for a moment before adding the wine. Let it evaporate a little, then add the tomato pulp, parsley, a nut of butter, the clam liquid, and a pinch of chilli powder (if you wish). Simmer this sauce gently for 10–15 minutes until it thickens slightly. Taste and adjust the seasoning when almost cooked. Remember if it cooks too long that the clams will be tough.

Cook the pasta *al dente* in plenty of boiling salted water. Drain, and serve topped with the sauce and decorated with the clams in their shells. A flake of butter is sometimes added to each portion, but no cheese.

Up and down the coast one finds *spaghetti del pescatore* – fisherman's spaghetti. It is made with the basic sauce used in the previous recipe, with perhaps a little garlic, and whatever combination of fresh shellfish is available. You can invent your own combinations and quantities, and a very passable version can be made with thawed frozen shellfish – mussels, clams, shrimps, prawns – added to the cooked sauce with their liquid for only long enough to heat them.

Strisce e ceci

Pasta with Chickpeas

A Florentine soup using inexpensive ingredients, but with a good flavour. For 6.

300g (11 oz) broken flat pasta	1 large handful parsley, chopped
500g (18 oz) dried chickpeas	2 cloves garlic, finely chopped
2 large onions, finely sliced	
4 tablespoons olive oil	1–2 tablespoons tomato paste

Methods and ingredients which may be unfamiliar are explained on pages 26–38.

Soak the chickpeas for 24 hours. Bring them to the boil in plenty of lightly salted water to which you've added a pinch of bicarbonate of soda for every 2 litre (4 pints) water. This helps tenderize them. Simmer steadily until the chickpeas are soft – which could be several hours if they're old. Then drain them, but keep the liquid.

Sauté the onions in the oil, in a large soup pan, until soft. Add the parsley and garlic. When the garlic begins to colour stir in the tomato paste, then add the chickpeas. Cook briefly together, add 1½ litre (3 pints) of the chickpea liquid, season to taste, bring to the boil, and add the pasta. When the pasta is cooked the soup is ready.

> . . . *air that smells of grass and spring onions, of parsley and garlic, chickpeas and salt cod, of corn and wood shavings, of oil and wine, of alleys freshly sprinkled on summer evenings before front doors.* . . .
>
> *Damned Tuscans*, Curzio Malaparte

Fresh tomato sauces, pasta and rosemary, and vegetable soups with beans, are the dishes you savour on the springtime air in Siena: especially beans, for in Tuscany beans are served after meat and game, and most of all in soup. They are so popular in this region that other Italians sometimes speak disdainfully of Florentines as *mangiafagioli* – bean eaters.

Minestrone alla toscana
Tuscan Minestrone

Tuscan soup is often served with large slices of toasted country bread, but this one is made with pasta. A substantial and economical lunch for 8 and an excellent way to use up the outside leaves of lettuce – but cabbage or Chinese lettuce can be substituted if you prefer. You can use whatever pasta you like, but broken fettuccine, pappardelle or lasagne are best of all.

There are often broken bits in boxes and packets and it is a good idea to save them for such soups.

200g (7 oz) pasta
350g (12 oz) dried haricot or
  black-eyed beans
a piece rosemary
a small bay leaf
350g (12 oz) outer leaves cos
  lettuce
1 small onion

1 stalk celery
1 handful parsley
3 tablespoons sunflower oil
200g (7 oz) fresh or tinned
  tomatoes, skinned and
  chopped
grated Parmesan cheese (or
  Cheddar)

Soak the beans in water overnight. Drain them, cover with water, bring to the boil and cook rapidly for 15 minutes. Throw away the water. Refill with water to come well above the beans, add the rosemary, bay leaf, and a little salt and simmer until the beans are cooked – the time varies greatly with the age of the beans; it could take all morning, and you may need to add water from time to time. Remove the rosemary and bay leaf and sieve, or liquidize, half the beans and return them to the pan before adding the cleaned and shredded lettuce leaves.

Sauté the finely chopped onion, celery and parsley gently in the oil until they begin to colour. Add the tomatoes, season with salt and simmer for 10 minutes before adding the mixture to the beans. Bring the bean pan to the boil, stirring occasionally to prevent the vegetables sticking, and adding more water if necessary. Then add the broken pasta and cook briskly until the pasta is *al dente*. Taste, and adjust the seasoning.

Let the soup stand a minute or two – minestrone is never served boiling hot – and serve passing round the pepper mill and grated cheese.

16 UMBRIA

'Greetings green Umbria', wrote Carducci, one of Italy's greatest poets, and to this day if Umbria is mentioned in conversation an Italian will often say, 'Ah, green Umbria!', because it is exactly so: gently, softly green, the only region of the peninsula that does not touch the sea; the heart of Italy. Its towns are gently medieval; there is nothing of the Dark Ages to be found in Perugia or Orvieto, nor in Assisi – town of St Francis – which stands on its mount, overlooking a wide plain, its silver stone tinged pink by the sun setting over the olive groves.

Made up of hills and valleys around the River Tiber, Umbria is an agricultural region producing vegetables and excellent oil. Most cottages have their own vegetable garden, and maybe a small olive grove, and enough vines for a year's wine. Its pasta sauces reflect this simplicity, with their fresh country ingredients – tender artichokes, asparagus, beans, nuts, wild mushrooms and, during the cold winter months, excellent sausages and *lonza* for which the region is famous.

But even Umbria has its touch of luxury – truffles. Not the white Piedmontese truffles, glory of Alba in the north, but round, rough-surfaced black truffles – like little coals – from Norcia. Prized by the Romans, they later garnished the dishes of the popes and nobles of Renaissance Italy. To Umbrians, finding these truffles is almost a rite. Using traditional lore, handed from father to son, they find them with the help of dogs, and pigs, and even by observing the direction in which flies pass over the ground. They make the most delicious dishes, their jet-black slices shining on heaps of pale cream pasta, rich with butter or oil.

Umbrians use the same exquisite combination of truffles, butter, and Parmesan for *Tagliatelle ai tartufi neri* that the Piedmontese use in *Tajarin con tartufi* – only the colour of the truffle is different. But Umbria has another prized truffle recipe.

Spaghetti ai tartufi neri
Spaghetti with Black Truffles

This curiously combines truffles with anchovies. It is one of those divisive dishes which you either adore or loathe, but unforgettable to those who love it. A first course for 3.

300g (11 oz) spaghetti
3 tablespoons best olive oil
1 anchovy fillet, drained of
  oil
1 garlic clove, slightly
  crushed
1 small fresh truffle (tinned
  will not do)

Cook the sauce over the lowest possible heat or in the top of a double saucepan. Warm the oil and pound in the anchovy. Add the garlic and let it give its flavour to the oil while you clean and finely peel the rough skin from the truffle.

Cook the pasta in plenty of boiling salted water. Meanwhile, remove the garlic and slice the truffle finely into the oil. Drain the pasta when *al dente*, place on a warm serving dish, and pour over the sauce.

Such luxuries as truffles only play a small part in Umbria's cooking: its real excellence lies in the use it makes of vegetables. *Fave* – broad beans – are very popular here, and Italians love to eat them raw, coupled with cheese. They take a bean from the pod and, putting it to their front teeth, nip it open, then with finger and thumb slip out the inner, tenderest part of the bean. Mouthfuls of sweet beans are punctuated by bites of pecorino, the hard salty sheep's cheese, crusty bread and wine.

That is the traditional picnic lunch on May Day, when everyone goes out into the country with friends and relatives. Sitting round wooden tables at a country inn in warm early sunshine, each will have his own pile of *fave*, a chunk of cheese, and a glass which will be kept constantly filled from pitchers of wine that, in ever-increasing numbers, arrive full only to take their place on the steadily growing piles of empties, and discarded bean pods.

Bavette con fave all'ortolano
Bavette the Kitchen Garden Way

Broad beans also go well with pasta, as in this traditional recipe. As its name suggests, this is a fresh-tasting sauce to be made with young vegetables in early summer, but not a dish to try with leathery, late season beans. A light lunch or first course for 4–5.

500g (18 oz) bavette, or
   linguine
1kg (2¼ lb) broad beans
60g (2 oz) unsmoked bacon, or
   ham
2–3 spring onions
3 tablespoons olive oil

1 tumbler dry white wine
enough fresh tomatoes to fill
   a large cup, when skinned
   and chopped
60g (2 oz) good Parmesan
   cheese, grated
black pepper

Shell the beans. Sauté the chopped bacon and spring onions in the oil, and when they begin to turn golden stir in the beans.

Cook a little, then pour in the wine. Let it bubble and evaporate slightly, then add the tomatoes. Season and simmer rapidly, stirring occasionally, until the beans are cooked. Taste and adjust the seasoning.

Cook the pasta *al dente* in plenty of boiling salted water. Drain, and mix with the sauce, adding grated cheese and a grind of black pepper.

Bavette con fave alla Perugina

Bavette with Broad Beans the Perugina Way

A richer dish than the previous one, but even easier to make. A light main course or rich first course for 4–6.

500g (18 oz) bavette, or linguine
1kg (2¼ lb) broad beans
2 spring onions
1 tablespoon good oil
1 tablespoon unsalted butter

60g (2 oz) thick ham, diced
1 cup chicken broth
150ml (6 fl oz) thick cream
60g (2 oz) good Parmesan cheese, grated
chopped parsley

Shell the beans. Sauté the chopped onions in the oil and butter, in a wide pan, until turning golden. Stir in the ham and cook for a minute or two. Mix in the beans, add the chicken broth, and cook rapidly until the beans are tender. Stir in the cream, and a grind of black pepper, and let the sauce bubble gently for a few minutes. Add the Parmesan. Taste and adjust the seasoning. Cover and keep warm.

Cook the pasta *al dente* in plenty of boiling salted water. Drain, mix it with the sauce, and serve topped with chopped parsley.

Methods and ingredients which may be unfamiliar are explained on pages 26–38.

From its hill Perugia has overlooked the gentle Umbrian landscape since long before Roman times when it was called Perusia, and in one of its winding shady streets, crossed by delicate arches, is a little trattoria called Old Perusia, where they use a delectable combination of cream and green beans as a sauce for short pasta.

Maccheroncelli alla Vecchia Perusia
Little Macaroni the Old Perugian Way

If you are roasting a joint it is worth remembering to set aside some of the juices for this lovely sauce which serves 4–5 as a light lunch or a rich first course. Frozen beans aren't nearly as good as fresh ones, but they can be used, and should go straight in the oil, without parboiling.

500g (18 oz) short macaroni, rigatoni, or shells
6–8 tablespoons juices from a roast, without fat
450g (16 oz) fresh French beans

1 small onion, finely chopped
2 tablespoons olive oil
400ml (¾ pint) thick cream
80g (3¾ oz) good Parmesan cheese, grated

The juices from the roast need to chill until the fat which rises is firm enough to be removed.

Top and tail the beans, cut them in 3cm (1 in) lengths, and cook very lightly in boiling salted water so that they remain slightly crisp. Sauté the onion in the oil, in a wide pan, until golden. Stir in the beans, meat juices, and cream. Cook the sauce gently until the cream begins to thicken. Season to taste. Then add a handful of Parmesan, stir, remove from the heat and cover.

Cook the pasta *al dente* in plenty of boiling salted water. Drain, toss carefully in the sauce, and serve, handing round extra Parmesan and the pepper mill – but don't overdo the pepper or this delicate sauce will be spoilt.

Penne con salsa di carciofi

Penne with Artichoke Sauce

To see the difference between Umbrian and Roman cooking compare this artichoke sauce with the one from Rome; this is both lighter and easier to make: a delicious first course for 4–5.

500g (18 oz) penne
4 small artichokes, or a
   substitute, see page 26
½ medium-sized onion, thinly
   sliced
3 tablespoons olive or
   sunflower oil

½–1 tablespoon capers
500g (18 oz) fresh tomatoes,
   skinned and chopped
1 tablespoon chopped parsley
2 tablespoons good Parmesan
   cheese, grated

Prepare the artichokes, see page 26. Gently brown the onions in the oil, add the sliced artichokes and turn them in the oil until they start to colour. Add the capers and chopped tomatoes. Season to taste, cover, and simmer gently until the artichokes are cooked and the sauce has thickened slightly. If it thickens too soon, add a spoonful or so of water or real chicken broth.

Have ready a large pan of boiling salted water and, when the sauce is almost ready, cook the pasta *al dente*. Drain, place in a warm bowl, top with the sauce, parsley and Parmesan, and mix lightly at table.

Linguine con asparagi

Linguine with Asparagus

This rich and unusual combination makes a quick dish which needs little more than salad, followed by fruit, to be a light meal for 5. In Umbria they use fine wild asparagus, so buy the thinnest you can find.

500g (18 oz) linguine, or
   spaghetti

1kg (2 lb 3 oz) slim asparagus,
   or tinned or frozen

50g (1¾ oz) unsalted butter	*100g (3½ oz) thick cream*
50g (1¾ oz) tinned tuna fish in oil	*good Parmesan cheese, grated*

Put a large pan of salted water to boil for the pasta. Rinse the fresh asparagus and cut into 3cm (1 in) lengths – discarding any parts which seem woody or tough. Parboil these for 5 minutes, and drain. Simply cut up tinned or frozen asparagus.

Sauté the asparagus gently in the butter in a wide shallow pan. After a minute or two, mix in the drained and flaked tuna fish, then add the cream. Season to taste and cook gently until the cream thickens. Meanwhile, cook the linguine *al dente* in plenty of boiling salted water. Drain, place on a warm serving dish and pour over the sauce. This is one of the few fish sauces to which Parmesan is sometimes added at table.

A far less rich asparagus sauce uses simply asparagus and tomatoes. To make *Spaghetti con punte di asparagi*, the amounts of pasta and asparagus, and their preparation, are the same as in the previous recipe. But sauté the asparagus in 5 tablespoons of olive oil instead of butter, then add 500g (18 oz) fresh tomatoes, skinned and chopped. Season, and simmer until the asparagus is tender.

In late autumn when the twisted skeletons of the vines are bare, the huge walnut trees of Umbria are shaken until the last nuts have been collected and stored for Christmas. But some of the nuts are used in the following weeks to make a fragrant nutty sauce for delicate egg noodles.

Fettuccelle con le noci
Fettuccelle with Walnut Sauce

A simple but unusual sauce which serves 6 as a first course. It needs the delicacy of freshly made pasta, but the walnuts don't have to be freshly gathered.

450g (1 lb) fresh fettuccelle (slim tagliatelle)
1 small onion, sliced
70g (2½ oz) unsalted butter
175g (6 oz) shelled walnuts
2 sticks celery, very finely chopped
4 tablespoons top of the milk
several handfuls good Parmesan cheese, grated

Put a large pan of salted water to boil for the pasta. Gently soften the onion in two thirds of the butter, and chop the nuts finely. Remove the onion and let the celery take colour in onion-flavoured butter. Add the chopped nuts and milk. Heat them together while you cook the pasta. Drain the pasta when *al dente*, place in a warm bowl and top with the sauce, the remaining butter in little flakes, and several tablespoons of the Parmesan. Extra seasoning is sometimes added and a few sprigs of parsley round the dish are attractive.

Picchiettini

Little Sticks

This typical homemade pasta isn't delicate, but it tastes good and is easy to make. It's usually served with a simple tomato sauce (see page 73). For 5.

Cutting picchiettini

egg pasta made from 500g (18 oz) plain flour but only 1 whole egg and 2 whites, see pages 17–19

Roll the pasta out fairly thinly, wrap it round and round the rolling pin, then with a sharp knife cut it from one end of the rolling pin to the other, and repeat on the other side, to make it into long strips. Stack the strips, and cut them the other way, in matchstick widths. Cook like other pasta.

Strangozzi di Spoleto

In Umbria they make another easy pasta with very little egg, or none at all. It looks rather like pappardelle. A filling pasta which serves 5–6.

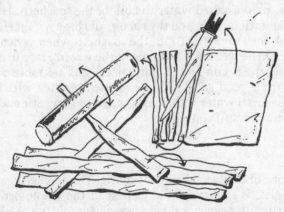

basic pasta made from 500g (18 oz) plain flour, water and perhaps 1 egg, see pages 17–19

Roll the pasta as thinly as this stiff paste will allow, and cut it into tapes 1cm (⅓ in) wide, and 15cm (6 in) long. Re-roll to make them thinner, and about two fingers wide. Cook these like other pasta, and serve with a good tomato sauce, see page 73.

Spaghetti grassi e magri

Fat and Lean Spaghetti

A homely dish from Perugia. Quick, warming and very inexpensive, it makes a surprisingly satisfying light lunch or supper for 4–5. In Umbria, various hard cheeses are used with pasta, so you may like to experiment.

500g (18 oz) spaghetti
1 tablespoon finely chopped
* bacon fat*
150g (5 oz) good thick
* unsmoked streaky bacon,*
* diced*

good Parmesan or pecorino
* cheese, grated*
freshly ground black pepper

Put a big pan of salted water to boil for the spaghetti. Heat the bacon fat until it runs. Add the bacon, and brown it nicely while you cook the spaghetti. Drain the spaghetti when *al dente*, but leave it a little wet and save some of the water. Place in a warm bowl, add the bacon and its pan juices, plus 2–3 tablespoons of cheese and a good grind of black pepper. Moisten with a little saved spaghetti water if the pasta seems too dry. Stir and serve, with extra cheese if you wish.

Pork is one of the specialities of Umbria. The *porchetta*, a whole roast piglet, is said to be the tastiest in the whole peninsula. Flavoured with pepper and wild fennel it is sold, on market and festival days, cut in thick slices and handed out on wedges of crusty white, unsalted bread for the farmers to enjoy, while they argue about politics and wine.

The town most famous for its pork is Norcia where the mountain air is perfect for curing hams and drying sausages. Dusty yellow fennel is gathered from the fields to soften the rich fattiness of the pork sausages, and the salami is a bright deep red,

Methods and ingredients which may be unfamiliar are explained on pages 26–38.

embedded with little black peppercorns. Norcia is also renowned for its black truffles and spaghetti with truffles is the dish for special occasions, but *pasta alla norcina* means pasta with pork of some kind. There are many recipes, some use small pieces of ham, *lonza* or local salami; some use cream, others mascarpone; but the simplest, most genuine way is with country sausages and fresh ricotta cheese.

Bombolotti alla norcina
Bombolotti the Pork Butcher's Way

A tasty, and extremely easy light main course for 4–5, provided the sausages are good (see page 36).

500g (18 oz) bombolotti, rigatoni, or other short thick pasta
3 really good meaty sausages, skinned

1 teaspoon unsalted butter
200g (7 oz) ricotta cheese
pecorino or good Parmesan cheese, grated
freshly ground black pepper

Put a large pan of salted water to boil for the pasta. Cut the sausages into small pieces and cook them gently in the butter without browning. Cover and keep warm.

When the water boils put in the pasta. Beat the ricotta to a cream in a warm pasta bowl with a spoonful of the pasta water, adding a handful of grated Parmesan and as much black pepper as you like. When the pasta is *al dente*, drain and transfer to the cheese mixture. Add the sausage pieces, mix well together and serve.

Tagliatelle di Quartilia
Quartilia's Tagliatelle

In the country around the town of Citta della Pieve, near the border with Tuscany, where the hillsides are thickly wooded and the clearings purple with heather and wild thyme, they still hunt Umbria's famous wild boars, and there are plenty of wood pigeons to make into pasta sauces such as this. A light main course for 3–4.

400g (14 oz) fresh tagliatelle
1 meaty sausage, skinned
1 pigeon
1 small egg
1 handful oven-baked
  breadcrumbs
1 tablespoon parsley,
  chopped

thyme and nutmeg
3 tablespoons olive oil
1 small onion
1 small celery stalk
600g (1 lb 5 oz) fresh or tinned
  tomatoes, skinned and
  chopped

Chop the pigeon's liver and mix it with half the sausage, the egg, and breadcrumbs, adding a little parsley, thyme and nutmeg and seasoning well. Stuff the bird with this. Dust it with salt and pepper and brown it lightly all over in the oil, in a small casserole, with the finely chopped onion and celery. Stir in the tomatoes and the remaining sausage, cover, and simmer very slowly until the bird is tender and a sauce has formed, which takes about 1½ hours.

Cook the pasta *al dente* in plenty of boiling salted water. Drain, place it on a warm serving dish, top with the sauce and a touch of parsley, and serve. A portion of pigeon is given to each person on a side plate – and often eaten in the fingers.

Every year an elderly woman in Rome is sent this chocolate cake by her old friend in Umbria. It used once to be made every Christmas in country districts of Umbria, as well as in remote parts of the Marches and Abruzzi. Today it is one of a tiny band of sweet pasta dishes which remain from the days when sweet pasta was popular, for most of their recipes have been lost.

Il dolce del contadino

Peasant's Cake

The idea of combining pasta with chocolate may not immediately appeal, but this cake is so remarkable that only the most conservative will dismiss the idea of sweet pasta once they've tried it. The original recipe was more extravagant and contained twice as many nuts, but it is extremely good like this. This quantity fills a soufflé dish the size of an average fruit cake, which should be plenty for 8. Whether you eat it as a cake or a dessert, and whether plain or – the ultimate gluttony – with whipped cream, is your choice. But a food processor to chop the nuts is almost essential.

250g (9 oz) lasagnette ricce, ricciutelle, or even farfalle
60g (2 oz) shelled hazelnuts
250g (9 oz) shelled walnuts
100g (3½ oz) blanched almonds
½ slice oven-dried bread
25g (1 oz) dark chocolate, grated finely

60g (2 oz) bitter cocoa powder
1 teaspoon powdered cinnamon
150g (5 oz) castor sugar
grated zest ½ an orange
grated zest ½ a lemon
1–2 tablespoons chopped candied peel
3 tablespoons rum

Remove the hazelnut skins by putting the hazelnuts in a warm oven for a little while, then shaking them in a bag.

Grind the nuts together, with the bread (to stop the nuts turning oily), until they form a thick paste. Put this in a bowl and mix it well with the chocolate, cocoa, cinnamon, sugar, orange and lemon zest and most of the candied peel and the rum. Check for sweetness, but don't make it too sweet.

Cook the pasta, so it is only slightly *al dente*, in plenty of boiling salted water, with a pinch of sugar. Drain and mix with a little of the nut paste. Spread a thin layer of the nut mixture in the bottom of a large soufflé dish, then a layer of pasta, then a thin layer of nut paste – and so on, ending with the nut mixture. Press down well, sprinkle on some rum, and decorate with the remaining candied peel and grated chocolate. Leave in a cool place overnight, decorate, then slice straight from the dish.

17 MOVABLE FEASTS

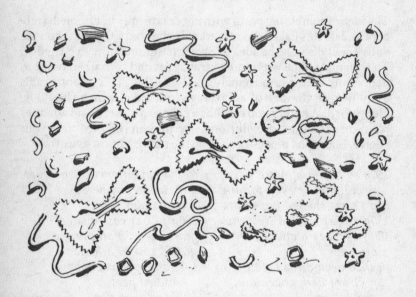

Although cooking in Italy is more egalitarian than in many countries, with peasant farmers and successful businessmen eating the same pasta and the same regional sauces, there are some dishes which have no regional origin: sauces that need foreign ingredients which are found in the big cities; dishes created recently by a particular cook; and those, such as pasta salads, which have only become popular during this century. Many of these recipes are too good to leave out of a book like this.

Farfalle estive di Serena

Serena's Summer Butterflies

This recipe comes from a beautiful blonde Italian girl called Serena. It was handed down by her grandmother, a romantic figure who eloped to India with the family doctor – and the family jewels – at the beginning of the century. A good dish for a buffet.

225g (8 oz) farfalle
celery, carrots, fennel,
   radishes
225g (8 oz) good mayonnaise,
   preferably homemade
1 handful chopped parsley

1 spring onion, or some
   chives
1 teaspoon capers
2cm (1 in) pickled gherkin
2–3 stalks watercress

You can balance the proportions of celery, carrots, fennel and radishes to your taste, but try about 2 tablespoons of each, cleaned, and cut in matchstick strips. Mix the finely chopped parsley, onion, capers, gherkin and watercress with the mayonnaise and adjust the seasoning. Cook the pasta *al dente* in plenty of boiling salted water, drain and mix with the other ingredients. Refrigerate till cold and decorate with a few slices of the vegetables.

Spaghetti estivi al tonno
Summery Spaghetti with Tuna Fish

A richer combination of pasta and mayonnaise, which makes a light main dish for 4–5, and is excellent for a buffet.

500g (18 oz) spaghetti
350g (12 oz) tinned tuna fish
   in oil
200g (7 oz) good mayonnaise
3–4 tablespoons milk
4 drops Tabasco sauce
1 tablespoon soya sauce
1 tablespoon sweet paprika

a very little finely chopped
   fresh chilli
a pinch castor sugar
1½ yellow pimentos
5 salad tomatoes, chopped
some parsley
3 spring onions, cleaned,
   trimmed and sliced

Drain the tuna fish oil into the mayonnaise. Mix it in, adding the milk, Tabasco, soya, chilli, sugar, salt and pepper. Put the pasta to cook in plenty of boiling salted water. Meanwhile, flake the tuna, and remove the stalk and seed from the peppers and cut them into very fine strips. Drain the pasta when *al dente*, and place it straight into a bowl with the other ingredients. Mix everything together delicately and chill. Decorate the dish with sprigs of parsley and slivers of pimento.

Penne all'uvetta
Penne with Raisins

An irresistible pasta salad: a sweet-sour combination with the special flavour of pine nuts – almonds are only second best. For 3–4.

250g (9 oz) penne or similar pasta	400g (14 oz) fresh tomatoes, skinned and chopped
70g (2½ oz) raisins	1 teaspoon sugar
4 tablespoons good olive oil	1–2 teaspoons vinegar
70g (2½ oz) pine kernels or blanched almonds	½ sharp eating apple

Soak the raisins in tepid water for at least 15 minutes. Warm the oil in a little pan and toss the pine nuts or slivered almonds in it until they begin to turn golden – beware, as they burn easily. Mix in the tomatoes, season with salt, and simmer for 10 minutes. Add the drained raisins, sugar and vinegar, and cook gently for 2 minutes. Taste and adjust the balance of sweet, sour and salt.

Cook the pasta in plenty of boiling salted water. Drain when *al dente*, mix with the sauce, and place on a serving dish. Serve cold but not chilled, mixing in the skinned and finely chopped apple just before serving.

Methods and ingredients which may be unfamiliar are explained on pages 26–38.

Rigatoni bianco, rosso, verde
Red, White and Green Rigatoni

One of the quickest pasta salads of all, but very good in a buffet or as a first course in summer. For 4.

400g (14 oz) rigatoni	fresh parsley and basil
8–10 firm ripe salad tomatoes	4 tablespoons soured cream
1 clove garlic	

Cook the pasta in plenty of boiling salted water. Meanwhile, chop the tomatoes without peeling them, combine with the garlic and a handful of parsley – both finely chopped – a few torn basil leaves, and the cream, and season to taste. Drain the pasta when *al dente* and mix into the sauce while hot. Cover and refrigerate until cold.

Lumache al prezzemolo
Pasta Snails with Parsley

The tang of lemon and fresh herbs makes this one of the most refreshing pasta sauces. You can either eat it with hot pasta or let the pasta get cold in the sauce and have it as a salad. A summery first course for 4–5, if you like simple food.

400g (14 oz) small lumache, or shells	1 spring onion (2-3 if tiny)
a few fresh basil leaves (optional)	8 tablespoons good olive oil
a large handful fresh parsley	1 tablespoon fresh lemon juice
a few celery leaves	4 tablespoons Parmesan cheese, grated

Trim, wash, dry and finely chop the basil, parsley, celery leaves and spring onion. Combine with the oil, lemon juice and a little salt. Taste and adjust the balance of oil and lemon. Store this sauce, covered, in the refrigerator until the meal.

Cook the pasta in plenty of boiling salted water. Drain when *al dente*, mix it with the cold sauce and Parmesan, and serve.

Frittata di pasta
Pasta Omelette

The Italian *frittata* resembles a Spanish omelette: thick, spongy, with a substantial filling, it turns out like a cake. Good cold, not at its best hot, it is ideal for picnics. It is also an excellent way to use up leftover pasta, for a favourite filling is any long pasta with a sauce of tomatoes, and perhaps other vegetables. This basic recipe serves 4–6.

4–6 large eggs
¼–½ teacup milk
1–1½ large cups pasta in vegetable sauce

1 tablespoon sunflower oil

Beat the eggs lightly with the milk, season, and mix in the cold pasta. Heat half the oil in an omelette pan, pour in the eggs, and lower the heat. Use a wooden spatula to pull at the mixture so that the egg trickles through the holes. Lift the edge occasionally, and when the underside looks golden put a plate upside down over the pan, hold it firmly in place, and turn the pan upside down so that the omelette lies on the plate. Heat the rest of the oil in the pan, slide in the omelette, uncooked side down, and continue on a low heat until it is cooked in the middle. Turn on to a plate and cool.

In Italy they turn the omelette several times but once will do, and if you haven't the strength to upturn an omelette pan at all just cook the upper surface under the grill: it won't look as elegant but it will still taste good.

Lasagnette col cavolfiore
Lasagnette with Cauliflower

The way the cauliflower is cooked in butter lifts this dish from being pasta and cauliflower cheese, to being very good indeed. A simple meal for 3–4, which also goes well with a chop.

400g (14 oz) lasagnette
1 medium cauliflower
1 tablespoon vinegar
100g (3½ oz) unsalted butter
1 rounded tablespoon flour

about ½ litre (1 pint) milk
4 tablespoons Parmesan, or
  other good cheese, grated
fresh black pepper

Break the cauliflower into florets, rinse well, and cook in boiling salted water with the vinegar. Drain while underdone, and sauté until golden, in an oven dish, in two-thirds of the butter. Make a white sauce, see page 37, with the remaining butter, the flour and milk. When it is cooked, stir in the grated cheese, pour over the cauliflower and place in a hot oven for 10–15 minutes.

Cook the lasagnette in plenty of boiling salted water, drain when *al dente*, place in a warm bowl and top with the cauliflower, adding extra cheese and black pepper.

Fusilli al verde
Fusilli with Green

This delicious and very simple sorrel sauce depends on the freshness of the ingredients. It cannot be made with dried herbs. A first course or light lunch for 4–5.

450g (1 lb) fusilli
450g (1 lb) sorrel or spinach or
  50:50
3 tablespoons olive oil
30g (1 oz) unsalted butter
1 tablespoon chopped parsley

1 tablespoon chopped fresh
  basil
5 tablespoons cream, or rich
  top of milk
good Parmesan cheese,
  grated

Put a large pan of salted water to boil for the pasta. Rinse the sorrel or spinach clean. Remove any large stalks and cook gently in a large, covered pan with a touch of salt but no water – enough remains on the leaves from washing. When tender drain and chop well.

Warm the oil and butter gently in a wide casserole, and add the sorrel or spinach and chopped herbs. Season to taste and cook over a low heat for 5 minutes. Stir in the cream and simmer the sauce gently for another 5 minutes. Meanwhile, cook the fusilli *al dente*. Drain, toss in the sauce, and serve with grated cheese.

Farfalle alle erbette

Farfalle with Spinach Beet

Don't dismiss this gentle and ludicrously simple little dish. With the right balance of nutmeg to other ingredients it makes an extraordinarily good first course or vegetarian lunch for 4–5.

400g (14 oz) farfalle
450g (1 lb) spinach beet or
  frozen spinach
50g (2 oz) unsalted butter
2 tablespoons rich cream

freshly grated nutmeg
80g (3 oz) ricotta cheese
1 handful grated pecorino or
  provolone cheese

Wash the spinach thoroughly, discarding thick stalks and damaged leaves. Cook gently, seasoned with salt, in a covered pan, with no water except that clinging to the leaves after washing, or cook frozen spinach according to its instructions. When tender, drain and chop it thoroughly.

Have ready a large pan of boiling salted water and put in the pasta. While it cooks, melt the butter in a wide pan and toss the spinach in it, adding the cream, and pepper, salt and grated nutmeg to taste. Cook gently together stirring constantly. Drain the farfalle when *al dente* and place them in a warm pasta bowl, dot with ricotta cheese, add the spinach sauce and a handful of grated cheese, toss together lightly and serve.

Sedani all'ortolano

Kitchen Gardener's Sedani

In this subtle and inexpensive sauce the spinach enhances the leeks beautifully. A light meal or first course for 4–5.

500g (18 oz) sedani, or similar
   short tubular pasta
3 fairly large leeks
350g (12 oz) fresh spinach, less
   if frozen

1 medium onion, finely
   chopped
90g (3 oz) unsalted butter
good Parmesan cheese,
   grated

Discard the root and damaged parts of the leeks, slice them very finely, using all but the toughest parts, and wash thoroughly removing every scrap of dirt. Do the same with the spinach and chop finely. Cook the onion gently in the butter, in a large pan, until it starts to colour, stir in the leeks and spinach, season with salt and cook the sauce extremely gently for about 20 minutes, until the vegetables are really tender.

Cook the pasta in plenty of boiling salted water. Drain when *al dente*, place in a warm bowl and top with the vegetables and a handful of cheese. Mix lightly.

Quadratoni in salsa di verdura

Pasta Squares in Vegetable Sauce

The large amount of celery and the way egg yolk is used to soften the taste of tomato make this a particularly good sauce. The squares of pasta can be homemade or you can simply break lasagne to the right size. You can even use other shapes such as shells or farfalle. A very easy light lunch or supper for 5, or a first course for 6.

500g (18 oz) lasagne	1 large carrot
850g (1 lb 13 oz) fresh or tinned tomatoes, skinned and chopped	3 large celery sticks (about 300g/10 oz)
	2 egg yolks
1 sage leaf	90g (3 oz) ham in a thick slice,
1 tablespoon olive oil	cut in strips
30g (1 oz) unsalted butter	good Parmesan cheese,
1 small onion	grated

Put the tomatoes, sage, oil, half the butter, and the finely chopped onion, carrot and celery in a heavy pan over a low heat. Season, cover, and simmer slowly for about 1 hour. Stir the mixture occasionally, adding a tablespoon or so of water if it gets dry, but don't make it watery. Taste and adjust the seasoning.

When the sauce is nearly cooked put a large pan of salted water to boil and break the pasta into 4cm (1½ in) squares – it doesn't matter if they aren't exactly square. When the water boils and the sauce is almost cooked, put 1 teaspoon of oil in the water, to stop the pasta sticking together, and drop in the pasta. Drain it when *al dente*, and place in a warm pasta bowl. Add the egg yolks, vegetable sauce, and remaining butter. Mix lightly, top with the strips of ham and serve immediately. Pass round the Parmesan at table.

Penne alla montanara

Mountaineer's Penne

In the Italian mountains they drink grappa constantly, the excuse being that it keeps out the cold, so it's not surprising that some gets into the pasta. It's a spirit made from the grape skins discarded after wine making: very strong, and with a wonderful aroma, nothing quite replaces it, but this dish is also good with vodka, or even brandy. A good first course for a supper party for 3–4.

Methods and ingredients which may be unfamiliar are explained on pages 26–38.

400g (14 oz) penne or fusilli
a handful dried porcini
  mushrooms
2 garlic cloves, crushed
45g (1½ oz) unsalted butter
1 tumbler aromatic white
  wine, not too dry
200g (7 oz) fresh or tinned
  tomatoes, skinned and
  chopped

a small handful chopped
  parsley
½ tumbler thick cream
2–3 tablespoons grappa
60g (2 oz) provolone or
  Parmesan cheese, grated
freshly ground black pepper

Soak the mushrooms in a little tepid water for 1–2 hours.

Sauté the garlic and porcini gently in the butter in a large shallow casserole for 5 minutes. Add the wine and reduce by half over a brisk heat. Add the tomatoes and half the parsley, and season to taste with salt. Turn down the heat and simmer for 30 minutes, adding the porcini water, strained through a muslin, if it gets dry.

Have ready a large pan of boiling salted water. Put in the pasta. While it cooks stir the cream rapidly into the sauce and simmer very gently until the pasta is cooked *al dente*. Drain the pasta, add the grappa to the sauce, stir quickly, remove from the heat and mix in the pasta. Grind over a little black pepper, sprinkle on the rest of the parsley and serve.

Conchiglie allo zafferano
Shells with Saffron

The lilac-coloured autumn crocus which provides saffron grows in Abruzzi and the Marches and finds its way into the cooking in dishes like this delicious golden mixture of chicken, cream and pasta. A lunch or a luxurious first course for a supper party for 4–5.

*400g (14 oz) medium-sized
 conchiglie (shells) or
 lumache*
*200g (7 oz) raw boneless
 chicken breast*
60g (2 oz) unsalted butter
real saffron powder

250ml (9 fl oz) thick cream
2 egg yolks
1 tablespoon chopped parsley
*60g (2 oz) provolone or
 Parmesan cheese, grated*

Put a large pan of salted water to boil for the pasta. Cut the
chicken into little strips, season with salt and freshly ground
pepper and sauté gently in the butter in a wide shallow casserole.
When almost cooked, stir in a pinch of saffron, then the cream.
Add a little more saffron if it is too pale, and simmer very gently
to thicken the cream slightly. While it thickens cook the pasta.
Taste the sauce, adjust the seasoning, remove from the heat and
lightly mix in the beaten yolks. Drain the pasta when *al dente*,
mix lightly with the sauce and serve sprinkled with parsley. Pass
round the cheese at table.

Orecchiette
con fagiolini
Little Ears with French Beans

You don't have to use orecchiette for this; any short, not too
chunky, pasta does well. In Italy it is served as a first course but
it also makes a delicious accompaniment to meat. To serve 5–6.

*450g (1 lb) homemade
 orecchiette (pages 53–4)
 or 350g (12 oz) packet
 pasta*
*350g (12 oz) French beans,
 fresh are best*
1 garlic clove, finely chopped

60g (2 oz) unsalted butter
150ml (6 fl oz) thick cream
*60g (2 oz) fontina or
 Emmenthal cheese, diced
 small*
*good Parmesan cheese,
 grated*

Top and tail the beans and cut them into 5cm (2 in) lengths. If they are fresh, half-cook them in boiling salted water for 3–4 minutes, and drain. Simply thaw frozen beans.

Put a large pan of salted water to boil for the pasta. Soften the garlic in the butter, over gentle heat, without browning. Add the beans and turn gently in the butter for 2 minutes, to absorb the flavour. Stir in the cream and let it thicken slightly. Put the pasta in the boiling water. Melt the fontina in the cream, then season to taste. Drain the pasta when *al dente*, place in a warm bowl and pour over the sauce. Serve immediately, mixing lightly and adding Parmesan at table.

Homemade orecchiette cook more slowly than packet pasta and would need to go into the water before you began cooking the sauce.

Tagliatelle dello scapolo
Bachelor's Tagliatelle

An ideal dish for bachelors of either sex to serve – it makes the maximum impression on the palate with a minimum of effort in the kitchen. There are two versions, and the second is probably the better, but if you choose good pâté, either is worthy of a special meal. A first course or light lunch for 2–3.

I

250g (8 oz) best-quality tagliatelle	110g (4 oz) fine pâté (taste before you buy)
25g (1 oz) unsalted butter	good Parmesan cheese, grated
150ml (¼ pint) thick cream	

Put the pasta to cook in boiling salted water and warm the pasta bowl on top with the butter in it. Meanwhile, mix the cream with the pâté, over gentle heat, seasoning to taste. Drain the pasta when *al dente*, place in the bowl, pour over the sauce, mix, and serve with a sprinkling of Parmesan on top. Add more Parmesan at table.

II

For a richer version, slice 100–150g (4–6 oz) cleaned button mushrooms finely, and cook them gently for 5 minutes in 2 tablespoons unsalted butter. Add half a teaspoon of crushed green peppercorns, and 1 tablespoon brandy, and let it bubble a moment. In another pan combine the pâté and cream as above, add the mushroom mixture, and warm gently together until the pasta is ready. Serve as before.

Paglia e fieno al salmone di Valeria

Valeria's Straw and Hay Noodles with Smoked Salmon

Smoked salmon is sold in all big cities and the Italians have, naturally, found an excellent way to use it in pasta. This is the dish a friend called Valeria created for a dinner on the Eve of St Laurence, 9 August; the night for seeing shooting stars, when everyone must make a wish. A first course for 4.

550g (19 oz) mixed green and cream tagliatelle, half of each colour, but same brand
40g (1½ oz) unsalted butter

1 smallish onion, very finely chopped
400ml (15 fl oz) thick cream
120g (4 oz) smoked salmon, or best smoked salmon pieces

Put a large pan of water to boil ready for the pasta. Melt the butter gently and let the onion turn transparent in it, without colouring. Stir in the cream, and season to taste with white pepper and a hint of salt. Let it thicken slightly over low heat while you cook the pasta and cut the salmon into little strips. When the pasta is almost cooked remove the sauce from the heat, and stir in the smoked salmon, saving a few pieces for decoration. Drain the pasta when *al dente*, toss in the sauce, place on a serving dish, and decorate with the pieces of salmon.

Tagliatelle alla Maria

Maria's Tagliatelle

A cream sauce can also be made with scallops, but here the white wine makes it less rich than the previous recipe and is an important part of the flavour. For 2–3.

300g (11 oz) fresh tagliatelle or 225g (8 oz) from a packet
2 large scallops or 4 small
30g (1 oz) unsalted butter
1 garlic clove

chopped parsley
⅔ tumbler good dry white wine
5 tablespoons thick cream, at room temperature

Rinse and clean the scallops, and cut them into slim strips. Put a large pan of salted water to boil for the pasta.

Rub a heavy casserole with garlic. Gently melt the butter in it and slowly cook the scallops and 1 tablespoon of chopped parsley, without letting the butter brown. After 2 minutes add the wine, turn up the heat and let it bubble fiercely for a minute. Remove from the heat, season to taste, and stir rapidly as you add the cream. Place over the lowest possible heat, for the cream to thicken slightly, while the tagliatelle cook. Drain the pasta when *al dente*, place on a warm dish, add the sauce and garnish with parsley.

Tortellini con funghi e panna

Tortellini with Mushrooms and Cream

This is the classic mushroom and cream sauce, used with tagliatelle and all sorts of meat-filled pastas. A rich first course or light meal for 4.

600g (1 lb 5 oz) tortellini
25g (1 oz) dried porcini
  mushrooms (optional)
300g (11 oz) button
  mushrooms
70g (2½ oz) unsalted butter

2 tablespoons good oil
150ml (6 fl oz) thick cream
chopped parsley
Parmesan cheese, grated
  (optional)

Soak the porcini in a little tepid water for 1–2 hours.

Rinse the button mushrooms and slice them finely. Sauté gently, in the butter and oil, with the drained porcini for 4 minutes. Add the porcini water, strained through a muslin, and bubble to reduce to a spoonful or so. Stir in the cream and cook very gently until it thickens slightly, seasoning to taste.

Have ready a large pan of boiling salted water. Cook the pasta *al dente*. Drain, place on a warm dish, add the sauce, and sprinkle with parsley. Serve, and pass round the Parmesan.

THE PASTA MENU

The dishes in this book range from the lightest of starters, through quick lunches and easy suppers, to roast joints and even sweet dishes. But in Italy there is no convention of the first course being smaller than the one that follows it, and pasta, of whatever kind, is eaten at the beginning of the meal. But to fit into the pattern of eating outside Italy its role needs to be more flexible. So this list is designed to make it easier to fit these dishes into a non-Italian pattern of eating. Of course, the divisions are slightly arbitrary, for very few dishes fit strictly into any one category – Italian soups, for example, are filling enough to make a hearty lunch, while the distinction between a light dish and a substantial one is partly a matter of personal taste. So our guidelines are simply a starting point from which to explore the place of pasta in meals of every kind. In addition, dishes which contain no meat are marked ▽.

Soups

Pasta for Pleasure

182 **MINESTRONE ALLA BORGHESE**
*a stylish minestrone with pimentos, courgettes, tomatoes
and celery*

239 **MINESTRONE ALLA TOSCANA** ▽
a Tuscan bean soup with onion, celery, tomato and pasta

122 **MINESTRONE CON CAZZETTINI D'ANGELI**
a hearty soup of beans, celery, courgettes, aubergines and pasta

210 **PAPPARDELLE E FEGATINI**
rich broth with pasta and chicken livers

214 **PASTA E FAGIOLI ALLA VENETA**
Venetian bean soup with onion, ham and cinnamon

78 **PASTA E PATATE**
a hearty soup of potatoes, onion, celery, bacon and tomatoes

238 **STRISCE E CECI** ▽
chickpea and onion soup with pasta

Salads

128 **BAVETTE IN INSALATA**
*long pasta with roast lamb and pork, cucumber, tomatoes
and onion*

254 **FARFALLE ESTIVE DI SERENA** ▽
*butterfly pasta with celery, radishes and fennel in green
mayonnaise*

257 **LUMACHE AL PREZZEMOLO** ▽
short pasta with onion, celery, parsley, oil and lemon juice

127 **MACCHERONCELLI IN INSALATA**
short pasta with tongue, salami, gherkin, tomatoes and cheese

The Pasta Menu

PENNE ALL'UVETTA ▽ 256
short pasta with a sweet-sour sauce of tomato, raisins and pine nuts

RIGATONI BIANCO ROSSO VERDE ▽ 257
short pasta with tomatoes, basil and sour cream

SPAGHETTI ESTIVI AL TONNO ▽ 255
spaghetti with tuna fish, tomatoes and pimentos in piquant mayonnaise

TAGLIOLINI MARINARI 126
a sophisticated pasta salad with salmon, palm hearts, shrimps and olives

First Courses or Very Light Main Courses

AVEMARIE ALLA LANGHIRANO 91
pasta beads with broad bean kernels, Parma ham and Parmesan

BIGOLI CON LE NOCI ▽ 208
brown spaghetti with walnuts, butter and cinnamon

BURRO E SALVIA ▽ 119
butter and sage sauce

BUCATINI E PEPERONCINI ▽ 134
bucatini with olive oil and lashings of garlic and chillies

CIARSCÓNS ALLA CARNIOLA ▽ 217
egg pasta stuffed with curd cheese, parsley and raisins

CAPLÉTT 96
egg pasta filled with turkey, ricotta and Parmesan

FETTUCCELLE CON LE NOCI ▽ 247
ribbon pasta with onion, celery and walnuts

271

Pasta for Pleasure

173   FETTUCCINE AL TRIPLO BURRO ▽
fettuccine in melted butter

57   FUSILLI DELLA RIVOLUZIONE ▽
a very easy oven-baked tomato sauce with short pasta

43   FUSILLI IN SALSA ▽
fusilli with a peppery sauce of tomato, basil and cheese

139   LASAGNE CON LA RICOTTA ▽
a delicate lasagne filled with creamy cheese and fresh basil

114   LASAGNETTE RICCE ALLE NOCI E GORGONZOLA ▽
*flat ribbons of pasta with cream cheese, Gorgonzola
and walnuts*

76–7   LINGUINE AGLIO OLIO E PEPERONCINO ▽
linguine in a sauce of olive oil, garlic and chillies

77   LINGUINE CON PEPERONI ▽
linguine with pimentos, onion and garlic

257   LUMACHE AL PREZZEMOLO ▽
*hot pasta with a cold sauce of onion, celery, parsley, oil
and lemon*

197   MACCHERONCELLI CON CAVOLFIORE ▽
*long macaroni with cauliflower, pine kernels, anchovy
and saffron*

264   ORECCHIETTE CON FAGIOLINI ▽
orecchiette with French beans, cream and melted cheese

54   ORECCHIETTE E BROCCOLETTI DI RAPE ▽
orecchiette with broccoli, anchovy and garlic

The Pasta Menu

PAGLIA E FIENO AL SALMONE DI VALERIA ▽   266
*mixed yellow and green tagliatelle with cream and
smoked salmon*

PANSÔTI DI RAPALLO ▽   109
*ravioli stuffed with cheese, spinach and eggs
in a walnut sauce*

PASTA AMMUDDICATA ▽   135
*long pasta in anchovies and oil, topped with
peppery breadcrumbs*

PASTA CON ZUCCHINE ▽   58
*pasta with courgettes, tomatoes, garlic,
and perhaps mozzarella*

PENNE AL GORGONZOLA ▽   113
short pasta with mild Gorgonzola and thick cream

PENNE ALL'UOVO E RICOTTA ▽   171
short pasta with eggs, cream and creamy cheese

PENNE CON SALSA DI CARCIOFI ▽   246
short pasta with artichokes, onions, tomatoes and capers

PESTO ▽   103
a sauce of fresh basil pounded with garlic, oil and pine kernels

QUADROTTI DUCA DI MANTOVA ▽   125
squares of pasta in a buttery leek sauce with Parmesan

SALSA DI NOCI ▽   109
a sauce of walnuts, ricotta and pine kernels

SEDANI ALL'ORTALANO ▽   261
short pasta with subtle sauce of leeks, spinach and onion

SPAGHETTI AGLIO, OLIO, PECORINO ▽   189
spaghetti with olive oil, garlic, pine kernels and pecorino cheese

Pasta for Pleasure

242   SPAGHETTI AI TARTUFI NERI ▽
spaghetti with oil, anchovy and truffle

179   SPAGHETTI ALLA PUTTANESCA ▽
spaghetti with tomatoes, anchovies, olives, garlic and capers

60   SPAGHETTI ALLA TARANTINA ▽
spaghetti with mussels cooked with white wine and garlic

73   SPAGHETTI AL POMODORO ▽
the classic tomato sauce with garlic and basil, plus variations

64   SPAGHETTI CHI VRUOCCOLI ARRIMINATA ▽
spaghetti with broccoli, tomatoes, pine nuts and raisins

247   SPAGHETTI CON PUNTE DI ASPARAGI ▽
spaghetti with a sauce of tomato and asparagus

74   SPAGHETTI CON SALSA A CRUDO ▽
*the classic raw tomato sauce with garlic and basil,
plus variations*

226   TAGLIATELLE AI FUNGHI PORCINI ▽
tagliatelle with porcini mushrooms, oil and garlic

128   TAGLIATELLE AL CAVIALE ▽
tagliatelle with unsalted butter and Danish caviar

155   TAGLIATELLE ALLA BIELLESE ▽
tagliatelle in a simple sauce of Parmesan, butter and nutmeg

90   TAGLIATELLE ALLA PANNA ▽
tagliatelle with the classic sauce of cream and Parmesan

160   TAGLIATELLE AL SUGO DI ARROSTO
tagliatelle with the juices from roast meat, and melted cheese

90   TAGLIATELLE AL PROSCIUTTO DI PARMA ▽
tagliatelle with butter and prosciutto

TAJARIN CON TARTUFI ▽   153
tagliatelle with truffles and Parmesan

TORTELLINI ALLA BOLOGNESE   93
tortellini filled with chicken, prosciutto and mortadella

TORTELLINI DI LUISA   95
tortellini filled with Parma ham, mortadella and Parmesan

TORTELLONI DA VIGILIA ▽   95
tortelloni filled with ricotta cheese, Parmesan and parsley

TRENETTE COL PESTO ALLA GENOVESE ▽   106
trenette and potatoes with pesto sauce

VERMICELLI AI CAPPERI ▽   75
*vermicelli with a cold sauce of black olives, capers, anchovies
and garlic*

VERMICELLI ALLA CALABRESE   63
*vermicelli in a sauce of pimentos, garlic and cheese, cooked in
lardo*

VERMICELLI ALL'ISOLA D'ISCHIA   74
*a cold sauce of tomatoes, onions, capers, olives, garlic
and parsley*

Light Main Courses or
Substantial First Courses

AGNOLOTTI DI SPINACI   157
*pasta stuffed with spinach, beef and cheese, in butter
and sage sauce*

Pasta for Pleasure

158   **AGNOLOTTI DI ANGELINO**
*oven-baked agnolotti with tomatoes, mushrooms, bacon
and melted cheese*

244   **BAVETTE CON FAVE ALLA PERUGINA**
long pasta with broad beans, ham, cream and Parmesan

243   **BAVETTE CON FAVE ALL'ORTOLANO**
*long pasta with broad beans, bacon, tomatoes, onions
and white wine*

116   **BAVETTE CON LE CIPOLLE ▽**
long narrow pasta with a rich onion sauce

236   **BUCATINI ALLA MANIERA DEL BUTTERO ▽**
oven-baked bucatini with potatoes, onion, cheese and tomato

168   **BUCATINI ALL'AMATRICIANA**
bucatini with bacon, tomato, onion and chilli

170   **BUCATINI CON LE SALSICCE**
a simple dish of pasta with sausages cooked in tomato sauce

82   **CANNELLONI ALLA MODA DI PARTENOPEA**
*delicate cheese and Parma ham stuffing with a light
tomato sauce*

230   **CANNELLONI ALLA MODA DI PORSENNA**
cannelloni filled with mushrooms and ham

212   **CANNELLONI ALLA VICENTINA**
*cannelloni filled with veal, pork, tongue, and spinach
and tomato*

227   **CANNELLONI RIPIENI DI CARNE**
cannelloni filled with mushrooms, veal and Parmesan

118   **CASONSEI DI BERGAMO**
very large homemade ravioli stuffed with beef, in butter and sage

The Pasta Menu

CHITARRELLI ALLA MARCHIGIANA   143
long pasta with a piquant sauce of tomatoes, bacon and capers

CICIONES   188
Sardinian gnocchetti with pork, onion, pimento and tomatoes

CONCHIGLIE ALLO ZAFFERANO   263
shell pasta in a sauce of chicken breast, cream, saffron and cheese

FARFALLE ALLE ERBETTE ▽   260
farfalle with spinach, cream and ricotta cheese

FETTUCCINE ALLA PAPALINA   174
ribbons of pasta with peas, ham, eggs and Parmesan

FETTUCCINE ALLA SQUARCIARELLA   173
ribbons of pasta with ham, onion, eggs and cream

FETTUCCINE CON RIGAGLIE   165
fettuccine with chicken livers, tomatoes and red wine

FREGNACCE   45
*lasagnette with tomatoes, bacon, pimento, prosciutto
and chillies*

FRITTATA DI PASTA ▽   258
a thick omelette made with leftover pasta in sauce

FUSILLI AL VERDE   259
fusilli with spinach, basil, butter and Parmesan

FUSILLI CON LUCANICA   136
fusilli with pimentos, onions, tomatoes and peppery sausages

I RAVIOLI DI SANT'ANTIOCO   190
*ravioli made of cheese, bone marrow and mountain ham,
with a pistachio sauce*

'L'AMATRICIANA' IN BIANCO   169
spaghetti with sausages, bacon, chilli and cheese

Pasta for Pleasure

154 **LASAGNETTE ALLA CAVOUR**
ribbon lasagne with chicken livers, brandy and Parmesan

259 **LASAGNETTE COL CAVOLFIORE** ▽
ribbon lasagne with cauliflower and cheese sauce

246 **LINGUINE CON ASPARAGI**
*long pasta with a rich sauce of tinned tuna fish, cream
and asparagus*

245 **MACCHERONCELLI ALLA VECCHIA PERUSIA**
*short paste with the juices from a roast, French beans, cream
and Parmesan*

115 **MACCHERONCINI AI QUATTRO FORMAGGI** ▽
macaroni with four types of melted cheese

67 **MACCHERONI ALLA CALABRESE**
a light tomato sauce well flavoured with Parma ham and cheese

42 **MACCHERONI ALLA CHITARRA CON POMODORO**
chitarra spaghetti with a peppery sauce of bacon and tomato

175 **MACCHERONI ALLA CIOCIARA**
long pasta with peas, bacon and Parmesan

186 **MALLOREDDUS**
Sardinian gnocchetti with tomato and peppery salami

180 **OCCI DI LUPO ALLA CAPPUCCETTO ROSSO**
short pasta with tomatoes, bacon, olives, celery and garlic

178 **PAGLIA E FIENO CON I CARCIOFI**
*mixed yellow and green tagliatelle with artichokes, bacon
and wine*

199 **PASTA A 'PICCHI-PACCHI'** ▽
*long pasta with a sauce of melted aubergines, tomato, basil
and anchovy*

The Pasta Menu

PASTA 'NCACIATA   202
short pasta with aubergines, eggs, salami and mozzarella, in tomato

PASTÉZZ ED CAPLÉTT   98
leftover cooked cappelletti oven-baked with tomato sauce

PENNE ALLA MONTANARA ▽   262
short pasta with mushrooms, tomatoes, cream, white wine and cheese

PENNE ALL'ARRABBIATA   233
short pasta with mushrooms, tomatoes, bacon, cheese and chillies

PENNE D'ORO ▽   177
short pasta with artichokes, mushrooms, peas and tomatoes

PIZZOCCHERI DELLA VALTELLINA ▽   124
buckwheat tagliatelle with onions, cabbage, potatoes and melted cheese

QUADRATONI IN SALSA DI VERDURA   261
pasta squares with celery and ham, in tomato sauce softened by egg

RIGATONI CON SALSICCE E UOVA   170
short pasta with meaty sausages, eggs and Parmesan

SPAGHETTI A 'CACIO E PEPE' ▽   171
spaghetti with lots of cheese and black pepper

SPAGHETTI AL FORNO CON LA FONTINA ▽   160
spaghetti with butter and melted cheese

SPAGHETTI ALLA CARBONARA   166
spaghetti with bacon, eggs and cheese, plus variations

Pasta for Pleasure

70   SPAGHETTI ALLA CARMELINA ▽
spaghetti with curls of squid in tomato, wine, garlic and chillies

200   SPAGHETTI ALLA NORMA ▽
*a decorative dish of spaghetti with aubergine slices and
tomato sauce*

111   SPAGHETTI ALLA PERASCA ▽
*spaghetti with a sauce of creamed cod and tomatoes with
black olives*

231   SPAGHETTI ALLA VACCARA
*spaghetti in a ham, bacon and tomato sauce, softened with
egg yolks*

237   SPAGHETTI ALLA VIAREGGINA ▽
spaghetti with clams in tomatoes and white wine

196   SPAGHETTI ALL'ISOLANA ▽
spaghetti with tinned tuna fish, olives, garlic and white wine

196   SPAGHETTI COL TONNO
spaghetti with tinned tuna fish and tomatoes

227   SPAGHETTI CON SALSA DI FUNGHI ▽
spaghetti with a rich mushroom and tomato sauce

211   SPAGHETTI CON SALSA DI QUAGLIA
spaghetti with quail sauce

179   SPAGHETTI 'ER ROSCIO'
*spaghetti with tomatoes, celery, onions, olives, salami, garlic
and chilli*

250   SPAGHETTI GRASSI E MAGRI
spaghetti with bacon, cheese and black pepper

154   TAGLIATELLE ALL'ALBESE
tagliatelle with chicken livers, mushrooms and wine

The Pasta Menu

TAGLIATELLE ALLA MARIA ▽   267
tagliatelle with scallops in cream and white wine

TAGLIATELLE DI QUARTILIA   251
tagliatelle with pigeon, sausage and tomato sauce

TAGLIATELLE DELLO SCAPOLO   265
*tagliatelle with cream, pâté and possibly mushrooms
and brandy*

TAGLIATELLE E GALLINACCI   156
tagliatelle with mushrooms, ham and melted cheese

TAGLIATELLE VERDI AI FUNGHI ▽   107
*tagliatelle with a copious sauce of mushrooms in tomatoes
and wine*

TIMBALLO DI BUCATINI CON MELANZANE ▽   201
*bucatini with tomatoes, Parmesan and aubergines
in a pastry case*

TIMBALLO DI MACCHERONI ▽   137
*oven-baked macaroni with aubergines, tomatoes
and cheese*

TORTELLINI CON FUNGHI E PANNA   268
stuffed pasta with the classic cream and mushroom sauce

TORTELLONI VERDI AL GORGONZOLA ▽   117
*green pasta stuffed with cheese and spinach in a mild
Gorgonzola sauce*

VERMICELLI ALLA POSILLIPO ▽   79
*a rich sauce of squid, clams, mussels and prawns with tomatoes
and wine*

VERMICELLI ALLA SICILIANA ▽   198
*vermicelli with a rich sauce of aubergines, pimentos, olives
and anchovy*

Pasta for Pleasure

81   VERMICELLI CON LE VONGOLE ▽
vermicelli with clams, garlic and parsley

195   VERMICELLI DELLA TONNARA ▽
*vermicelli with fresh tuna fish, tomatoes, capers
and white wine*

Substantial Dishes

209   BIGOLI CON SALSA D' ANITRA
brown spaghetti with duck sauce

49   COSCIOTTO D'AGNELLO ALL'ABRUZZESE CON
FETTUCCINE
*leg of lamb with garlic, bacon and tomatoes on a bed
of fettuccine*

282   BOMBOLOTTI ALLA NORCINA
short pasta with sausages and curd cheese

203   FARSUMAGRU
*tagliatelle and a roll of stuffed beef pot roasted with wine
and tomato*

138   FUSILLI E INVOLTINI DI EMILIA
*fusilli and beef rolls in tomato sauce with bacon, celery
and chillies*

84   LA GENOVESE
pasta with a pot roast beef or pork in a rich onion sauce

46   LASAGNE ABRUZZESI
*lasagne with beef, tomatoes, mushrooms, cheese, eggs
and prosciutto*

145   LASAGNE AL FORNO
lasagne made with chicken, pork, beef, tomatoes and prosciutto

LASAGNE ALLA MANIERA DI RAGUSA   206
a light lasagne with cooked veal, curd cheese and tomatoes

LASAGNE ALLA NAVIGLIA   130
lasagne with courgettes, salami, tomatoes, cheese
and white wine

LASAGNE DI SAN FREDIANO   229
lasagne with mushrooms, veal and ham and white wine

MACCHERONCINI DI CAMPOFILONE   142
fine egg pasta with two rich beef and tomato sauces

LASAGNE VERDI ALLA MODENESE   100
the classic lasagne combining a meaty Bolognese sauce
and white sauce

LE PENNE DEL GERMANO   224
short pasta with wild duck, tomatoes, wine and cinnamon

MACCARONES CON LA RICOTTA   188
homemade macaroni with a joint of pork, tomatoes, wine and
curd cheese

MACCHERONCELLI UBRIACHI   159
short pasta with meaty sausages, cream, wine and brandy

MACCHERONI ALLA CARRETTAIA   68
homemade or packet pasta with a simple beef sauce

MACCHERONI ALLA CHITARRA
CON PEPERONCINO   40
chitarra spaghetti with a peppery sauce of lamb, onions and
pimentos

MACCHERONI ALLA CHITARRA E SUGO
DI AGNELLO   41
chitarra spaghetti with a peppery sauce of lamb, tomatoes
and rosemary

69   MACCHERONI ALLA SALSICCIA
*long macaroni with cabbage, wine, cheese
and spicy sausages*

47   MILLEFOGLIE ALLA 'GUARDIESE'
*lasagne with veal, tomatoes, peas, mushrooms
and cheese*

55   ORECCHIETTE AL POMODORO
orecchiette with pork or lamb, onion and tomatoes

56   ORECCHIETTE DEL TRULLO
orecchiette with meat balls in tomato sauce

225   PAPPARDELLE ALLA CACCIATORA
*pappardelle with joints of chicken, onion, tomato
and Marsala*

222   PAPPARDELLE CON LA LEPRE
pappardelle in a rich sauce of hare and red wine

44   PASTA ALLA PECORARA
*a decorative and spicy dish of fusilli with meat and
various vegetables*

193   PASTA CON LE SARDE ▽
*long macaroni with pilchards, fennel, onions, anchovies
and pine nuts*

234   PENNE ALLA TOSCANA
short pasta with sausages, tomato, onion and spinach

148   PINCINELLE ALL'ANCONETANA
*rustic egg pasta with a joint of beef, pot roasted in wine
and tomatoes*

50   RAGÙ PER MACCHERONI CARRATI
*a sauce from pot roast veal with mushrooms, tomatoes
and chicken livers*

The Pasta Menu

RIGATONI ALL'ERBA MAGICA   235
*rigatoni with beef, sausages and tomatoes, flavoured
with mace*

ROTOLO DI PASTA E SPINACI   144
*a unique dish of fresh pasta, cheese and ham
in a meat sauce*

SCALOPPINE DI ANIMELLA ALLA MILANESE
CON FETTUCCINE AL BURRO   129
*fried escalope of veal sweetbreads with
buttery fettuccine*

SPAGHETTI AI FRUTTI DI MARE ▽   60
*a sauce of clams, mussels, shrimps and conger eel in
tomatoes and garlic*

TAGLIATELLE BOLOGNESE   88
the classic rich Bolognese sauce

TAGLIATELLE ALLA PIEMONTESE   161
tagliatelle with pot roast beef and veal in a wine sauce

TIMBALLO DI CAVOLO E MOZZARELLA   131
*lasagne with a delicate mixture of beef, cabbage
and cheese*

TIMBALLO DI MACCHERONI
ALLA ROMAGNOLA   99
*a pie with macaroni, pigeon, veal, sweetbreads and
mushrooms in a rich sauce*

VERMICELLI AL SUGO DI CARNE   65
*a meaty sauce of beef and pork with mushrooms, onion and
pine kernels*

VINCISGRASSI   147
*a very rich lasagne of sweetbreads, chicken livers
and mushrooms*

Pasta for Pleasure

83 ZITI CO'O RAGÙ
pasta with rich, pot roasted beef and pork in wine
and tomatoes

Sweet Pasta Dishes

219 CIALZÓNS DI PAINURA
pasta stuffed with plums and served with melted butter

253 IL DOLCE DEL CONTADINO
a cake with a rich chocolate and nut paste between thin
layers of pasta

218 LASAGNETTE AI SEMI DI PAPAVERO
ribbon pasta with melted butter, sugar and poppy seeds

183 RIGATONI CON LA RICOTTA
short pasta with curd cheese, sugar and cinnamon

119 TORTELLI ALLA CREMASCA
egg pasta stuffed with amaretti, brandy and egg

121 TORTELLI DI ZUCCA
egg pasta stuffed with pumpkin, candied fruit
and amaretti

SPECIALIST SHOPS

The popularity of pasta is growing so fast that new fresh pasta shops are opening every month, and the list of shops and supermarkets which sell fresh chilled pasta increases almost daily. Some shops are also now stocking the more unusual ingredients needed for pasta sauces. A list of all such shops would be a book in itself, but the following is a selection of places which can supply most of the ingredients used in these recipes. Some of these shops also stock Italian wine and some will supply fresh herbs, such as basil, on request. Fresh ingredients, like herbs or ricotta cheese, may only be available on certain days of the week, or to order, so it could be worth checking by phone.

The fact that a shop appears in this list should not be taken as a guarantee of the quality of its products: the standard of fresh pasta varies widely, and the recipes and ingredients being used by these shops for pasta are subject to changes which the authors cannot predict.

The symbols indicate the following:

OFP – own fresh pasta made on the premises
CP – fresh chilled pasta is sold
P – a good range of dried pasta is sold
I – most ingredients for sauces stocked or available to order

La Bottega   CP,P,I
30 Wells Road
Bath

Bath 20672

Pasta Galore   OFP,I
4 Broad Street
Bath

Bath 64060

La Bottega   OFP,P,I
51 Commercial Road
Bedford

Bedford 52361

Tony's Food & Wine   CP,P,I
118 St Michael's Hill
Cotham
Bristol

Bristol 291

P. Balzano   P,I
26 Ainsworth Street
Cambridge

Cambridge 62988

Berni's Delicatessen   OFP,P,I
57 Wellfield Road
Roath
Cardiff

Cardiff 490358

C. Forgione   CP,P,I
6 Shurdington Road
Cheltenham
Glos.

Cheltenham 514213

Specialist Shops

Continental Foods (Wrexham) Ltd 5 Watergate Street Chester Chester 25773	CP,P,I
Valvona and Crolla Ltd 19 Elm Row Edinburgh Edinburgh 556 6066	OFP,P,I
Fazzi Brothers Ltd 232 Clyde Street Glasgow Glasgow 221 9411	OFP,P,I
Hampers 163–5 Telegraph Road Heswall Wirral Heswall 342 7683	CP,P,I
Mirapol Delicatessen 62 North Street Keighley West Yorkshire Keighley 69006	CP,P,I
A. & B. Suffredini 24 Dean Street Kilmarnock Ayrshire Kilmarnock 22063	P,I

Mazurska   P, I
18 Guildhall Street
Lincoln

Lincoln 25304

Fratelli Camisa   OFP, P, I
1a Berwick Street
London, W1

I. Camisa   OFP, P, I
61 Old Compton Street
London, W1

01-437 4686

Harrods Ltd   OFP, I
Knightsbridge
London, SW1

01-730 1234

Lina Stores   OFP, P, I
18 Brewer Street
London, W1

01-437 6482

Luigi's Delicatessen   OFP, P, I
349 Fulham Road
London, SW10

01-352 7739

also 60 New King's Road, SW6
and 23 Barrett Street, W1

Specialist Shops

Pasta Factory   OFP
261 Kings Road
London, SW3

01-352 8573

Pasta Pasta   OFP,P,I
52 Pimlico Road
London, SW1

01-730 1435

also 102 Marylebone High Street, NW1

01-935 4650

Pronto Pasta   OFP,P,I
66 Old Brompton Road
London, SW7

01-589 1760

The Pasta Place   OFP,P,I
42 Heath Street
London, NW3

01-431 0018

Pasta Pasta   OFP,P,I
29 Little Clarendon Street
Oxford

Jordans   CP,P,I
8 Upper High Street
Thame
Oxon

Thame 2056

Giorgio Continental Stores   CP,P,I
127 Sneinton Dale
Nottingham

Nottingham 55447

Katsouris Delicatessen   CP,P,I
11–13 The Square
Market Hall
Bury
Greater Manchester

Manchester 764 4382

C. C. & M. V. Brook   CP,P,I
26 Church Road
Cheadle Hulme
Nr Manchester

Manchester 485 1548

Giovanna Delicatessen   CP,P,I
42 Market Place
Rochdale
Greater Manchester

Rochdale 359559

Arne Pasta   Fresh pasta to
The Old Tavern   order
Compton Dundon
Somerton
Somerset

0458 42347

Amalfi Delicatessen   P,I
17 Queensway
Southampton

Southampton 28635

Ceci
59 Wyldes Lane
Worcester

Worcester 353602

P, I

C. Carnevale
107 Blundell Street
London, N7

01-607 8777

Wholesaler of
Italian cheese,
pasta and meat
products and will
gladly supply
details of the
nearest stockist

Rossi's Pasta
McVitie's Frozen Foods
Ashley Trading Estate
Ashley Parade
Bristol

Manufacture
chilled fresh pasta
sold in many
supermarkets and
will supply details
of your nearest
stockist

Pasta Information Centre
26 Fitzroy Square
London, W1

01-388 7421

May be able to
supply details of
new fresh pasta
shops

EQUIPMENT

Divertimenti
68–72 Marylebone Lane
London, W1

01-935 0689

Good
pasta-making
equipment. Mail
order catalogue
£1.50 (incl. p & p)

Some items for pasta-making are also available at most branches
of John Lewis.

AUSTRALIA Shops which may be able to supply fresh pasta or the ingredients for these dishes.

Nature's Harvest
20 Napoleon Street
Cottesloe
Perth

Passello
5 Transvaal Avenue
Double Bay
NSW

Interfoods Deli
14 South Terrace
Fremantle
Perth

The Pasta House
413 Parramatta Road
Leichhardt
Sydney

The Ravioli and Lasagne Kitchen
77 Military Road
Neutral Bay
Sydney

Donnini's Home-Made Pasta
398 Lygon Street
Carlton
Victoria

L'Emiliana Pasta Products
76 Acland Street
St Kilda
Victoria

Pasta Fresca
4 Close Street
Canterbury
Sydney

Supplies fresh pasta to shops in region; will supply details of stockists

INDEX

Numbers in bold type denote pages for reference rather than recipes

Index

Index

Index

Index

Index